FURTHER REFLECTIONS
ON THE REVOLUTION IN FRANCE

EDMUND BURKE

FURTHER REFLECTIONS ON THE REVOLUTION IN FRANCE

————

EDMUND BURKE

EDITED BY DANIEL E. RITCHIE

Liberty Fund

Frontispiece photo courtesy of the National Portrait Gallery, London. Portrait from the studio of Joshua Reynolds.

Library of Congress Cataloging-in-Publication Data

Burke, Edmund, 1729–1797.
Further reflections on the revolution in France / Edmund Burke ; edited by Daniel E. Ritchie.
    p.   cm.
Includes bibliographical references and index.
ISBN 0-86597-098-x (hardcover).—ISBN 0-86597-099-8 (pbk.)
1. Burke, Edmund, 1729–1797—Correspondence. 2. France—History—Revolution, 1789–1799—Foreign public opinion, British. 3. Public opinion—Great Britain—History—18th century. 4. Burke, Edmund, 1729–1797. Reflections on the Revolution in France. I. Ritchie, Daniel E. II. Title.

DC150.B8 1992
944.04—dc20   91-33265

08 21 22 23 24 C 7 6 5 4 3
21 22 23 24 25 P 8 7 6 5 4

CONTENTS

FOREWORD

In the two hundred years since Edmund Burke produced his writings on the French Revolution, the question of how to achieve liberty within a good society has remained a pressing one. Simon Schama's masterful chronicle of the French Revolution, *Citizens*, argues that the Revolution attempted to create two entities, "a potent state and . . . a community of free citizens," whose interests were irreconcilable. It was impossible, Schama states, to serve one without damaging the other.[1]

Burke's alternative to revolutionary freedom and the revolutionary state may be found throughout this volume, especially in his description of what liberty is. "Practical liberty," as Burke calls it in the first work printed here, differs in almost every respect from the revolutionary liberty of the French on both the individual and corporate levels. The individual that Burke describes is the "gentleman," a member of a "natural aristocracy." This gentleman is educated to respect the ancients, for they anticipate the errors of the moderns, and to revere God. His upbringing includes a respect for parents, for we "begin our public affections in our families," as Burke says in *Reflections on the Revolution in France*.[2] The gentleman enjoys his liberties in and through his social, economic, religious, and political institutions. They mediate his liberties through his obligations to them. Those obligations are not at war with the Englishman's liberties: rather, they provide the means for him to develop fully into the virtuous, free human being that God intended (p. 161). Aware of the hostility of the revolutionaries to the ideal of the gentleman, Burke writes: "The great object of your tyrants is to destroy the gentlemen of France. . . " (p. 54).

By contrast, the individual suited for revolutionary liberty is the "citizen." To quote Schama on the cultural construction of the French citizen: "In this new world [of the French citizen,] heart

[1] Simon Schama, *Citizens: A Chronicle of the French Revolution* (New York: Knopf, 1989), p. 15.

[2] Edmund Burke, *Reflections on the Revolution in France*, ed. Conor Cruise O'Brien (Harmondsworth: Penguin, 1968), p. 315. Subsequent references to this work will be given as *Reflections*.

was to be preferred to head; emotion to reason; nature to culture. . . . To possess *un coeur sensible* (a feeling heart) was the precondition for morality."[3] Rousseau, the chief educator of the revolutionary generation of French citizens, taught that liberty was to be enjoyed after the individual had *removed* his existing social, economic, religious, and political obligations.

Practical liberty differs from revolutionary liberty in its corporate construction also. This difference is epitomized by the distinction between Burke's "Constitution" and the French Declaration of the Rights of Man. Burke's critics, such as Thomas Paine, jeered that Britain lacked a constitution altogether, for there was no single piece of paper with that title. Burke's defense of the Constitution, especially in *An Appeal from the New to the Old Whigs* and *A Letter to a Noble Lord*, shows the simple-mindedness of Paine's criticism. Paper declarations and manifestoes of "universal" rights for abstract "man" do nothing to further liberty, argued Burke. Burke's words on the American crisis in 1775 are apropos. The Americans, he said,

> are not only devoted to liberty, but to liberty according to English ideas, and on English principles. Abstract liberty, like other mere abstractions, is not to be found. Liberty inheres in some sensible object; and every nation has formed to itself some favourite point, which by way of eminence becomes the criterion of their happiness.[4]

By the "sensible objects" of liberty, Burke means the actual practices of the assemblies, courts, churches, and commercial institutions of an actual people. The liberty pursued by Burke and the other Rockingham Whigs, he says in *A Letter to a Noble Lord*, "was a Liberty inseparable from order, from virtue, from morals, and from religion. . ." (p. 287). Burke consistently denied the possibility of discussing liberty in abstract terms and denied that liberty and constitutional law could ever truly be separate.

A fundamentally different approach to reality underlies the contrast between the practical liberty enjoyed by the gentleman under the British Constitution and the revolutionary liberty of the

[3] Schama, p. 149.

[4] Edmund Burke, *Speech on Conciliation*, in *The Works of the Right Honourable Edmund Burke*, 9 vols. (London: Henry G. Bohn, 1854–62), I:464. Subsequent references to this collection will be given as *Works*, Bohn.

French citizen. To Burke, every principle such as liberty must be *mediated* by actual practices. To put it another way, a spiritual truth becomes real only insofar as it becomes flesh. By contrast, the revolutionary finds that the limitations of the flesh enchain the spirit, and he therefore attempts to strip away appearances—conventions, habits, prejudices, customs, and traditions—in order to recover the essential reality beneath them, as Jeffrey Hart has explained.[5] The spirit of revolutionary liberty is disembodied, and pervades an international atmosphere, inspiring universal movements now in one place, now in another, requiring universal declarations of the rights of man now in one time, now in another. Bodies, whether they are legislatures, churches, families, or individual persons, are merely accidental. Indeed, they have always been, throughout history, the limiting factor in the revolutionary's achievement of his goals. The revolutionary envisions an immediate liberty with no social institutions outside the self to limit his freedoms.

Burke never believed that the achievement of liberty, in historical time, could enable men somehow to transcend their human nature. The sort of liberty he envisioned enables men to realize their nature to the imperfect degree that it is possible on earth, but not to overcome their natural limitations. The paradoxical truth is that those fleshly limitations, especially as they are mediated by the artificial institutions of society, are the very means by which men achieve such liberty as they can. "Art is man's nature," writes Burke in *An Appeal*. In contrast to the sentimental French citizen, who saw art as opposed to nature, Burke writes:

> The state of civil society . . . is a state of nature; and much more truly so than a savage and incoherent mode of life. For man is by nature reasonable; and he is never perfectly in his natural state, but when he is placed where reason may be best cultivated, and most predominates. Art is man's nature. We are as much, at least, in a state of nature in formed manhood, as in immature and helpless infancy. [p. 168]

Burke had argued against the revolutionary notion of a "natural society"—a society constructed with reference to an *im*mediate "nature" and without reference to the actual practices of govern-

5 Jeffrey Hart, *Acts of Recovery* (Hanover, N.H.: University Press of New England, 1989), pp. 228-232.

ment—ever since his first published work, the satirical *Vindication of Natural Society* (1756).

The belief that our liberties must be mediated to be enjoyed has consequences for both the individual and the corporate construction of freedom. In the earliest work printed here, the letter to Depont, Burke lays out the conditions for judging when a nation has achieved a "real *practical* liberty, with a government powerful to protect, [and] impotent to evade it. . ." (p. 11; Burke's emphasis). He does not believe these conditions preclude a strong government, as Schama believes they did in France. On the contrary, practical liberty requires strong government. The individual, Burke writes, needs security of property, a free market for labor, freedom from confiscatory taxation, and freedom of expression. The corporate body, the state, needs a constitution which affirms the rule of law according to precedent, administers equal justice by an independent judiciary, gives control of the armed forces to a freely chosen legislative body, and provides for the security of ancient, prescriptive rights.

Toward the end of the letter to Depont, Burke begins to develop another individual precondition for practical liberty: virtue. The pursuit of virtue is what Burke means by "education" in the widest sense. In *Letter to William Elliot*, Burke says that the educated gentleman would not use his freedom as a pretext for throwing off morality (p. 274). Rather, morality and liberty are dependent upon each other, as he explains in yet another text:

> Men are qualified for civil liberty, in exact proportion to their disposition to put moral chains upon their own appetites. . . . Society cannot exist unless a controlling power upon will and appetite be placed somewhere, and the less of it there is within, the more there must be without. It is ordained in the eternal constitution of things, that men of intemperate minds cannot be free. Their passions forge their fetters. [*A Letter to a Member of the National Assembly,* p. 69]

As Burke well knew, the literary culture preceding the Revolution rejected as stultifying or unnatural, artificial or scholastic, the kind of moral reasoning he recommended. He knew that passion—whether the romantic passion of Rousseau's *La Nouvelle Héloïse* or the political passion of the revolutionary—was thought to justify itself by its own intensity and sincerity. The sympathies elicited by

FOREWORD

Rousseau's novel and his other works, especially *Emile* and the *Confessions*, were, again, very different from those that Burke considered necessary to an educated gentleman, and he profoundly disagreed with a revolutionary education. Yet it would be a mistake to suppose that while the revolutionary citizen preferred the heart to the head, the Burkean gentleman preferred the head to the heart. In *Letter to Philip Francis*, where Burke responds to the criticism that his famous remembrance of the Queen of France is "pure foppery" and that her moral failings made her unworthy of Burke's attention, he protests that Francis's "natural sympathies" are disordered:

> What! Are not high rank, great splendour of descent, great personal elegance and outward accomplishments, ingredients of moment in forming the interest we take in the misfortunes of men? The minds of those who do not feel thus, are not even systematically right. "What's Hecuba to him, or he to Hecuba, that he should weep for her?" Why, because she was Hecuba, the queen of Troy, the wife of Priam, and suffered, in the close of life, a thousand calamities! I felt too for Hecuba, when I read the fine tragedy of Euripides upon her story. . . . [p. 23]

An education in Shakespeare and Euripides, Burke implies, teaches one how to feel for a queen. This is not to say, however, that all feeling is good, regardless of its object; Burke's opponents would be more likely to maintain that view. He maintains his preoccupation with the gentleman's proper mode of feeling from the first to the last in this volume, concluding *A Letter to a Noble Lord* with a meditation on how one of his friends would have felt, in 1796, had he witnessed the Revolution.

The debilitating effect of *false* sympathy, created by a misguided education, is explained in *A Letter to a Member of the National Assembly*. Burke warns against the Assembly's "scheme of educating the rising generation, the principles which they intend to instil, and the sympathies which they wish to form in the mind, at the season in which it is the most susceptible. . . . Rousseau is their canon of holy writ; in his life he is their canon of *Polycletus*; he is their standard figure of perfection" (pp. 46–47). The "natural" education of Emile and of Julie (in *La Nouvelle Héloïse*) removes them from a sympathy with their families and previous social relations. Reflecting on Julie's illicit passion for her tutor, Saint-Preux, which commanded the sympathies of Rousseau's readers, Burke comments, "That no means may exist of confederating against their tyranny, by the false sympathies of this Nouvelle Eloise, they endeavour to subvert those principles of domestic trust and fidelity, which form the discipline of social life" (p. 54).

Burke had already written in the *Reflections* that "[w]e begin our public affections in our families. No cold relation is a zealous citizen."[6] By sending out their children to the Foundling Hospital and refusing to form a family, that most demanding and rewarding of all social relations, Rousseau and his mistress became for Burke the very antithesis of society's guardians. The Rousseauian education, charges Burke, teaches "[b]enevolence to the whole species, and want of feeling for every individual. . . ." The revolutionary citizen is prepared to exercise compassion among the liberated, universal masses, but as to individual Frenchmen, particularly family and neighbors, that's quite a different story. Beginning with the repudiation of actual family relations that should (according to the ancients quoted in *A Letter to a Member*) naturally elicit one's sympathies, the modern, revolutionary citizen ends with nothing more than a promise of redirecting his sympathies toward an abstract concept: the masses. By re-educating his sympathies away from the traditional and the familial, the habitual and the customary, the revolutionary citizen "liberated" himself from the very circumstances in which most ordinary citizens enjoyed their liberty.

One final contrast between the education of the gentleman and that of the citizen, with large consequences for the constitutional Parliamentarian, as against the passionate revolutionary, has to do with their attitudes about the past. Burke, like many of the great British writers of the eighteenth century, was profoundly skeptical of the Enlightenment and its claim to a moral and political wisdom greater than that of the ancients. "The author of the Reflections has *heard* a great deal concerning the modern lights," writes Burke of himself, "but he has not yet had the good fortune to *see* much of them. . . . Where the old authors whom he has read, and the old men whom he has conversed with, have left him in the dark, he is in the dark still" (p. 147).

Burke's strategy—which we may call a "useful fiction," as long as we recall that the deepest truths are often conveyed by fiction—is to discover modern advances latent in the wisdom of the ancients.

[6] *Reflections*, p. 315.

Burke is confident, for instance, that the constitutional settlement of the Glorious Revolution (1688–89) was a reassertion of *ancient* laws and that the Bill of Rights (1689) was merely declarative of pre-existing liberties and rights. To Thomas Paine, who in this respect may serve as a model for the revolutionary citizen, Burke's "referring to musty records and moldy parchments" was beneath contempt.

In *An Appeal*, Burke pleaded guilty as charged: "It is current that these old politicians [at the time of the Glorious Revolution] knew little of the rights of men; that they lost their way by groping about in the dark, and fumbling among rotten parchments and musty records" (p. 147). Not only does Burke argue that the ancients' understanding of liberty was superior to Paine's, he finds that they anticipated modern *errors* as well. He discovers in ancient (and medieval) letters the very categories of the revolutionary rhetoric of liberty that the moderns mistakenly believe they have invented. He continues by comparing the language of Paine with that of John Ball, a leader in the Peasant Revolt in 1381, and he quotes Tacitus on the Germans' invasion of the Gallic provinces: the invaders used the cant of liberty, but their real motives for war were lust, avarice, and a wish to leave their homes. The ancients, Burke suggests, can teach us to distinguish practical from revolutionary liberty.

The dispute between ancients and moderns is a clear case of an individual matter—education—with corporate consequences. Burke expounds these consequences in *Letter to William Elliot*, where he calls for a new Maccabeus to "assert the honor of the antient law." Also, in *Letter to a Member*, he marshals the authority of Juvenal and Cicero in his dispute with Rousseau over "natural" affections (pp. 50–51). In *Thoughts on French Affairs*, Burke refers with horror to the offer of Condorcet to serve as the dauphin's tutor. A year later, Condorcet's Report on Education (April 1792) would conclude that a profound knowledge of Greek and Latin was too difficult to attain to justify it as a goal for the French citizen, that classical literature was "full of errors," that the citizen's education should be secular, and that the teaching of moral principles was to be derived directly from natural sentiment and reason, rather than mediated by religion.

Burke, by contrast, argues that for a man to be free from the fear of any earthly master, he needs to learn to fear God. The alliance between liberty and piety is thus fundamental: "[Despots]

know," he writes in *A Letter to a Member*, "that he who fears God fears
nothing else; and therefore they eradicate from the mind, through
their Voltaire, their Helvetius, and the rest of that infamous gang,
that only sort of fear which generates true courage. Their object is,
that their fellow citizens may be under the dominion of no awe, but
that of their committee of research, and of their lanterne" (p. 55).
Condorcet's goal for education was to form citizens who were free,
equal, and serviceable to the *Patrie*. The older ideal of the gentleman is, ironically, more individual and, submitting to instruction
from Greeks and Romans, Jews and Christians, more cosmopoli-
tan. Contradictory as it may seem, Burke suggests that English liberty requires gentlemen whose education is decidedly "non-En-
glish": their natural sympathies for English authors can be
assumed, but their sympathies for others separated by great dis-
tances of time and space must be cultivated.

After education, perhaps the clearest link between the individual and the corporate requirements for practical liberty is property.
Of all the institutions that mediate between the British Constitution
and the British gentleman, property and property rights summon
up a number of Burke's most characteristic images and deepest
thoughts.

Burke maintains that the security of property, especially landed property passed down through generations, is essential to a free
people. The security of property does not guarantee liberty, but it
serves as a precondition for liberty. For instance, Burke invites his
opponents to reflect whether "under that domination [of the
French absolute monarchs], though personal liberty has been precarious and insecure, property at least was ever violated." Property
seems to be a necessary, though not sufficient, characteristic of a
free society.

In Burke's thought, the propertied classes are represented by
the Whig grandees of the Glorious Revolution and the rest of the
landed gentry. Why are English liberties safer with propertied men
as leaders, rather than with unpropertied men? Propertied men are
not desperate men, as Harvey Mansfield comments, and their political ambitions are therefore somewhat more limited and trustwor-
thy than those of unpropertied, politically ambitious ideologues.[7]

---

[7] Harvey Mansfield, *Statesmanship and Party Government: A Study of Burke and
Bolingbroke* (Chicago: University of Chicago Press, 1965), p. 185.

FOREWORD

"We know that parties must ever exist in a free country," Burke says in *A Speech on Conciliation*.[8] The Constitution could safely incorporate party government, Burke thought, if party leaders were drawn from the landed gentry, because they would be as careful of constitutional rights as they were of their own property rights.

In addition to security of property, Burke believed that practical, constitutional liberty required that a free people be led by a "natural aristocracy"—a term that seems intentionally to contrast with "hereditary aristocracy." Burke's later works defended the constitutional rights of hereditary aristocrats, who made up the House of Lords, even though he trusted them less than he did the landed gentry. In the final two works printed here, Burke delights in the irony of a commoner defending noblemen whose radical sentiments would overthrow their own rights. In 1795, he wrote *Letter to William Elliot* in response to an attack by the Duke of Norfolk, earl marshal of England and the eighth-ranking nobleman in the land. That work was but a trial run, however, for *A Letter to a Noble Lord*, a withering response to the Duke of Bedford and Earl of Lauderdale, who had attacked Burke's pension. "These noble persons," Burke replies with scorn, "have lost no time in conferring upon me, that sort of honour, which it is alone within their competence, and which it is certainly most congenial to their nature and their manners to bestow" (p. 279). Despite his disdain for these aristocrats, particularly for their delusive self-images as radicals, Burke describes the leaders needed by a free people as a natural aristocracy. Here, the connection between the individual and corporate requirements of practical liberty is again very close, and it explains the prerequisites necessary for the individual to be "naturally" suited for political leadership:

> To be bred in a place of estimation; To see nothing low and sordid from one's infancy; To be taught to respect one's self; To be habituated to the censorial inspection of the public eye; To look early to public opinion . . . To have leisure to read, to reflect, to converse; To be enabled to draw the court and attention of the wise and learned wherever they are to be found . . . To be taught to despise danger in the pursuit of honour and duty . . . These are the circumstances of men, that form what I should call a *natural* aristocracy, without which there is no nation. [*An Appeal*, p. 168]

[8] *Works*, Bohn, I:506.

Foreword

For a nation to maintain that it protects and enjoys liberty, it must be so constituted as to cultivate a natural aristocracy for its ruling class. This natural aristocracy is inseparable from the state, he says: "It is the soul to the body, without which the man does not exist." Only a nation that functions under its direction, Burke believes, deserves to be called "a people." A people is therefore neither the revolutionary mob addressed by John Ball, nor the counter-revolutionary mob that burned the home of Burke's opponent, Joseph Priestley, nor any "majority of men, told by the head." "The idea of a people is the idea of a corporation. It is wholly artificial"—just as, one might add, all of society is artificial (p. 163). Burke's natural aristocracy, which itself depends upon the artificial structures of a civilization, becomes the crucial term in his definition of a people: "When great multitudes act together, under *that discipline of nature*, I recognize the PEOPLE" (p. 169, italics added). "That discipline" is the direction of the multitudes by the natural aristocracy. Apparently, then, a merely hereditary, wealthy aristocracy does not lead to a virtuous liberty any more certainly than, as Burke recognized, a good education does. It is a help, like a good education, but not a guarantee. "Aristocrat" becomes, in Burke's language, a designation for the virtuous gentleman.

Burke finds an analogy for the political rights enjoyed under the British Constitution in the rights that accrue over time to the uncontested holders of lands—"prescriptive" rights. Whereas the revolutionary desires an *im*mediate enjoyment of his liberty and submits to a government only upon sufferance, Burke believed that liberty, proceeding from God as natural law, is mediated through the established, prescriptive laws, usages, and customs of a people. Property rights are the outward and most visible manifestation of prescriptive rights.

The origins of property rights, like the origins of virtually every historical government, are shrouded in antiquity and even rooted in injustice. They cannot survive revolutionaries' continual questions concerning the legitimacy of their authority, especially if the revolutionaries suppose that the only legitimacy comes from the simple majority of a people at any given moment. But if, over time, a government fulfills the purposes of civil society—namely, the development of man's moral and reasonable nature—then the government (like the property holder) acquires a prescriptive authority. By the same token, the citizens of that land acquire all the rights that have accrued to them over time, through custom, legal precedent, royal charter, and Parliamentary law.

If the defender of revolutionary liberty finds this explanation of prescriptive rights unconvincing, Burke invites him to consider the ultimate consequences of his own argument: "Who are they who claim [land] by prescription and descent from certain gangs of banditti called Franks," he asks of the revolutionaries, ". . . whilst at the very time they tell me, that prescription and long possession form no title to property?" (p. 166). Were he to nullify the force of prescriptive law, the citizen would nullify his right to his own land and citizenship in France. The rotten parchments and musty records of the statute books, which guarantee property and prescriptive rights, arouse Burke's imagination as much as natural right arouses Thomas Paine's. Against the natural rights asserted to be the foundation of revolutionary liberty, Burke defended prescriptive rights, found in actual statutes and sanctioned by custom, as the best guarantee for a just, constitutional liberty. Burke "is resolved not 'to be wise beyond what is written' in the legislative record and practice; that when doubts arise on them, he endeavours to interpret one statute by another; and to reconcile them all to established recognized morals, and to the general antient known policy of the laws of England" (p. 134). The object of this submission to precedent is not legalism, but liberty. "They did not wish," writes Burke of the Rockingham Whigs, "that Liberty, in itself one of the first of blessings, should in it's perversion become the greatest curse which could fall upon mankind. To preserve the Constitution entire, . . . in all it's parts, was to them the first object" (p. 287). Burke knew that the inchoate tyrant begins by asserting an "extravagant liberty" against existing, repressive laws, and ends by ruling for his own pleasure (p. 119). The language of the statute books is not extravagant, but what it obtains, it keeps. The rotten parchments cannot compete with the promises of revolutionary liberty, but duly constituted courts guarantee what the tribunal must put off until the revolution is finally over.

The system of practices which govern the citizen and regulate Britain's mixed government of Kings, Lords, and Commons Burke calls the Constitution. Its prescriptions are authoritative, regardless of what a simple majority of persons living in England at any given time may think. The Constitution will change over time, as all living systems change, but its changes will come from its internal life and not, to repeat, from being acted upon by a majority maintaining that majority dictates alone possess legitimacy.

In Burke's view of practical liberty, the Constitution is where one must seek a resolution of the tension between principle and actuality. Or, rather, it is where one must seek a paradox at its most intense, as when Burke merges Windsor Castle with the Temple of Jerusalem as a symbol for the Constitution:

> But as to *our* country and *our* race, as long as the well compacted structure of our church and state, the sanctuary, the holy of holies of that ancient law, defended by reverence, defended by power, a fortress at once and a temple, shall stand inviolate on the brow of the British Sion—as long as the British Monarchy, not more limited than fenced by the orders of the State, shall, like the proud Keep of Windsor . . . oversee and guard the subjected land . . . [a]s long as our Sovereign Lord the King, and his faithful subjects, the Lords and Commons of this realm, the triple cord, which no man can break; the solemn, sworn, constitutional frank-pledge of this nation . . . [a]s long as these endure, so long the Duke of Bedford is safe: and we are all safe together. . . . [*Letter to a Noble Lord*, p. 310]

Burke is symbolizing the Constitution as Coleridge defines "symbol": the Constitution/Temple/Castle is characterized by the "translucence of the Eternal through and in the Temporal. It always partakes of the Reality which it renders intelligible. . . ."9 The individual elements of the nation (King, Lords, Commons) participate in the unity of the Constitution without losing their identity. Or, as Coleridge said of Burke's metaphorical language in another place, this language expresses "meaning, image, and passion *triunely*."10 Here, in Burke's example, one sees the merging of meaning and image, of ideal and concrete. There is always something beyond—in this example, the Sion that is not merely British. Yet Burke also leaves the reader whose sympathies derive from a Burkean rather than a Rousseauian education with the conviction

9 Samuel Taylor Coleridge, *The Statesman's Manual*, ed. E.R. White, in *The Collected Works of Samuel Taylor Coleridge*, 16 vols., ed. Kathleen Coburn, et al. (Princeton: Princeton University Press, 1969–), VI:30.

10 Samuel Taylor Coleridge, *The Notebooks of Samuel Taylor Coleridge*, 3 vols., ed. Kathleen Coburn (New York: Pantheon, 1957), III:2431f4. The quotation is from 1805, only nine years after Burke's words were written. The emphasis is Coleridge's.

that he has participated in a union of the spirit and the flesh, liberated within history to the highest degree possible.

Nothing in Burke is immediate. The experience of liberty is not the immediate one that the revolutionary citizen wishes for. Practical liberty is mediated through a Constitution, which *A Letter to a Noble Lord* represents by the mediating symbols of Windsor Castle and the Temple. Nature is mediated through art, natural law through social institutions, the acts of a people through the leadership of a natural aristocracy. Burke's view of practical liberty is complex, but its complexities are those of human life. Its satisfactions are limited, but its limitations are those of human life as well.

DANIEL E. RITCHIE
Bethel College

EDITOR'S NOTE

Regarding the texts used for this edition, the letters to Charles-Jean-François Depont and Philip Francis come from *Correspondence of the Right Honourable Edmund Burke between the Year 1744, and the Period of his Decease, in 1797*, eds. Charles William Wentworth-Fitzwilliam, 5th Earl Fitzwilliam, and Sir Richard Bourke, 4 vols. London: Francis and John Rivington, 1844. They have been compared with the Copeland edition of Burke's *Correspondence*. The other texts have been chosen in accordance with William B. Todd's *Bibliography of Edmund Burke* (London: Rupert Hart-Davis, 1964) to represent the most authoritative version of each work.

The text of *A Letter to a Member of the National Assembly* is that of the first impression of the first English edition on 21 May 1791.

The text of *An Appeal from the New to the Old Whigs*, first published on 3 August 1791, comes from the fourth impression of the first edition.

Thoughts on French Affairs, written in December 1791, comes from the first impression of the first edition, published on 7 September 1797, in *Three Memorials on French Affairs*.

Letter to William Elliot, dated 26 May 1795, comes from the first impression of the first edition of *Two Letters on the Conduct of Our Domestick Parties, With Regard to French Politicks*, published on 31 October 1797.

The text of *A Letter to a Noble Lord*, first published on 24 February 1796, comes from the thirteenth impression.

Minor errors of spelling have been silently corrected, although the eighteenth-century orthography of the texts has been preserved. One or two minor doubtful readings have been revised for greater clarity, in accordance with the Bohn and Oxford editions, and other variants have been compared. Burke's eighteenth-century Greek has been modernized. Quotation marks surround translations from Latin if the quote is direct or fairly direct; quotation marks do not surround translations of proverbial Latin sayings and very indirect (or untraceable) Latin quotations. The editor's foot-

EDITOR'S NOTE

notes are bracketed to distinguish them from Burke's, which have all been retained.

I wish to express appreciation to the staffs of the Beinecke Rare Book Room at the Yale University Library and of the Boston Athenaeum for providing the needed texts. Professor Jeremiah Reedy of Macalester College provided the long translation from Walsingham in *An Appeal from the New to the Old Whigs* and gave useful advice on many of the Latin translations.

Burke scholars will recognize the influence of Francis Canavan and Peter Stanlis in my Foreword, and to them I express gratitude.

This book is dedicated to my wife, Judith C. Ritchie:

> *Esse sacerdotes delubraque vestra tueri*
> *Poscimus; et quoniam concordes egimus annos,*
> *Auferat hora duos eadem, nec conjugis unquam*
> *Busta meae videam, neu sim tumulandus ab illa.*

LIST OF SHORT TITLES

Works, Bohn

The Works of the Right Honourable Edmund Burke. 9 vols. London: Henry G. Bohn, 1854–62.

Corr., Copeland

Copeland, Thomas W., et al., eds. *The Correspondence of Edmund Burke.* 10 vols. Chicago and Cambridge: Chicago and Cambridge University Presses, 1958–78.

Corr., 1844

Burke, Edmund. *Correspondence of the Right Honourable Edmund Burke between the Year 1744, and the Period of his Decease, in 1797,* eds. Charles William Wentworth-Fitzwilliam, 5th Earl Fitzwilliam, and Sir Richard Bourke. 4 vols. London: Francis and John Rivington, 1844.

Parliamentary Register

Parliamentary Register: of History of the Proceedings and Debates of the House of Commons (and House of Lords) . . . , 112 vols., London, 1775–1813.

Parliamentary History

The Parliamentary History of England from the Norman Conquest in 1066 to the year 1803, ed. W. Cobbett. 36 vols. London: 1806–20.

Reflections

O'Brien, Conor Cruise, ed. *Reflections on the Revolution in France.* Harmondsworth: Penguin, 1968.

Writings and Speeches

Langford, Paul, et al., eds. *The Writings and Speeches of Edmund Burke.* 12 vols. Oxford: Clarendon Press, 1981–.

FURTHER REFLECTIONS
ON THE REVOLUTION IN FRANCE

1

LETTER TO CHARLES-JEAN-FRANÇOIS DEPONT

November 1789

*E*dmund *Burke's letter to Charles-Jean-François Depont (1767–1796) is his first extensive analysis of the French Revolution. Written just four months after the fall of the Bastille, when many Englishmen were uncertain in their opinions of the events in France, the letter is striking for the certainty of its judgments. Burke did not send this letter immediately, for he believed it might endanger Depont, but the young Frenchman continued to urge Burke to send his views of the Revolution (Corr. Copeland 6:59-61). Burke probably sent the letter below in early 1790. Burke's more important, much longer* Reflections on the Revolution in France *also takes the form of a letter to Depont. In its language and in its themes of constitutional government, prudence, and abstract versus "practical" liberty, the letter below is in some respects an early draft of the* Reflections.

The date of this letter is supplied by Alfred Cobban and Robert A. Smith, editors of volume six of the Copeland edition of the Correspondence.

LETTER TO CHARLES-JEAN-FRANÇOIS DEPONT

November 1789

DEAR SIR,

We are extremely happy in your giving us leave to promise ourselves a renewal of the pleasure we formerly had in your company at Beconsfield[1] and in London. It was too lively to be speedily forgotten on our part; and we are highly flattered to find that you keep so exactly in your memory all the particulars of the few attentions which you were so good to accept from us during your stay in England. We indulge ourselves in the hope that you will be able to execute what you intend in our favour; and that we shall be more fortunate in the coming spring, than we were in the last.

You have reason to imagine that I have not been as early as I ought, in acquainting you with my thankful acceptance of the correspondence you have been pleased to offer. Do not think me insensible to the honour you have done me. I confess I did hesitate for a time, on a doubt, whether it would be prudent to yield to my earnest desire of such a correspondence.

Your frank and ingenuous manner of writing would be ill answered by a cold, dry, and guarded reserve on my part. It would, indeed, be adverse to my habits and my nature, to

---

[1] [Burke's home was located about a mile from the small village of Beconsfield, or Beaconsfield. Depont had visited the Burkes in 1785.]

LETTER TO CHARLES-JEAN-FRANÇOIS DEPONT

make use of that sort of caution in my intercourse with any friend. Besides, as you are pleased to think that your splendid flame of liberty was first lighted up at my faint and glimmering taper, I thought you had a right to call upon me for my undisguised sentiments on whatever related to that subject. On the other hand, I was not without apprehension, that in this free mode of intercourse I might say something, not only disagreeable to your formed opinions upon points on which, of all others, we are most impatient of contradiction, but not pleasing to the power which should happen to be prevalent at the time of your receiving my letter. I was well aware that, in seasons of jealousy, suspicion is vigilant and active; that it is not extremely scrupulous in its means of inquiry; not perfectly equitable in its judgments; and not altogether deliberate in its resolutions. In the ill-connected and inconclusive logic of the passions, whatever may appear blameable is easily transferred from the guilty writer to the innocent receiver. It is an awkward as well as unpleasant accident; but it is one that has sometimes happened. A man may be made a martyr to tenets the most opposite to his own. At length a friend of mine, lately come from Paris, informed me that heats are beginning to abate, and that intercourse is thought to be more safe. This has given me some courage; and the reflection that the sentiments of a person of no more consideration than I am, either abroad or at home, could be of little consequence to the success of any cause or any party, has at length decided me to accept of the honour you are willing to confer upon me.

You may easily believe, that I have had my eyes turned, with great curiosity, to the astonishing scene now displayed in France. It has certainly given rise in my mind to many reflections, and to some emotions. These are natural and unavoidable; but it would ill become me to be too ready in forming a positive opinion upon matters transacted in a country, with the correct political map of which I must be very imperfectly acquainted. Things, indeed, have already happened so much beyond the scope of all speculation, that persons of infinitely more sagacity than I am, ought to be ashamed of any thing like confidence in their reasoning upon the operation of any principle, or the effect of any measure. It would become me, least of all, to be so confident, who ought, at my time of life, to have well learned the important lesson of self-distrust, a lesson of no small value in company with the best information, but which alone can make any sort of amends for our not having learned other lessons so well as it was our business to learn them. I beg you, once for all, to apply this corrective of the diffidence I have, on my own judgment, to whatever I may happen to say with more positiveness than suits my knowledge and situation. If I should seem any where to express myself in the language of disapprobation, be so good as to consider it as no more than the expression of doubt.

You hope, sir, that I think the French deserving of liberty. I certainly do. I certainly think that all men who desire it, deserve it. It is not the reward of our merit, or the acquisition of our industry. It is our inheritance. It is the birthright of our species. We cannot forfeit our right to it, but by what forfeits our title to the privileges of our kind. I mean the abuse, or oblivion, of our rational faculties, and a ferocious indocility which makes us prompt to wrong and violence, destroys our social nature, and transforms us into something little better than the description of wild beasts. To men so degraded, a state of strong constraint is a sort of necessary substitute for freedom; since, bad as it is, it may deliver them in some measure from the worst of all slavery—that is, the despotism of their own blind and brutal passions.

You have kindly said, that you began to love freedom from your intercourse with me. Permit me then to continue our conversation, and to tell you what the freedom is that I love, and that to which I think all men entitled. This is the more necessary, because, of all the loose terms in the world, liberty is the most indefinite. It is not solitary, unconnected, individual, selfish liberty, as if every man was to regulate the whole of his conduct by his own will. The liberty I mean is *social* freedom. It is that state of things in which liberty is secured by the equality of restraint. A constitution of things in which the liberty of no one man, and no body of men, and no number of men, can find means to trespass on the liberty of any person, or any description of persons, in the society. This kind of liberty is, indeed, but another name for justice; ascertained by wise laws, and secured by well-constructed institutions. I am sure that liberty, so incorporated, and in a manner identified with justice, must be infinitely dear to every one who is capable of conceiving what it is. But whenever a separation is made between liberty and justice, neither is, in my opinion, safe. I do not believe that men ever did submit, certain I am that they never ought to have submitted, to the arbitrary pleasure of one man; but, under circumstances in which the arbitrary pleasure of many persons in the community pressed with an intolerable hardship upon the just and equal rights of their fellows, such a choice might be made, as among evils. The moment *will* is set above reason and justice, in any community, a great question may arise in sober minds, in what part or portion of the community that dangerous dominion of *will* may be the least mischievously placed.

If I think all men who cultivate justice, entitled to liberty, and, when joined in states, entitled to a constitution framed to perpetuate and secure it, you may be assured, sir, that I think your countrymen eminently worthy of a blessing which is peculiarly adapted to noble, generous, and humane natures. Such I found the French, when, more than fifteen years ago, I had the happiness, though but for too short a time, of visiting your country; and I trust their character is not altered since that period.

I have nothing to check my wishes towards the establishment of a solid and rational scheme of liberty in France. On the subject of the relative power of nations, I may have my prejudices; but I envy internal freedom, security, and good order, to none. When, therefore, I shall learn that, in France, the citizen, by whatever description he is qualified, is in a perfect state of legal security, with regard to his life, to his property, to the uncontrolled disposal of his person, to the free use of his industry and his faculties: When I hear that he is protected in the beneficial enjoyment of the estates to which, by the course of settled law, he was born, or is provided with a fair compensation for them; that he is maintained in the full fruition of the advantages belonging to the state and condition of life in which he had lawfully engaged himself, or is supplied with a substantial, equitable, equivalent: When I am assured that a simple citizen may decently express his sentiments upon public affairs, without hazard to his life or safety, even though against a predominant and fashionable opinion: When I know all this of France, I shall be as well pleased as every one must be, who has not forgot the general communion of mankind, nor lost his natural sympathy, in local and accidental connexions.

If a constitution is settled in France upon those principles, and calculated for those ends, I believe there is no man in this country whose heart and voice would not go along with you. I am sure it will give me, for one, a heartfelt pleasure when I hear that, in France, the great public assemblies, the natural securities for individual freedom, are perfectly free themselves; when there can be no suspicion that they are under the coercion of a military power of any description; when it may be truly said, that no armed force can be seen, which is not called into existence by their creative voice, and which must not instantly disappear at their dissolving word; when such assemblies, after being freely chosen, shall proceed with the weight of magistracy, and not with the arts of candidates; when they do not find themselves under the necessity of feeding one part of the community at the grievous charge of other parts, as necessitous as those who are so fed; when they are not obliged (in order to flatter those who have their lives in their disposal) to tolerate acts of doubtful influence on commerce and on agriculture; and for the sake of a precarious relief, under temporary scarcity, to sow (if I may be allowed the expression) the seeds of lasting want; when they are not compelled daily to stimulate an irregular and juvenile imagination for supplies, which they are not in a condition firmly to demand; when they are not obliged to diet the state from

LETTER TO CHARLES-JEAN-FRANÇOIS DEPONT

hand to mouth, upon the casual alms of choice, fancy, vanity, or caprice, on which plan the value of the object to the public which receives, often bears no sort of proportion to the loss of the individual who gives; when they are not necessitated to call for contributions to be estimated on the conscience of the contributor, by which the most pernicious sorts of exemptions and immunities may be established, by which virtue is taxed and vice privileged, and honour and public spirit are obliged to bear the burdens of craft, selfishness, and avarice; when they shall not be driven to be the instruments of the violence of others from a sense of their own weakness, and from a want of authority to assess equal and proportioned charges upon all, they are not compelled to lay a strong hand upon the possessions of a part; when, under the exigencies of the state (aggravated, if not caused, by the imbecility of their own government, and of all government), they are not obliged to resort to *confiscation* to supply the defect of *taxation*, and thereby to hold out a pernicious example, to teach the different descriptions of the community to prey upon one another; when they abstain religiously from all general and extra-judicial declarations concerning the property of the subject; when they look with horror upon all arbitrary decisions in their legislative capacity, striking at prescriptive right, long undisturbed possession, opposing an uninterrupted stream of regular judicial determinations, by which sort of decisions they are conscious no man's possession could be safe, and individual property, to the very idea, would be extinguished; when I see your great sovereign bodies, your now supreme power, in this condition of deliberative freedom, and guided by these or similar principles in acting and forbearing, I shall be happy to behold in assemblies whose name is venerable to my understanding and dear to my heart, an authority, a dignity, a moderation, which, in all countries and governments, ought ever to accompany the collected reason and representative majesty of the commonwealth.

I shall rejoice no less in seeing a judicial power established in France, correspondent to such a legislature as I have presumed to hint at, and worthy to second it in its endeavours to secure the freedom and property of the subject. When your courts of justice shall obtain an ascertained condition, before they are made to decide on the condition of other men; when they shall not be called upon to take cognizance of public offences, whilst they themselves are considered only to exist as a tolerated abuse; when, under doubts of the legality of their rules of decision, their forms and modes of proceeding, and even of the validity of that system of authority to which they owe their existence; when, amidst circumstances of suspense, fear, and humiliation, they shall not be put to judge on the lives, liberties, properties, or estimation of their fellow-citizens; when they are not called upon to put any man to his trial upon undefined crimes of state, not ascertained by any previous rule, statute, or course of precedent; when victims shall not be snatched from the fury of the people, to be brought before a tribunal, itself subject to the effects of the same fury, and where the acquittal of the parties accused, might only place the judge in the situation of the criminal; when I see tribunals placed in this state of independence of every thing but law, and with a clear law for their direction, as a true lover of equal justice (under the shadow of which alone true liberty can live), I shall rejoice in seeing such a happy order established in France, as much as I do in my consciousness that an order of the same kind, or one not very remote from it, has been long settled, and I hope on a firm foundation, in England. I am not so narrow-minded as to be unable to conceive that the same object may be attained in many ways, and perhaps in ways very different from those which we have followed in this country. If this real *practical* liberty, with a government powerful to protect, impotent to evade it, be established, or is in a fair train of being established in the democracy, or rather collection of democracies, which seem to be chosen for the future frame of society in France, it is not my having long enjoyed a sober share of freedom, under a qualified monarchy, that shall render me incapable of admiring and praising your system of republics. I should rejoice, even though England should hereafter be reckoned only as one among the happy nations, and should no longer retain her proud distinction, her monopoly of fame for a practical constitution, in which the grand secret had been found, of reconciling a government of real energy for all foreign and all domestic purposes, with the most perfect security to the liberty and safety of individuals. The government, whatever its name or form may be, that shall be found substantially and practically to unite these advantages, will most merit the applause of all discerning men.

But if (for in my present want of information I must only speak hypothetically) neither your great assemblies, nor your judicatures, nor your municipalities, act, and forbear to act, in the particulars, upon the principles, and in the spirit that I have stated, I must delay my congratulations on your acquisition of liberty. You may have made a revolution, but not a reformation. You may have subverted monarchy, but not recovered freedom.

You see, sir, that I have merely confined myself in my few observations on what has been done and is doing in France, to the topics of the liberty, property, and safety of the subjects. I have not said much on the influence of the present measures upon your country, as a state. It is not my business, as a citizen of the world; and it is unnecessary to take up much time about it, as it is sufficiently visible.

You are now to live in a new order of things, under a plan of government of which no man can speak from experience. Your talents, your public spirit, and your fortune, give you fair pretensions to a considerable share in it. Your settlement may be at hand; but that it is still at some distance, is more likely. The French may be yet to go through more transmigrations. They may pass, as one of our poets says, "through many varieties of untried being,"[2] before their state obtains its

---

[2] [Joseph Addison, *Cato*, V.i.11:

Through what variety of untried being,
Through what new scenes and changes must we pass!]

final form. In that progress through chaos and darkness, you will find it necessary (at all times it is more or less so) to fix rules to keep your life and conduct in some steady course. You have theories enough concerning the rights of men; it may not be amiss to add a small degree of attention to their nature and disposition. It is with man in the concrete; it is with common human life, and human actions, you are to be concerned. I have taken so many liberties with you, that I am almost got the length of venturing to suggest something which may appear in the assuming tone of advice. You will, however, be so good as to receive my very few hints with your usual indulgence, though some of them, I confess, are not in the taste of this enlightened age; and, indeed, are no better than the late ripe fruit of mere experience. Never wholly separate in your mind the merits of any political question, from the men who are concerned in it. You will be told, that if a measure is good, what have you to do with the character and views of those who bring it forward. But designing men never separate their plans from their interests; and, if you assist them in their schemes, you will find the pretended good, in the end, thrown aside or perverted, and the interested object alone compassed, and that, perhaps, through your means. The power of bad men is no indifferent thing.

At this moment you may not perceive the full sense of this rule; but you will recollect it when the cases are before you; you will then see and find its use. It will often keep your virtue from becoming a tool of the ambition and ill designs of others. Let me add what I think has some connexion with the rule I mentioned, that you ought not to be so fond of any political object, as not to think the means of compassing it a serious consideration. No man is less disposed than I am to put you under the tuition of a petty pedantic scruple, in the management of arduous affairs. All I recommend is, that whenever the sacrifice of any subordinate point of morality, or of honour, or even of common liberal sentiment and feeling is called for, one ought to be tolerably sure that the object is worth it. Nothing is good, but in proportion and with reference. There are several who give an air of consequence to very petty designs and actions, by the crimes through which they make their way to their objects. Whatever is obtained smoothly and by easy means, appears of no value in their eyes. But when violent measures are in agitation, one ought to be pretty clear that there are no others to which we can resort, and that a predilection from character to such methods is not the true cause of their being proposed. The state was reformed by Sylla and by Caesar; but the Cornelian law and the Julian law were not worth the proscription. The pride of the Roman nobility deserved a check; but I cannot, for that reason, admire the conduct of Cinna, and Marius, and Saturninus.[3]

I admit that evils may be so very great and urgent, that other evils are to be submitted to for the mere hope of their removal. A war, for instance, may be necessary, and we know what are the rights of war; but before we use those rights, we ought to be clearly in the state which alone can justify them; and not, in the very fold of peace and security, by a bloody sophistry, to act towards any persons at once as citizens and as enemies, and, without the necessary formalities and evident distinctive lines of war, to exercise upon our countrymen the most dreadful of all hostilities. Strong party contentions, and a very violent opposition to our desires and opinions, are not war, nor can justify any one of its operations.

One form of government may be better than another, and this difference may be worth a struggle. I think so. I do not mean to treat any of those forms which are often the contrivances of deep human wisdom (not the rights of men,

---

[3] [Burke here refers to the "reforms" of Lucius Cornelius Sulla ("Sylla," 138–78 B.C.) and Julius Caesar (100–44 B.C.). The "proscription" refers to Sulla's list of men who were "legally" put to death. The positive good done by Caesar and Sulla was overbalanced by their violent, extra-constitutional methods, a lesson Burke could have inferred from his reading of Plutarch. Cinna, Marius, and Saturninus were contemporaries of Sulla, notable for their opposition to the power of the nobles. Plutarch's treatment of them, however, is characteristically skeptical.]

as some people, in my opinion, not very wisely, talk of them) with slight or disrespect; nor do I mean to level them.

A positively vicious and abusive government ought to be changed—and, if necessary, by violence—if it cannot be (as sometimes it is the case) reformed. But when the question is concerning the more or the less *perfection* in the organization of a government, the allowance to *means* is not of so much latitude. There is, by the essential fundamental constitution of things, a radical infirmity in all human contrivances; and the weakness is often so attached to the very perfection of our political mechanism, that some defect in it—something that stops short of its principle, something that controls, that mitigates, that moderates it—becomes a necessary corrective to the evils that the theoretic perfection would produce. I am pretty sure it often is so; and this truth may be exemplified abundantly.

It is true that every defect is not of course such a corrective as I state; but supposing it is not, an imperfect good is still a good. The defect may be tolerable, and may be removed at some future time. In that case, prudence (in all things a virtue, in politics, the first of virtues) will lead us rather to acquiesce in some qualified plan, that does not come up to the full perfection of the abstract idea, than to push for the more perfect, which cannot be attained without tearing to pieces the whole contexture of the commonwealth, and creating a heart-ache in a thousand worthy bosoms. In that case, combining the means and end, the less perfect is the more desirable. The *means* to any end being first in order, are *immediate* in their good or their evil; they are always, in a manner, *certainties*. The *end* is doubly problematical; first, whether it is to be attained; then, whether, supposing it attained, we obtain the true object we sought for.

But allow it in any degree probable, that theoretic and practical perfection may differ, that an object pure and absolute may not be so good as one lowered, mixed, and qualified; then, what we abate in our demand, in favour of moderation and justice, and tenderness to individuals, would be neither more nor less than a real improvement which a wise legislator would make, if he had no collateral motive whatsoever, and only looked, in the formation of his scheme, to its own independent ends and purposes. Would it then be right to make way, through temerity and crime, to a form of things which, when obtained, evident reason, perhaps imperious necessity, would compel us to alter, with the disgrace of inconsistency in our conduct, and of want of foresight in our designs?

Believe me, sir, in all changes in the state, moderation is a virtue, not only amiable but powerful. It is a disposing, arranging, conciliating, cementing virtue. In the formation of new constitutions, it is in its province. Great powers reside in those who can make great changes. Their own moderation is their only check; and if this virtue is not paramount in their minds, their acts will taste more of their power than of their wisdom, or their benevolence. Whatever they do will be in extremes; it will be crude, harsh, precipitate. It will be submitted to with grudging and reluctance. Revenge will be smothered and hoarded, and the duration of schemes marked in that temper, will be as precarious as their establishment was odious. This virtue of moderation (which times and situations will clearly distinguish from the counterfeits of pusillanimity and indecision) is the virtue only of superior minds. It requires a deep courage, and full of reflection, to be temperate when the voice of multitudes (the specious mimic of fame and reputation) passes judgment against you. The impetuous desire of an unthinking public will endure no course, but what conducts to splendid and perilous extremes. Then, to dare to be fearful, when all about you are full of presumption and confidence, and when those who are bold at the hazard of others would punish your caution and disaffection, is to show a mind prepared for its trial; it discovers, in the midst of general levity, a self-possessing and collected character, which, sooner or later, bids fair to attract every thing to it, as to a centre. If, however, the tempest should prove to be so very violent, that it would make public prudence itself unseasonable, and, therefore, little less than madness for the individual and the public too; perhaps a young man could not do better than to retreat for a while into study, to leave the field to those whose duty or inclination, or the necessities of their condition, have put them in possession of it, and wait for the settlement of such a commonwealth as an honest man may act in with satisfaction and credit. This he can never do when those who counsel the public, or the prince, are under terror, let the authority under which they are made to speak other than the dictates of their conscience, be never so imposing in its name and attributes.

This moderation is no enemy to zeal and enthusiasm. There is room enough for them; for the restraint is no more than the restraint of principle, and the restraint of reason.

I have been led further than I intended; but every day's account shows more and more, in my opinion, the ill-consequence of keeping good principles, and good general views, within no bounds. Pardon the liberty I have taken; though it seems somewhat singular that I, whose opinions have so little weight in my own country, where I have some share in a public trust, should write as if it were possible they should affect one man with regard to affairs in which I have no concern. But, for the present, my time is my own, and to tire your patience is the only injury I can do you.

I am, &c.

EDM. BURKE

2

LETTER TO PHILIP FRANCIS

February 20, 1790

*B*urke grew increasingly alarmed over his colleagues'
*favorable view of the French Revolution. His friend and political ally
Philip Francis apparently gave credence to the poisonous propaganda that had been issuing for a decade about the sexual appetite of the
Queen of France—the ironic result of her attempt to act in a more
"natural" and less regal manner—as if a great civilization should be
razed if the queen were found guilty of fornication. Other interpreters
compared the events in France to Britain's Glorious Revolution of
1688–89 in order to serve contemporary revolutionary purposes. On
November 4, 1789, the Revolution Society, formed originally to commemorate the Glorious Revolution, heard this comparison made by
Dr. Richard Price, a Unitarian minister and promoter of the American War of Independence. Price is mentioned in the letter below,
along with William Petty, 2nd Earl of Shelburne and Marquis of
Lansdowne, who was an old antagonist of Burke and the Rockingham Whigs.*

*Burke had known Philip Francis since at least 1770, and from
1785 Francis had assisted Burke in the prosecution of Warren Hastings, Governor-General of India. Burke had sent Francis a short
portion of the* Reflections *in draft form, and Francis had written
back disapprovingly. He believed that the best hope of dissuading
Burke from proceeding with the* Reflections *was to argue that combat
with the English admirers of the French Revolution was beneath him
and to warn Burke of the pamphlet war that would ensue. Of the*

famous purple patch on Marie Antoinette, Francis's comment was brutal: "pure foppery." Burke responds by explaining the sympathies that a suffering queen should evoke in a properly educated gentleman. Those sympathies contrast markedly with the revolutionary sympathies that inspired Price, Shelburne, and their "set."

Letter to Philip Francis

Gerard-street, February 20, 1790

My dear Sir,

I sat up rather late at Carlton-house, and on my return hither,
I found your letter on my table. I have not slept since. You
will, therefore, excuse me if you find any thing confused, or
otherwise expressed than I could wish, in speaking upon a
matter which interests you from your regard to me. There are
some things in your letter for which I must thank you; there
are others which I must answer; some things bear the mark of
friendly admonition; others bear some resemblance to the
tone of accusation.

You are the only friend I have who will dare to give me
advice; I must, therefore, have something terrible in me,
which intimidates all others who know me from giving me the
only unequivocal mark of their regard. Whatever this rough
and menacing manner may be, I must search myself upon it;
and when I discover it, old as I am, I must endeavour to correct it. I flattered myself, however, that you at least would not
have thought my other friends justified in withholding from
me their services of this kind. You certainly do not always
convey to me your opinions with the greatest tenderness and
management; and yet I do not recollect, since I first had the
pleasure of your acquaintance, that there has been a heat or a
coolness of a single day's duration, on my side, during that

whole time. I believe your memory cannot present to you an instance of it. I ill deserve friends, if I throw them away on account of the candour and simplicity of their good nature. In particular you know, that you have in some instances favoured me with your instructions relative to things I was preparing for the public. If I did not in every instance agree with you, I think you had, on the whole, sufficient proofs of my docility, to make you believe that I received your corrections, not only without offence, but with no small degree of gratitude.

Your remarks upon the first two sheets of my Paris letter, relate to the composition and the matter. The composition, you say, is loose, and I am quite sure of it: I never intended it should be otherwise. For, purporting to be, what in truth it originally was, a letter to a friend, I had no idea of digesting it in a systematic order. The style is open to correction, and wants it. My natural style of writing is somewhat careless, and I should be happy in receiving your advice towards making it as little vicious as such a style is capable of being made. The general character and colour of a style, which grows out of the writer's peculiar turn of mind and habit of expressing his thoughts, must be attended to in all corrections. It is not the insertion of a piece of stuff, though of a better kind, which is at all times an improvement.

Your main objections are, however, of a much deeper nature, and go to the political opinions and moral sentiments of the piece; in which I find, though with no sort of surprise, having often talked with you on the subject, that we differ only in every thing. You say, "the mischief you are going to do yourself, is to my apprehension palpable; I snuff it in the wind, and my taste sickens at it." This anticipated stench, that turns your stomach at such a distance, must be nauseous indeed. You seem to think I shall incur great (and not wholly undeserved) infamy, by this publication. This makes it a matter of some delicacy to me, to suppress what I have written; for I must admit in my own feelings, and in that of those who have seen the piece, that my sentiments and opinions deserve the infamy with which they are threatened. If they do not, I know nothing more than that I oppose the prejudices and inclinations of many people. This I was well aware of from the beginning; and it was in order to oppose those inclinations and prejudices, that I proposed to publish my letter. I really am perfectly astonished how you could dream, with my paper in your hand, that I found no other cause than the beauty of the queen of France (now, I suppose, pretty much faded) for disapproving the conduct which has been held towards her, and for expressing my own particular feelings. I am not to order the natural sympathies of my own heart, and of every honest breast, to wait until all the jokes of all the anecdotes of the coffee-houses of Paris, and of the dissenting meeting-houses of London, are scoured of all the slander of those who calumniate persons, that, afterwards, they may murder them with impunity. I know nothing of your story of Messalina.[1] Am I obliged to prove juridically the virtues of all those I shall see suffering every kind of wrong, and contumely, and risk of life, before I endeavour to interest others in their sufferings, and before I endeavour to excite horror against midnight assassins at back-stairs, and their more wicked abettors in pulpits? What! Are not high rank, great splendour of descent, great personal elegance and outward accomplishments, ingredients of moment in forming the interest we take in the misfortunes of men? The minds of those who do not feel thus, are not even systematically right. "What's Hecuba to him, or he to Hecuba, that he should weep for her?"[2] Why, because she was Hecuba, the queen of Troy, the wife of Priam, and suffered, in the close of life, a thousand calamities! I felt too for Hecuba, when I read the fine tragedy of Euripides upon her story; and I never inquired into the anecdotes of the court

[1] [Francis had written, "[I]t is in vain to expect that I or any reasonable man shall regret the sufferings of a Messalina, as I should those of a Mrs Crewe or a Mrs Burke, I mean of all that is beautiful or virtuous amongst women" (*Corr.* Copeland 6:87). French pornographic publications had been comparing Marie Antoinette to famous sexual profligates, including Messalina, for many years.]

[2] [*Hamlet* II.ii.559–560.]

LETTER TO PHILIP FRANCIS

or city of Troy, before I gave way to the sentiments which the author wished to inspire; nor do I remember that he ever said one word of her virtue. It is for those who applaud or palliate assassination, regicide, and base insult to women of illustrious place, to prove the crimes (in sufferings)[3] which they allege, to justify their own. But if they have proved fornication on any such woman, taking the manners of the world, and the manners of France, I shall never put it in a parallel with assassination! No: I have no such inverted scale of faults, in my heart or my head.

You find it perfectly ridiculous, and unfit for me in particular, to take these things as my ingredients of commiseration. Pray why is it absurd in me to think, that the chivalrous spirit which dictated a veneration for women of condition and of beauty, without any consideration whatever of enjoying them, was the great source of those manners which have been the pride and ornament of Europe for so many ages? And am I not to lament that I have lived to see those manners extinguished in so shocking a manner, by means of speculations of finance, and the false science of a sordid and degenerate philosophy? I tell you again, that the recollection of the manner in which I saw the queen of France, in the year 1774, and the contrast between that brilliancy, splendour, and beauty, with the prostrate homage of a nation to her, and the abominable scene of 1789, which I was describing, *did* draw tears from me and wetted my paper. These tears came again into my eyes, almost as often as I looked at the description; they may again. You do not believe this fact, nor that these are my real feelings; but that the whole is affected, or, as you express it, downright foppery. My friend, I tell you it is truth; and that it is true, and will be truth, when you and I are no more; and will exist as long as men with their natural feelings shall exist. I shall say no more on this foppery of mine. Oh! by the way, you ask me how long I have been an admirer of German ladies? Always the same. Present me the idea of such massacres about

---

[3] [The Copeland text of the *Correspondence* (6:90) reads "in the sufferers" in place of the words in parentheses.]

LETTER TO PHILIP FRANCIS

any German lady here, and such attempts to assassinate her, and such a triumphant procession from Windsor to the Old Jewry, and I assure you, I shall be quite as full of natural concern and just indignation.[4]

As to the other points, they deserve serious consideration, and they shall have it. I certainly cannot profit quite so much by your assistance, as if we agreed. In that case, every correction would be forwarding the design. We should work with one common view. But it is impossible that any man can correct a work according to its true spirit, who is opposed to its object, or can help the expression of what he thinks should not be expressed at all.

I should agree with you about the vileness of the controversy with such miscreants as the "Revolution Society," and the "National Assembly"; and I know very well that they, as well as their allies, the Indian delinquents, will darken the air with their arrows. But I do not yet think they have the advowson of reputation. I shall try that point. My dear sir, you think of nothing but controversies; "I challenge into the field of battle and retire defeated, &c." If their having the last word be a defeat, they most assuredly will defeat me. But I intend no controversy with Dr. Price, or Lord Shelburne, or any other of their set. I mean to set in full view the danger from their wicked principles and their black hearts. I intend to state the true principles of our constitution in church and state, upon grounds opposite to theirs. If any one be the better for the example made of them, and for this exposition, well and good. I mean to do my best to expose them to the hatred, ridicule, and contempt of the whole world; as I always shall expose such calumniators, hypocrites, sowers of sedition, and approvers of murder and all its triumphs. When I have done

[4] [Burke is imagining a procession in which a noblewoman is forced from her rightful home, such as Windsor Palace, to the location of her opposition, in this case the Meeting House in the Old Jewry, where Richard Price delivered his "Discourse on the love of our country." He is alluding to the events of October 5–6, 1789, when the apartments of the French royal family at Versailles were invaded and the King and Queen forced to travel to Paris.]

LETTER TO PHILIP FRANCIS

that, they may have the field to themselves; and I care very little how they triumph over me, since I hope they will not be able to draw me at their heels, and carry my head in triumph on their poles.

I have been interrupted, and have said enough. Adieu! Believe me always sensible of your friendship; though it is impossible that a greater difference can exist on earth, than, unfortunately for me, there is on those subjects, between your sentiments and mine.

EDM. BURKE

3

A LETTER TO A MEMBER OF THE
NATIONAL ASSEMBLY

May 1791

*T*he recipient of A Letter to a Member of the National Assembly *was François-Louis-Thibaut de Menonville. The opening
paragraphs, which refer to Menonville's response (Corr. Copeland
6:162–169) to Burke's* Reflections, *acknowledge and then dismiss
most of Menonville's criticisms.*

By the time he wrote A Letter, *in January 1791, Burke had come
to a deep understanding of the modern revolutionary mind and its
method of defending itself: atrocities were to be set down as "excesses"
provoked by its opponents; revolutionary speakers were not to be held
to the same ethical standards as others, since their motives were, after
all, the best; and no amount of actual suffering in the present could
call into question the revolutionary's hope for a bright future. Burke
clearly believed that the revolutionary enterprise was international in
character and had to be opposed by force. He was soon to be bitterly
disappointed by the irresolute and fractious European coalitions
formed for this purpose.*

*This work is famous for its consideration of Jean-Jacques Rous-
seau and is noteworthy as well for its opposition to the new-modeling
of education and sentiment which Rousseau's works, especially*
Emile, *portended. Burke had begun reading Rousseau by 1759 at the
latest, when he reviewed the* Letter . . . to M. d'Alembert *for the*
Annual Register. *He refers in that review to two of the* Discourses.
In 1762, he reviewed Emile. *As for Rousseau himself, his highly pub-*

licized trip to England between January *1766* and May *1767*—espe-cially his quarrel with his host, David Hume—impressed the English with his vanity and ingratitude.

In A Letter, *and continuing in* An Appeal from the New to the Old Whigs, *one can see Burke allying himself with the ancients, with classical modes of education and feeling, against the Enlighten-ment.*

A Letter to a Member of the National Assembly

May 1791

Sɪʀ,

I had the honour to receive your letter of the 17th of November last, in which, with some exceptions, you are pleased to consider favourably the letter I have written on the affairs of France. I shall ever accept any mark of approbation, attended with instruction, with more pleasure than general and un-qualified praises. The latter can serve only to flatter our vanity; the former, whilst it encourages us to proceed, may help to improve us in our progress.

Some of the errors you point out to me in my printed letter are really such. One only I find to be material. It is corrected in the edition which I take the liberty of sending to you. As to the cavils which may be made on some part of my remarks, with regard to the *gradations* in your new constitution, you observe justly, that they do not affect the substance of my objections. Whether there be a round more or less in the ladder of representation, by which your workmen ascend from their parochial tyranny to their federal anarchy, when the whole scale is false, appears to me of little or no importance.

I published my thoughts on that constitution, that my countrymen might be enabled to estimate the wisdom of the plans which were held out to their imitation. I conceived that the true character of those plans would be best collected from the committee appointed to prepare them. I thought that the scheme of their building would be better comprehended in the design of the architects than in the execution of the masons. It was not worth my reader's while to occupy himself with the alterations by which bungling practice corrects absurd theory. Such an investigation would be endless: because every day's past experience of impracticability has driven, and every day's future experience will drive, those men to new devices as exceptionable as the old; and which are no otherwise worthy of observation than as they give a daily proof of the delusion of their promises, and the falsehood of their professions. Had I followed all these changes, my letter would have been only a gazette of their wanderings; a journal of their march from error to error, through a dry dreary desert, unguided by the lights of heaven, or by the contrivance which wisdom has invented to supply their place.

I am unalterably persuaded, that the attempt to oppress, degrade, impoverish, confiscate, and extinguish the original gentlemen, and landed property of an whole nation, cannot be justified under any form it may assume. I am satisfied beyond a doubt, that the project of turning a great empire into a vestry, or into a collection of vestries, and of governing it in the spirit of a parochial administration, is senseless and absurd, in any mode, or with any qualifications. I can never be convinced, that the scheme of placing the highest powers of the state in churchwardens and constables, and other such officers, guided by the prudence of litigious attornies and Jew brokers, and set in action by shameless women of the lowest condition, by keepers of hotels, taverns, and brothels, by pert apprentices, by clerks, shop-boys, hair-dressers, fidlers, and dancers on the stage (who, in such a commonwealth as your's, will in future overbear, as already they have overborne, the sober incapacity of dull uninstructed men, of useful but laborious occupations), can never be put into any shape, that must not be both disgraceful and destructive. The whole of this project, even if it were what it pretends to be, and was not in reality the dominion, through that disgraceful medium, of half a dozen, or perhaps fewer, intriguing politicians, is so mean, so low-minded, so stupid a contrivance, in point of wisdom, as well as so perfectly detestable for its wickedness, that I must always consider the correctives which might make it in any degree practicable, to be so many new objections to it.

In that wretched state of things, some are afraid that the authors of your miseries may be led to precipitate their further designs, by the hints they may receive from the very arguments used to expose the absurdity of their system, to mark the incongruity of its parts, and its inconsistency with their own principles; and that your masters may be led to render their schemes more consistent, by rendering them more mischievous. Excuse the liberty which your indulgence authorises me to take, when I observe to you, that such apprehensions as these would prevent all exertion of our faculties in this great cause of mankind.

A rash recourse to *force* is not to be justified in a state of real weakness. Such attempts bring on disgrace; and, in their failure, discountenance and discourage more rational endeavours. But *reason* is to be hazarded, though it may be perverted by craft and sophistry; for reason can suffer no loss nor shame, nor can it impede any useful plan of future policy. In the unavoidable uncertainty, as to the effect, which attends on every measure of human prudence, nothing seems a surer antidote to the poison of fraud than its detection. It is true the fraud may be swallowed after this discovery; and perhaps even swallowed the more greedily for being a detected fraud. Men sometimes make a point of honour not to be disabused; and they had rather fall into an hundred errors than confess one. But after all, when neither our principles nor our dispositions, nor, perhaps, our talents, enable us to encounter delusion with delusion, we must use our best reason to those that ought to be reasonable creatures, and to take our chance for the event. We cannot act on these anomalies in the minds of men. I do not conceive that the persons who have contrived

A LETTER TO A MEMBER OF THE NATIONAL ASSEMBLY

these things can be made much the better or the worse for any thing which can be said to them. *They* are reason proof. Here and there, some men, who were at first carried away by wild good intentions, may be led, when their first fervors are abated, to join in a sober survey of the schemes into which they have been deluded. To those only (and I am sorry to say they are not likely to make a large description) we apply with any hope. I may speak it upon an assurance almost approaching to absolute knowledge, that nothing has been done that has not been contrived from the beginning, even before the states had assembled. *Nulla nova mihi res inopinave surgit.*[1] They are the same men and the same designs that they were from the first, though varied in their appearance. It was the very same animal that at first crawled about in the shape of a caterpillar, that you now see rise into the air, and expand his wings to the sun.

Proceeding, therefore, as we are obliged to proceed, that is upon an hypothesis that we address rational men, can false political principles be more effectually exposed, than by demonstrating that they lead to consequences directly inconsistent with and subversive of the arrangements grounded upon them? If this kind of demonstration is not permitted, the process of reasoning called *deductio ad absurdum*, which even the severity of geometry does not reject, could not be employed at all in legislative discussions. One of our strongest weapons against folly acting with authority, would be lost.

You know, Sir, that even the virtuous efforts of you patriots to prevent the ruin of your country have had this very turn given to them. It has been said here, and in France too, that the reigning usurpers would not have carried their tyranny to such destructive lengths, if they had not been stimulated and provoked to it by the acrimony of your opposition. There is a dilemma to which every opposition to successful iniquity

[1] [Burke is quoting Aeneas's response to the Cumaean Sibyl, who has just predicted suffering and hardship for him in Latium:

no terror to my view,
No frightful face of danger can be new. (*Aeneid* 6:103–104)]

must, in the nature of things, be liable. If you lie still, you are considered as an accomplice in the measures in which you silently acquiesce. If you resist, you are accused of provoking irritable power to new excesses. The conduct of a losing party never appears right: at least it never can possess the only infallible criterion of wisdom to vulgar judgments—success.

The indulgence of a sort of undefined hope, an obscure confidence, that some lurking remains of virtue, some degree of shame, might exist in the breasts of the oppressors of France, has been among the causes which have helped to bring on the common ruin of king and people. There is no safety for honest men, but by believing all possible evil of evil men, and by acting with promptitude, decision, and steadiness on that belief. I well remember, at every epocha of this wonderful history, in every scene of this tragic business, that when your sophistic usurpers were laying down mischievous principles, and even applying them in direct resolutions, it was the fashion to say, that they never intended to execute those declarations in their rigour. This made men cautious in their opposition, and remiss in early precaution. By holding out this fallacious hope, the impostors deluded sometimes one description of men, and sometimes another, so that no means of resistance were provided against them, when they came to execute in cruelty what they had planned in fraud.

There are cases in which a man would be ashamed not to have been imposed on. There is a confidence necessary to human intercourse, and without which men are often more injured by their own suspicions than they could be by the perfidy of others. But when men, whom we *know* to be wicked, impose upon us, we are something worse than dupes. When we know them, their fair pretences become new motives for distrust. There is one case, indeed, in which it would be madness not to give the fullest credit to the most deceitful of men, that is, when they make declarations of hostility against us.

I find, that some persons entertain other hopes, which I confess appear more specious than those by which at first so many were deluded and disarmed. They flatter themselves that the extreme misery brought upon the people by their folly, will at last open the eyes of the multitude, if not of their leaders. Much the contrary, I fear. As to the leaders in this system of imposture, you know, that cheats and deceivers never can repent. The fraudulent have no resource but in fraud. They have no other goods in their magazine. They have no virtue or wisdom in their minds, to which, in a disappointment concerning the profitable effects of fraud and cunning, they can retreat. The wearing out of an old, serves only to put them upon the invention of a new delusion. Unluckily too, the credulity of dupes is as inexhaustible as the invention of knaves. They never give people possession; but they always keep them in hope. Your state doctors do not so much as pretend that any good whatsoever has hitherto been derived from their operations, or that the public has prospered in any one instance, under their management. The nation is sick, very sick, by their medicines. But the *charlatan* tells them that what is past cannot be helped; they have taken the draught, and they must wait its operation with patience; that the first effects indeed are unpleasant, but that the very sickness is a proof that the dose is of no sluggish operation; that sickness is inevitable in all constitutional revolutions; that the body must pass through pain to ease; that the prescriber is not an empirick who proceeds by vulgar experience, but one who grounds his practice on[2] the sure rules of art, which cannot possibly fail. You have read Sir, the last Manifesto, or Mountebank's bill, of the National Assembly. You see their presumption in their promises is not lessened by all their failures in the performance. Compare this last address of the Assembly, and the present state of your affairs with the early engagements of that body; engagements which, not content with declaring, they solemnly deposed upon oath, swearing lustily that if they were supported they would make their

[2] It is said in the last quackish address of the National Assembly to the people of France; that they have not formed their arrangements upon vulgar practice; but on a theory which cannot fail, or something to that effect.

A Letter to a Member of the National Assembly

country glorious and happy; and then judge whether those who can write such things, or those who can bear to read them, are of *themselves* to be brought to any reasonable course of thought or action.

As to the people at large, when once these miserable sheep have broken the fold, and have got themselves loose, not from the restraint, but from the protection of all the principles of natural authority, and legitimate subordination, they became the natural prey of impostors. When they have once tasted of the flattery of knaves, they can no longer endure reason, which appears to them only in the form of censure and reproach. Great distress has never hitherto taught, and whilst the world lasts it never will teach, wise lessons to any part of mankind. Men are as much blinded by the extremes of misery as by the extremes of prosperity. Desperate situations produce desperate councils, and desperate measures. The people of France, almost generally, have been taught to look for other resources than those which can be derived from order, frugality, and industry. They are generally armed; and they are made to expect much from the use of arms. *Nihil non arrogant armis.*[3] Besides this, the retrograde order of society has something flattering to the dispositions of mankind. The life of adventurers, gamesters, gipsies, beggars, and robbers, is not unpleasant. It requires restraint to keep men from falling into that habit. The shifting tides of fear and hope, the flight and pursuit, the peril and escape, the alternate famine and feast, of the savage and the thief, after a time, render all course of slow, steady, progressive, unvaried occupation, and the prospect only of a limited mediocrity at the end of long labour, to the last degree tame, languid, and insipid. Those who have been once intoxicated with power, and have derived any kind of emolument from it, even though but for one year, never can willingly abandon it. They may be distressed in the midst of all their power; but they will never look to any thing but power for their relief. When did

---

[3] ["They think everything must yield to arms." Horace, *The Art of Poetry*, I.122]

distress ever oblige a prince to abdicate his authority? And what effect will it have upon those who are made to believe themselves a people of princes?

The more active and stirring part of the lower orders having got government, and the distribution of plunder, into their hands, they will use its resources in each municipality to form a body of adherents. These rulers, and their adherents, will be strong enough to overpower the discontents of those who have not been able to assert their share of the spoil. The unfortunate adventurers in the cheating lottery of plunder will probably be the least sagacious, or the most inactive and irresolute of the gang. If, on disappointment, they should dare to stir, they will soon be suppressed as rebels and mutineers by their brother rebels. Scantily fed for a while, with the offal of plunder, they will drop off by degrees; they will be driven out of sight, and out of thought; and they will be left to perish obscurely, like rats, in holes and corners.

From the forced repentance of invalid mutineers and disbanded thieves, you can hope for no resource. Government itself, which ought to constrain the more bold and dextrous of these robbers, is their accomplice. Its arms, its treasures, its all, are in their hands. Judicature, which above all things should awe them, is their creature and their instrument. Nothing seems to me to render your internal situation more desperate than this one circumstance of the state of your judicature. Many days are not past since we have seen a set of men brought forth by your rulers for a most critical function. Your rulers brought forth a set of men, steaming from the sweat and drudgery, and all black with the smoak and soot of the forge of confiscation and robbery—*ardentis massae fuligine lippos*,[4] a set of men brought forth from the trade of hammering arms of proof, offensive and defensive, in aid of the enterprizes, and for the subsequent protection of housebreakers, murderers, traitors, and malefactors; men, who had their minds seasoned with theories perfectly comformable to their

---

[4] ["Blinded by the soot of the fiery mass." Juvenal, *Satires* 10:130]

practice, and who had always laughed at possession and pre-scription, and defied all the fundamental maxims of jurisprudence. To the horror and stupefaction of all the honest part of this nation, and indeed of all nations who are spectators, we have seen, on the credit of those very practices and principles, and to carry them further into effect, these very men placed on the sacred seat of justice in the capital city of your late kingdom. We see, that in future, you are to be destroyed with more form and regularity. This is not peace; it is only the introduction of a sort of discipline in their hostility. Their tyranny is complete, in their justice; and their lanthorn is not half so dreadful as their court.

One would think that out of common decency they would have given you men who had not been in the habit of trampling upon law and justice in the assembly, neutral men, or men apparently neutral, for judges, who are to dispose of your lives and fortunes.

Cromwell, when he attempted to legalize his power, and to settle his conquered country in a state of order, did not look for his dispensers of justice in the instruments of his usurpation. Quite the contrary. He sought out with great sollicitude and selection, and even from the party most opposite to his designs, men of weight, and decorum of character; men un-stained with the violence of the times, and with hands not fouled with confiscation and sacrilege: for he chose an *Hales*[5] for his chief justice, though he absolutely refused to take his civic oaths, or to make any acknowledgment whatsoever of the legality of his government. Cromwell told this great lawyer, that since he did not approve his title, all he required of him was, to administer, in a manner agreeable to his pure sentiments and unspotted character, that justice without which human society cannot subsist: that it was not his partic-

---

[5] [Sir Matthew Hale (1609–1676) was notable for the neutrality with which he approached the law during the decades of the English Civil War and Cromwell's rule, when he was made Justice of Common Pleas. He had an active role in forwarding the Restoration and was made Chief Justice of the King's Bench in 1671.]

ular government, but civil order itself, which as a judge he wished him to support. Cromwell knew how to separate the institutions expedient to his usurpation from the administration of the public justice of his country. For Cromwell was a man in whom ambition had not wholly suppressed, but only suspended the sentiments of religion, and the love (as far it could consist with his designs) of fair and honourable reputation. Accordingly, we are indebted to this act of his for the preservation of our laws, which some senseless assertors of the rights of men were then on the point of entirely erasing, as relicks of feudality and barbarism. Besides, he gave in the appointment of that man, to that age, and to all posterity, the most brilliant example of sincere and fervent piety, exact justice, and profound jurisprudence.[6] But these are not the things in which your philosophic usurpers choose to follow Cromwell.

One would think, that after an honest and necessary Revolution (if they had a mind that theirs should pass for such) your masters would have imitated the virtuous policy of those who have been at the head of revolutions of that glorious character. Burnet tells us, that nothing tended to reconcile the English nation to the government of King William so much as the care he took to fill the vacant bishoprics with men who had attracted the public esteem by their learning, eloquence, and piety, and above all, by their known moderation in the state. With you, in your purifying Revolution, whom have you chosen to regulate the church? Mr. Mirabeau is a fine speaker—and a fine writer—and a fine—a very fine man; but really nothing gave more surprize to every body here, than to find him the supreme head of your ecclesiastical affairs. The rest is of course. Your Assembly addresses a manifesto to France in which they tell the people, with an insulting irony, that they have brought the church to its primitive condition. In one respect their declaration is undoubtedly true; for they have brought it to a state of poverty and persecution.

[6] See Burnet's life of Hales.

A LETTER TO A MEMBER OF THE NATIONAL ASSEMBLY

What can be hoped for after this? Have not men (if they deserve the name) under this new hope and head of the church, been made bishops, for no other merit than having acted as instruments of atheists; for no other merit than having thrown the children's bread to dogs; and in order to gorge the whole gang of usurers; pedlars, and itinerant Jew-discounters at the corners of streets, starved the poor of their Christian flocks, and their own brother pastors? Have not such men been made bishops to administer in temples, in which (if the patriotic donations have not already stripped them of their vessels) the churchwardens ought to take security for the altar plate, and not so much as to trust the chalice in their sacrilegious hands, so long as Jews have assignats on ecclesiastic plunder, to exchange for the silver stolen from churches?

I am told, that the very sons of such Jew-jobbers have been made bishops; persons not to be suspected of any sort of *Christian* superstition, fit colleagues to the holy prelate of Autun;[7] and bred at the feet of that Gamaliel. We know who it was that drove the money-changers out of the temple. We see too who it is that brings them in again. We have in London very respectable persons of the Jewish nation, whom we will keep: but we have of the same tribe others of a very different description, housebreakers, and receivers of stolen goods, and forgers of paper currency, more than we can conveniently hang. These we can spare to France, to fill the new episcopal thrones: men well versed in swearing; and who will scruple no oath which the fertile genius of any of your reformers can devise.

In matters so ridiculous, it is hard to be grave. On a view of their consequences it is almost inhuman to treat them lightly. To what a state of savage, stupid, servile insensibility must your people be reduced, who can endure such proceedings in their church, their state, and their judicature, even for a moment! But the deluded people of France are like other

[7] [Talleyrand.]

madmen, who, to a miracle, bear hunger, and thirst, and cold, and confinement, and the chains and lash of their keeper, whilst all the while they support themselves by the imagination that they are generals of armies, prophets, kings, and emperors. As to a change of mind in these men, who consider infamy as honour, degradation as preferment, bondage to low tyrants as liberty, and the practical scorn and contumely of their upstart masters, as marks of respect and homage, I look upon it as absolutely impracticable. These madmen, to be cured, must first, like other madmen, be subdued. The sound part of the community, which I believe to be large, but by no means the largest part, has been taken by surprize, and is disjointed, terrified, and disarmed. That sound part of the community must first be put into a better condition, before it can do any thing in the way of deliberation or persuasion. This must be an act of power, as well as of wisdom; of power, in the hands of firm, determined patriots, who can distinguish the misled from traitors, who will regulate the state (if such should be their fortune) with a discriminating, manly, and provident mercy; men who are purged of the surfeit and indigestion of systems, if ever they have been admitted into the habit of their minds; men who will lay the foundation of a real reform, in effacing every vestige of that philosophy which pretends to have made discoveries in the *terra australis* of morality; men who will fix the state upon these bases of morals and politics, which are our old, and immemorial, and, I hope, will be our eternal possession.

This power, to such men, must come from *without*. It may be given to you in pity; for surely no nation ever called so pathetically on the compassion of all its neighbours. It may be given by those neighbours on motives of safety to themselves. Never shall I think any country in Europe to be secure, whilst there is established, in the very centre of it, a state (if so it may be called) founded on principles of anarchy, and which is, in reality, a college of armed fanatics, for the propagation of the principles of assassination, robbery, rebellion, fraud, faction, oppression, and impiety. *Mahomet*, hid, as for a time he was, in

_____

the bottom of the sands of Arabia, had his spirit and character been discovered, would have been an object of precaution to provident minds. What if he had erected his fanatic standard for the destruction of the Christian religion in *luce Asiae*, in the midst of the then noon-day splendour of the then civilized world? The princes of Europe, in the beginning of this century, did well not to suffer the monarchy of France to swallow up the others. They ought not now, in my opinion, to suffer all the monarchies and commonwealths to be swallowed up in the gulph of this polluted anarchy. They may be tolerably safe at present, because the comparative power of France for the present is little. But times and occasions make dangers. Intestine troubles may arise in other countries. There is a power always on the watch, qualified and disposed to profit of every conjuncture, to establish its own principles and modes of mischief, wherever it can hope for success. What mercy would these usurpers have on other sovereigns, and on other nations, when they treat their own king with such unparalleled indignities, and so cruelly oppress their own countrymen?

The king of Prussia, in concurrence with us, nobly interfered to save Holland from confusion. The same power, joined with the rescued Holland and with Great Britain, has put the emperor in the possession of the Netherlands; and secured, under that prince, from all arbitrary innovation, the antient, hereditary constitution of those provinces. The chamber of Wetzlar has restored the Bishop of Leige, unjustly dispossessed by the rebellion of his subjects. The king of Prussia was bound by no treaty, nor alliance of blood, nor had any particular reasons for thinking the emperor's government would be more mischievous or more oppressive to human nature than that of the Turk; yet on mere motives of policy that prince has interposed with the threat of all his force, to snatch even the Turk from the pounces of the imperial eagle. If this is done in favour of a barbarous nation, with a barbarous neglect of police, fatal to the human race, in favour of a nation, by principle in eternal enmity with the Chris-

tian name; a nation which will not so much as give the saluta-
tion of peace (Salam) to any of us; nor make any pact with any
Christian nation beyond a truce; if this be done in favour of
the Turk, shall it be thought either impolitic, or unjust, or
uncharitable, to employ the same power, to rescue from captivity a virtuous monarch (by the courtesy of Europe considered as Most Christian) who, after an intermission of 175
years, had called together the states of his kingdom, to reform
abuses, to establish a free government, and to strengthen his
throne; a monarch, who at the very outset, without force,
even without sollicitation, had given to his people such a
Magna Charta of privileges, as never was given by any king to
any subjects? Is it to be tamely borne by kings who love their
subjects, or by subjects who love their kings, that this monarch, in the midst of these gracious acts, was insolently and
cruelly torn from his palace, by a gang of traitors and assassins, and kept in close prison to this very hour, whilst his royal
name and sacred character were used for the total ruin of
those whom the laws had appointed him to protect?

The only offence of this unhappy monarch towards his
people, was his attempt, under a monarchy, to give them a
free constitution. For this, by an example hitherto unheard of
in the world, he has been deposed. It might well disgrace
sovereigns to take part with a deposed tyrant. It would suppose in them a vitious sympathy. But not to make a common
cause with a just prince, dethroned by traitors and rebels, who
proscribe, plunder, confiscate, and in every way cruelly oppress their fellow citizens, in my opinion is to forget what is
due to the honour, and to the rights of all virtuous and legal
government.

I think the king of France to be as much an object both of
policy and compassion as the Grand Seignor or his states. I do
not conceive, that the total annihilation of France (if that
could be effected) is a desirable thing to Europe; or even to
this its rival nation. Provident patriots did not think it good
for Rome, that even Carthage should be quite destroyed; and
he was a wise Greek, wise for the general Grecian interests, as

---

well as a brave Lacedemonian enemy, and generous conqueror, who did not wish, by the destruction of Athens, to pluck out the other eye of Greece.

However, Sir, what I have here said of the interference of foreign princes is only the opinion of a private individual, who is neither the representative of any state, nor the organ of any party; but who thinks himself bound to express his own sentiments with freedom and energy in a crisis of such importance to the whole human race.

I am not apprehensive that in speaking freely on the subject of the King and Queen of France, I shall accelerate (as you fear) the execution of traiterous designs against them. You are of opinion, Sir, that the usurpers may, and that they will, gladly lay hold of any pretext to throw off the very name of a king; assuredly I do not wish ill to your king; but better for him not to live (he does not reign) than to live the passive instrument of tyranny and usurpation.

I certainly meant to shew, to the best of my power, that the existence of such an executive officer, in such a system of republic as theirs, is absurd in the highest degree. But in demonstrating this—to *them*, at least, I can have made no discovery. They only held out the royal name to catch those Frenchmen to whom the name of king is still venerable. They calculate the duration of that sentiment; and when they find it nearly expiring, they will not trouble themselves with excuses for extinguishing the name, as they have the thing. They used it as a sort of navel-string to nourish their unnatural offspring from the bowels of royalty itself. Now that the monster can purvey for its own subsistence, it will only carry the mark about it, as a token of its having torn the womb it came from. Tyrants seldom want pretexts. Fraud is the ready minister of injustice; and whilst the currency of false pretence and sophistic reasoning was expedient to their designs, they were under no necessity of drawing upon me to furnish them with that coin. But pretexts and sophisms have had their day; and have done their work. The usurpation no longer seeks plausibility. It trusts to power.

A LETTER TO A MEMBER OF THE NATIONAL ASSEMBLY

Nothing that I can say, or that you can say, will hasten them by a single hour, in the execution of a design which they have long since entertained. In spite of their solemn declarations, their soothing addresses, and the multiplied oaths which they have taken, and forced others to take, they will assassinate the king when his name will no longer be necessary to their designs; but not a moment sooner. They will probably first assassinate the queen, whenever the renewed menace of such an assassination loses its effect upon the anxious mind of an affectionate husband. At present, the advantage which they derive from the daily threats against her life, is her only security for preserving it. They keep their sovereign alive for the purpose of exhibiting him, like some wild beast at a fair; as if they had a Bajazet in a cage.[8] They choose to make monarchy contemptible by exposing it to derision, in the person of the most benevolent of their kings.

In my opinion, their insolence appears more odious even than their crimes. The horrors of the 5th and 6th of October were less detestable than the festival of the 14th of July.[9] There are situations (God forbid I should think that of the 5th and 6th of October one of them) in which the best men may be confounded with the worst, and in the darkness and confusion, in the press and medley of such extremities, it may not be so easy to discriminate the one from the other. The necessities created, even by ill designs, have their excuse. They may be forgotten by others, when the guilty themselves do not choose to cherish their recollection, and by ruminating their offences, nourish themselves through the example of their past, to the perpetration of future crimes. It is in the relaxa-

[8] [Bajazet, the eponymous hero of a tragedy by Racine, was executed by his brother, Sultan Murad IV of Turkey, who was "an Ottoman Nero," in the words of one commentator.]

[9] [Burke's references to the 5th and 6th of October 1789 recall the Paris mob's forcing of the royal family from Versailles to the Tuileries, where they were, for all practical purposes, prisoners. The first anniversary of the fall of the Bastille, whose celebrations began on July 14, 1790, and continued for a week, is discussed in Mona Ozouf, *Festivals and the French Revolution*, trans. Alan Sheridan (Cambridge, Mass.: Harvard University Press, 1988).]

tion of security, it is in the expansion of prosperity, it is in the hour of dilatation of the heart, and of its softening into festivity and pleasure, that the real character of men is discerned. If there is any good in them, it appears then or never. Even wolves and tygers, when gorged with their prey, are safe and gentle. It is at such times that noble minds give all the reins to their good-nature. They indulge their genius even to intemperance, in kindness to the afflicted, in generosity to the conquered; forbearing insults, forgiving injuries, overpaying benefits. Full of dignity themselves, they respect dignity in all, but they feel it sacred in the unhappy. But it is then, and basking in the sunshine of unmerited fortune, that low, sordid, ungenerous, and reptile souls swell with their hoarded poisons; it is then that they display their odious splendor, and shine out in the full lustre of their native villainy and baseness. It is in that season that no man of sense or honour can be mistaken for one of them. It was in such a season, for them of political ease and security, tho' their people were but just emerged from actual famine, and were ready to be plunged into a gulph of penury and beggary, that your philosophic lords chose, with an ostentatious pomp and luxury, to feast an incredible number of idle and thoughtless people collected with art and pains, from all quarters of the world. They constructed a vast amphitheatre in which they raised a species of pillory.[10] On this pillory they set their lawful king and queen, with an insulting figure over their heads. There they exposed these objects of pity and respect to all good minds, to the derision of an unthinking and unprincipled multitude, degenerated even from the versatile tenderness which marks the irregular and capricious feelings of the populace. That their cruel insult might have nothing wanting to complete it, they chose the anniversary of that day in which they exposed the life of their prince to the most imminent dangers, and the vilest indignities, just following the instant when the assassins, whom they had hired without owning, first openly took

[10] The pillory (carcan) in England is generally made very high, like that raised for exposing the King of France.

up arms against their king, corrupted his guards, surprized his castle, butchered some of the poor invalids of his garrison, murdered his governor, and, like wild beasts, tore to pieces the chief magistrate of his capital city, on account of his fidelity to his service.

Till the justice of the world is awakened, such as these will go on, without admonition, and without provocation, to every extremity. Those who have made the exhibition of the 14th of July, are capable of every evil. They do not commit crimes for their designs; but they form designs that they may commit crimes. It is not their necessity, but their nature, that impels them. They are modern philosophers, which when you say of them, you express every thing that is ignoble, savage, and hard-hearted.

Besides the sure tokens which are given by the spirit of their particular arrangements, there are some characteristic lineaments in the general policy of your tumultuous despotism, which, in my opinion, indicate beyond a doubt that no revolution whatsoever *in their disposition* is to be expected. I mean their scheme of educating the rising generation, the principles which they intend to instil, and the sympathies which they wish to form in the mind, at the season in which it is the most susceptible. Instead of forming their young minds to that docility, to that modesty, which are the grace and charm of youth, to an admiration of famous examples, and to an averseness to any thing which approaches to pride, petulance, and self-conceit (distempers to which that time of life is of itself sufficiently liable), they artificially foment these evil dispositions, and even form them into springs of action. Nothing ought to be more weighed than the nature of books recommended by public authority. So recommended, they soon form the character of the age. Uncertain indeed is the efficacy, limited indeed is the extent of a virtuous institution. But if education takes in *vice* as any part of its system, there is no doubt but that it will operate with abundant energy, and to an extent indefinite. The magistrate, who in favour of freedom thinks himself obliged to suffer all sorts of publications, is under a stricter duty than any other, well to consider what sort of writers he shall authorize; and shall recommend, by the strongest of all sanctions, that is, by public honours and rewards. He ought to be cautious how he recommends authors of mixed or ambiguous morality. He ought to be fearful of putting into the hands of youth writers indulgent to the peculiarities of their own complexion, lest they should teach the humours of the professor, rather than the principles of the science. He ought, above all, to be cautious in recommending any writer who has carried marks of a deranged understanding; for where there is no sound reason, there can be no real virtue; and madness is ever vitious and malignant.

The National Assembly proceeds on maxims the very reverse of these. The Assembly recommends to its youth a study of the bold experimenters in morality. Every body knows that there is a great dispute amongst their leaders, which of them is the best resemblance to Rousseau.[11] In truth, they all resemble him. His blood they transfuse into their minds and into their manners. Him they study; him they meditate; him they turn over in all the time they can spare from the laborious mischief of the day, or the debauches of the night. Rousseau is their canon of holy writ; in his life he is their canon of *Polycletus*; he is their standard figure of perfection. To this man and this writer, as a pattern to authors and to Frenchmen, the founderies of Paris are now running for statues, with the kettles of their poor and the bells of their churches. If an author had written like a great genius on geometry, though his practical and speculative morals were vitious in the extreme, it might appear that in voting the statue, they honoured only the geometrician. But Rousseau is a moralist, or he is nothing. It is impossible, therefore, putting the circumstances together, to mistake their design in choosing

[11] [Like most contemporary readers, Burke became acquainted with Rousseau largely through *La Nouvelle Héloïse, Emile, Confessions*, and the *Discourses*. See Joan McDonald, *Rousseau and the French Revolution* (London: University of London Press, 1965) and Carol Blum, *Rousseau and the Republic of Virtue: The Language of Politics in the French Revolution* (Ithaca, New York: Cornell University Press, 1986).]

the author, with whom they have begun to recommend a course of studies.

Their great problem is to find a substitute for all the principles which hitherto have been employed to regulate the human will and action. They find dispositions in the mind, of such force and quality, as may fit men, far better than the old morality, for the purposes of such a state as theirs, and may go much further in supporting their power, and destroying their enemies. They have therefore chosen a selfish, flattering, seductive, ostentatious vice, in the place of plain duty. True humility, the basis of the Christian system, is the low, but deep and firm foundation of all real virtue. But this, as very painful in the practice, and little imposing in the appearance, they have totally discarded. Their object is to merge all natural and all social sentiment in inordinate vanity. In a small degree, and conversant in little things, vanity is of little moment. When full grown, it is the worst of vices, and the occasional mimick of them all. It makes the whole man false. It leaves nothing sincere or trust-worthy about him. His best qualities are poisoned and perverted by it, and operate exactly as the worst. When your lords had many writers as immoral as the object of their statue (such as Voltaire and others) they chose Rousseau; because in him that peculiar vice which they wished to erect into a ruling virtue, was by far the most conspicuous.

We have had the great professor and founder of *the philosophy of vanity* in England. As I had good opportunities of knowing his proceedings almost from day to day, he left no doubt in my mind, that he entertained no principle either to influence his heart, or to guide his understanding, but *vanity*. With this vice he was possessed to a degree little short of madness. It is from the same deranged eccentric vanity, that this, the insane *Socrates* of the National Assembly, was impelled to publish a mad Confession of his mad faults, and to attempt a new sort of glory, from bringing hardily to light the obscure and vulgar vices which we know may sometimes be blended with eminent talents. He has not observed on the nature of vanity, who does not know that it is omnivorous; that it has no choice in its food; that it is fond to talk even of its own faults and vices, as what will excite surprize and draw attention, and what will pass at worst for openness and candour. It was this abuse and perversion, which vanity makes even of hypocrisy, which has driven Rousseau to record a life not so much as chequered, or spotted here and there, with virtues, or even distinguished by a single good action. It is such a life he chooses to offer to the attention of mankind. It is such a life, that with a wild defiance, he flings in the face of his Creator, whom he acknowledges only to brave. Your Assembly, knowing how much more powerful example is found than precept, has chosen this man (by his own account without a single virtue) for a model. To him they erect their first statue. From him they commence their series of honours and distinctions.

It is that new-invented virtue which your masters canonize, that led their moral hero constantly to exhaust the stores of his powerful rhetoric in the expression of universal benevolence; whilst his heart was incapable of harbouring one spark of common parental affection. Benevolence to the whole species, and want of feeling for every individual with whom the professors come in contact, form the character of the new philosophy. Setting up for an unsocial independence, this their hero of vanity refuses the just price of common labour, as well as the tribute which opulence owes to genius, and which, when paid, honours the giver and the receiver; and then he pleads his beggary as an excuse for his crimes. He melts with tenderness for those only who touch him by the remotest relation, and then, without one natural pang, casts away, as a sort of offal and excrement, the spawn of his disgustful amours, and sends his children to the hospital of foundlings. The bear loves, licks, and forms her young; but bears are not philosophers. Vanity, however, finds its account in reversing the train of our natural feelings. Thousands admire the sentimental writer; the affectionate father is hardly known in his parish.

A LETTER TO A MEMBER OF THE NATIONAL ASSEMBLY

Under this philosophic instructor in the *ethics of vanity*, they have attempted in France a regeneration of the moral constitution of man. Statesmen, like your present rulers, exist by every thing which is spurious, fictitious, and false; by every thing which takes the man from his house, and sets him on a stage, which makes him up an artificial creature, with painted theatric sentiments, fit to be seen by the glare of candlelight, and formed to be contemplated at a due distance. Vanity is too apt to prevail in all of us, and in all countries. To the improvement of Frenchmen it seems not absolutely necessary that it should be taught upon system. But it is plain that the present rebellion was its legitimate offspring, and it is piously fed by that rebellion, with a daily dole.

If the system of institution, recommended by the Assembly, is false and theatric, it is because their system of government is of the same character. To that, and to that alone, it is strictly conformable. To understand either, we must connect the morals with the politics of the legislators. Your practical philosophers, systematic in every thing, have wisely began at the source. As the relation between parents and children is the first among the elements of vulgar, natural morality,[12] they erect statues to a wild, ferocious, low-minded, hard-hearted father, of fine general feelings; a lover of his kind, but a hater of his kindred. Your masters reject the duties of this vulgar relation, as contrary to liberty; as not founded in the social compact; and not binding according to the rights of men; because the relation is not, of course, the result of *free*

[12] Filiola tua te delectari laetor et probari tibi στοργήν φυσικήν esse τὴν πρὸς τὰ τέκνα: etenim, si haec non est, nulla potest homini esse ad hominem naturae adjunctio: qua sublata vitae societas tolletur. Valete Patron [Rousseau] et tui condiscipuli! [L'Assemblée Nationale].

Cic. Ep. ad Atticum

["I am glad you take delight in your baby daughter, and have satisfied yourself that a desire for children is natural. For, if it is not, there can be no natural tie between man and man; remove that tie, and social life is destroyed." Burke then adds the following: "Hail Patron [Rousseau] and your disciples! [The National Assembly]." Cicero, *Letters to Atticus* 7.2 (Loeb Classical Library)]

election; never so on the side of the children, not always on the part of the parents.

The next relation which they regenerate by their statues to Rousseau, is that which is next in sanctity to that of a father. They differ from those old-fashioned thinkers, who considered pedagogues as sober and venerable characters, and allied to the parental. The moralists of the dark times, *preceptorem sancti voluere parentis esse loco.*[13] In this age of light, they teach the people, that preceptors ought to be in the place of gallants. They systematically corrupt a very corruptible race (for some time a growing nuisance amongst you), a set of pert, petulant, literators, to whom, instead of their proper, but severe, unostentatious duties, they assign the brilliant part of men of wit and pleasure, of gay, young, military sparks, and danglers at toilets. They call on the rising generation in France, to take a sympathy in the adventures and fortunes, and they endeavour to engage their sensibility on the side of pedagogues, who betray the most awful family trusts, and vitiate their female pupils. They teach the people, that the debauchers of virgins, almost in the arms of their parents, may be safe inmates in their house, and even fit guardians of the honour of those husbands who succeed legally to the office which the young literators had pre-occupied, without asking leave of law or conscience.

Thus they dispose of all the family relations of parents and children, husbands and wives. Through this same instructor, by whom they corrupt the morals, they corrupt the taste. Taste and elegance, though they are reckoned only among the smaller and secondary morals, yet are of no mean importance in the regulation of life. A moral taste is not of force to turn vice into virtue; but it recommends virtue with something like the blandishments of pleasure; and it infinitely abates the evils of vice. Rousseau, a writer of great force and vivacity, is totally destitute of taste in any sense of the word. Your masters, who are his scholars, conceive that all refine-

[13] ["They wanted the teacher to be in the place of a revered parent." Juvenal, *Satires* 7:209–210]

ment has an aristocratic character. The last age had exhausted all its powers in giving a grace and nobleness to our natural appetites, and in raising them into higher class and order than seemed justly to belong to them. Through Rousseau, your masters are resolved to destroy these aristocratic prejudices. The passion called love, has so general and powerful an influence; it makes so much of the entertainment, and indeed so much the occupation of that part of life which decides the character for ever, that the mode and the principles on which it engages the sympathy, and strikes the imagination, become of the utmost importance to the morals and manners of every society. Your rulers were well aware of this; and in their system of changing your manners to accommodate them to their politics, they found nothing so convenient as Rousseau. Through him they teach men to love after the fashion of philosophers; that is, they teach to men, to Frenchmen, a love without gallantry; a love without any thing of that fine flower of youthfulness and gentility, which places it, if not among the virtues, among the ornaments of life. Instead of this passion, naturally allied to grace and manners, they infuse into their youth an unfashioned, indelicate, sour, gloomy, ferocious medley of pedantry and lewdness; of metaphysical speculations, blended with the coarsest sensuality. Such is the general morality of the passions to be found in their famous philosopher, in his famous work of philosophic gallantry, the *Nouvelle Eloise*.

When the fence from the gallantry of preceptors is broken down, and your families are no longer protected by decent pride, and salutary domestic prejudice, there is but one step to a frightful corruption. The rulers in the National Assembly are in good hopes that the females of the first families in France may become an easy prey to dancing-masters, fidlers, pattern-drawers, friseurs, and valets de chambre, and other active citizens of that description, who having the entry into your houses, and being half-domesticated by their situation, may be blended with you by regular and irregular relations. By a law, they have made these people your equals. By

adopting the sentiments of Rousseau, they have made them
your rivals. In this manner, these great legislators complete
their plan of levelling, and establish their rights of men on a
sure foundation.

I am certain that the writings of Rousseau lead directly to
this kind of shameful evil. I have often wondered how he
comes to be so much more admired and followed on the continent than he is here. Perhaps a secret charm in the language
may have its share in this extraordinary difference. We certainly perceive, and to a degree we feel, in this writer, a style
glowing, animated, enthusiastic; at the same time that we find
it lax, diffuse, and not in the best taste of composition; all the
members of the piece being pretty equally laboured and expanded, without any due selection or subordination of parts.
He is generally too much on the stretch, and his manner has
little variety. We cannot rest upon any of his works, though
they contain observations which occasionally discover a considerable insight into human nature. But his doctrines, on the
whole, are so inapplicable to real life and manners, that we
never dream of drawing from them any rule for laws or conduct, or for fortifying or illustrating any thing by a reference
to his opinions. They have with us the fate of older paradoxes,

> Cum ventum ad *verum* est *sensus moresque* repugnant,
> Atque ipsa utilitas justi prope mater et aequi.[14]

Perhaps bold speculations are more acceptable, because
more new to you than to us, who have been long since satiated
with them. We continue, as in the two last ages, to read more
generally, than I believe is now done on the continent, the
authors of sound antiquity. These occupy our minds. They
give us another taste and turn; and will not suffer us to be
more than transiently amused with paradoxical morality. It is
not that I consider this writer as wholly destitute of just no-

---

[14] ["When it comes to the truth of the matter, one's instincts and mores are
repelled, and so even is utility, which is virtually the mother of justice and
right." Horace, *Satires* 1.3:98–99]

tions. Amongst his irregularities, it must be reckoned, that he is sometimes moral, and moral in a very sublime strain. But the *general spirit and tendency* of his works is mischievous; and the more mischievous for this mixture: For, perfect depravity of sentiment is not reconcileable with eloquence; and the mind (though corruptible, not complexionally vitious) would reject and throw off with disgust, a lesson of pure and unmixed evil. These writers make even virtue a pander to vice.

However, I less consider the author, than the system of the Assembly in perverting morality, through his means. This I confess makes me nearly despair of any attempt upon the minds of their followers, through reason, honour, or conscience. The great object of your tyrants, is to destroy the gentlemen of France; and for that purpose they destroy, to the best of their power, all the effect of those relations which may render considerable men powerful or even safe. To destroy that order, they vitiate the whole community. That no means may exist of confederating against their tyranny, by the false sympathies of this Nouvelle Eloise, they endeavour to subvert those principles of domestic trust and fidelity, which form the discipline of social life. They propagate principles by which every servant may think it, if not his duty, at least his privilege, to betray his master. By these principles, every considerable father of a family loses the sanctuary of his house. *Debet sua cuique domus esse perfugium tu tissimum,*[15] says the law, which your legislators have taken so much pains first to decry, then to repeal. They destroy all the tranquillity and security of domestic life; turning the asylum of the house into a gloomy prison, where the father of the family must drag out a miserable existence, endangered in proportion to the apparent means of his safety; where he is worse than solitary in a croud of domestics, and more apprehensive from his servants and inmates, than from the hired blood-thirsty mob without doors, who are ready to pull him to the lanterne.

[15] [The house of each man ought to be the safest possible refuge.]

A LETTER TO A MEMBER OF THE NATIONAL ASSEMBLY

It is thus, and for the same end, that they endeavour to destroy that tribunal of conscience which exists independently of edicts and decrees. Your despots govern by terror. They know, that he who fears God fears nothing else; and therefore they eradicate from the mind, through their Voltaire, their Helvetius, and the rest of that infamous gang, that only sort of fear which generates true courage. Their object is, that their fellow citizens may be under the dominion of no awe, but that of their committee of research, and of their lanterne.

Having found the advantage of assassination in the formation of their tyranny, it is the grand resource in which they trust for the support of it. Whoever opposes any of their proceedings, or is suspected of a design to oppose them, is to answer it with his life, or the lives of his wife and children. This infamous, cruel, and cowardly practice of assassination, they have the impudence to call *merciful*. They boast that they have operated their usurpation rather by terror than by force; and that a few seasonable murders have prevented the bloodshed of many battles. There is no doubt they will extend these acts of mercy whenever they see an occasion. Dreadful, however, will be the consequences of their attempt to avoid the evils of war, by the merciful policy of murder. If, by effectual punishment of the guilty, they do not wholly disavow that practice, and the threat of it too, as any part of their policy; if ever a foreign prince enters into France, he must enter it as into a country of assassins. The mode of civilized war will not be practised: nor are the French who act on the present system entitled to expect it. They, whose known policy it is to assassinate every citizen whom they suspect to be discontented by their tyranny, and to corrupt the soldiery of every open enemy, must look for no modified hostility. All war, which is not battle, will be military execution. This will beget acts of retaliation from you; and every retaliation will beget a new revenge. The hell-hounds of war, on all sides, will be uncoupled and unmuzzled. The new school of murder and barbarism, set up in Paris, having destroyed (so far as in it lies) all the other manners and principles which have hitherto civilized Europe, will destroy also the mode of civilized war, which, more than any thing else, has distinguished the Christian world. Such is the approaching golden age, which the Virgil of your Assembly has sung to his Pollios![16]

In such a situation of your political, your civil, and your social morals and manners, how can you be hurt by the freedom of any discussion? Caution is for those who have something to lose. What I have said to justify myself in not apprehending any ill consequence from a free discussion of the absurd consequences which flow from the relation of the lawful King to the usurped constitution, will apply to my vindication with regard to the exposure I have made of the state of the army under the same sophistic usurpation. The present tyrants want no arguments to prove, what they must daily feel, that no good army can exist on their principles. They are in no want of a monitor to suggest to them the policy of getting rid of the army, as well as of the King, whenever they are in a condition to effect that measure. What hopes may be entertained of your army for the restoration of your liberties, I know not. At present, yielding obedience to the pretended orders of a King, who, they are perfectly apprised, has no will, and who never can issue a mandate, which is not intended, in the first operation, or in its certain consequences, for his own destruction, your army seems to make one of the principal links in the chain of that servitude of anarchy, by which a cruel usurpation holds an undone people at once in bondage and confusion.

You ask me what I think of the conduct of General Monk.[17] How this affects your case, I cannot tell. I doubt whether you possess, in France, any persons of a capacity to serve the French monarchy in the same manner in which

---

[16] Mirabeau's speech concerning universal peace.

[17] [Menonville had written to Burke that Jacobin writers had been defending the worst acts of Cromwell's Parliament and criticizing the actions of the Presbyterian General George Monck (1608–1670). Monck made common cause with the followers of the executed Charles I to bring about the restoration of the English monarchy in 1660, when King Charles II came to the throne. See *Corr.* Copeland 6:164.]

A Letter to a Member of the National Assembly

Monk served the monarchy of England. The army which Monk commanded had been formed by Cromwell to a perfection of discipline which perhaps has never been exceeded. That army was besides of an excellent composition. The soldiers were men of extraordinary piety after their mode, of the greatest regularity, and even severity of manners; brave in the field, but modest, quiet and orderly, in their quarters; men who abhorred the idea of assassinating their officers or any other persons; and who (they at least who served in this island) were firmly attached to those generals, by whom they were well treated and ably commanded. Such an army, once gained, might be depended on. I doubt much, if you could now find a Monk, whether a Monk could find, in France, such an army.

I certainly agree with you, that in all probability we owe our whole constitution to the restoration of the English monarchy. The state of things from which Monk relieved England, was however by no means, at that time, so deplorable in any sense, as yours is now, and under the present sway is likely to continue. Cromwell had delivered England from anarchy. His government, though military and despotic, had been regular and orderly. Under the iron, and under the yoke, the soil yielded its produce. After his death, the evils of anarchy were rather dreaded than felt. Every man was yet safe in his house and in his property. But it must be admitted, that Monk freed this nation from great and just apprehensions both of future anarchy and of probable tyranny in some form or other. The king whom he gave us was indeed the very reverse of your benignant sovereign, who in reward for his attempt to bestow liberty on his subjects, languishes himself in prison. The person given to us by Monk was a man without any sense of his duty as a prince; without any regard to the dignity of his crown; without any love to his people; dissolute, false, venal, and destitute of any positive good quality whatsoever, except a pleasant temper, and the manners of a gentleman. Yet the restoration of our monarchy, even in the person of such a prince, was every thing to us; for without monarchy in England, most certainly we never can enjoy either peace or liberty. It was under this conviction that the very first regular step which we took on the Revolution of 1688, was to fill the throne with a real king; and even before it could be done in due form, the chiefs of the nation did not attempt themselves to exercise authority so much as by *interim*. They instantly requested the Prince of Orange to take the government on himself. The throne was not effectively vacant for an hour.

Your fundamental laws, as well as ours, suppose a monarchy. Your zeal, Sir, in standing so firmly for it as you have done, shews not only a sacred respect for your honour and fidelity, but a well-informed attachment to the real welfare and true liberties of your country. I have expressed myself ill, if I have given you cause to imagine, that I prefer the conduct of those who have retired from this warfare to your behaviour, who, with a courage and constancy almost supernatural, have struggled against tyranny, and kept the field to the last. You see I have corrected the exceptionable part in the edition which I now send you. Indeed in such terrible extremities as yours, it is not easy to say, in a political view, what line of conduct is the most adviseable. In that state of things, I cannot bring myself severely to condemn persons who are wholly unable to bear so much as the sight of those men in the throne of legislation, who are only fit to be the objects of criminal justice. If fatigue, if disgust, if unsurmountable nausea, drive them away from such spectacles, *ubi miseriarum pars non minima erat, videre et aspici*,[18] I cannot blame them. He must have an heart of adamant who could hear a set of traitors puffed up with unexpected and undeserved power, obtained by an ignoble, unmanly, and perfidious rebellion, treating their honest fellow citizens as *rebels*, because they refused to bind themselves through their conscience, against the dictates of conscience itself, and had declined to swear an active compliance with their own ruin. How could a man of common flesh and blood endure, that those, who but the

[18] [Where it was not the smallest part of one's miseries to see and be seen.]

other day had skulked unobserved in their antichambers, scornfully insulting men, illustrious in their rank, sacred in their function, and venerable in their character, now in decline of life, and swimming on the wrecks of their fortunes, that those miscreants should tell such men scornfully and outrageously, after they had robbed them of all their property, that it is more than enough if they are allowed what will keep them from absolute famine, and that for the rest, they must let their grey hairs fall over the plough, to make out a scanty subsistence with the labour of their hands! Last, and worst, who could endure to hear this unnatural, insolent, and savage despotism called liberty? If, at this distance, sitting quietly by my fire, I cannot read their decrees and speeches without indignation, shall I condemn those who have fled from the actual sight and hearing of all these horrors? No, no! mankind has no title to demand that we should be slaves to their guilt and insolence; or that we should serve them in spite of themselves. Minds, sore with the poignant sense of insulted virtue, filled with high disdain against the pride of triumphant baseness, often have it not in their choice to stand their ground. Their complexion (which might defy the rack) cannot go through such a trial. Something very high must fortify men to that proof. But when I am driven to comparison, surely I cannot hesitate for a moment to prefer to such men as are common, those heroes, who in the midst of despair perform all the tasks of hope; who subdue their feelings to their duties; who, in the cause of humanity, liberty, and honour, abandon all the satisfactions of life, and every day incur a fresh risque of life itself. Do me the justice to believe that I never can prefer any fastidious virtue (virtue still) to the unconquered perseverance, to the affectionate patience of those who watch day and night, by the bed-side of their delirious country, who, for their love to that dear and venerable name, bear all the disgusts, and all the buffets they receive from their frantic mother. Sir, I do look on you as true martyrs; I regard you as soldiers who act far more in the spirit of our Commander in chief, and the Captain of our salvation, than those who have left you; though I must first bolt myself very thoroughly, and know that I could do better, before I can censure them. I assure you, Sir, that, when I consider your unconquerable fidelity to your sovereign, and to your country, the courage, fortitude, magnanimity, and long-suffering of yourself, and the Abbé Maury, and of Mr. Cazales, and of many worthy persons of all orders, in your Assembly, I forget, in the lustre of these great qualities, that on your side has been displayed an eloquence so rational, manly, and convincing, that no time or country, perhaps, has ever excelled. But your talents disappear in my admiration of your virtues.

As to Mr. Mounier and Mr. Lally,[19] I have always wished to do justice to their parts, and their eloquence, and the general purity of their motives. Indeed I saw very well from the beginning, the mischiefs which, with all these talents and good intentions, they would do to their country, through their confidence in systems. But their distemper was an epidemic malady. They were young and inexperienced; and when will young and inexperienced men learn caution and distrust of themselves? And when will men, young or old, if suddenly raised to far higher power than that which absolute kings and emperors commonly enjoy, learn any thing like moderation? Monarchs in general respect some settled order of things, which they find it difficult to move from its basis, and to which they are obliged to conform, even when there are no positive limitations to their power. These gentlemen conceived that they were chosen to new model the state, and even the whole order of civil society itself. No wonder that *they* entertained dangerous visions, when the King's ministers, trustees for the sacred deposit of the monarchy, were so in-

[19] [The Comte de Lally-Tollendal had favored the plenary courts that the French government proposed shortly before the Revolution in an effort to strip the French Parlements of much of their historic authority, which was increasingly being used against the monarchy. Joseph Mounier, most famous for suggesting the Tennis Court Oath, proposed a bicameral legislature on the British model. Both men were members of the National Assembly, and both ultimately left France. See Simon Schama, *Citizens* (New York: Knopf, 1989): 269, 443.]

fected with the contagion of project and system (I can hardly think it black premeditated treachery) that they publicly advertised for plans and schemes of government, as if they were to provide for the rebuilding of an hospital that had been burned down. What was this, but to unchain the fury of rash speculation amongst a people, of itself but too apt to be guided by a heated imagination, and a wild spirit of adventure?

The fault of Mr. Mounier and Mr. Lally was very great; but it was very general. If those gentlemen stopped when they came to the brink of the gulph of guilt and public misery, that yawned before them in the abyss of these dark and bottomless speculations, I forgive their first error; in that they were involved with many. Their repentance was their own.

They who consider Mounier and Lally as deserters, must regard themselves as murderers and as traitors: for from what else than murder and treason did they desert? For my part, I honour them for not having carried mistake into crime. If, indeed, I thought that they were not cured by experience; that they were not made sensible that those who would reform a state, ought to assume some actual constitution of government which is to be reformed; if they are not at length satisfied that it is become a necessary preliminary to liberty in France, to commence by the re-establishment of order and property of *every* kind, through the re-establishment of their monarchy, of every one of the old habitual distinctions and classes of the state; if they do not see that these classes are not to be confounded in order to be afterwards revived and separated; if they are not convinced that the scheme of parochial and club governments takes up the state at the wrong end, and is a low and senseless contrivance (as making the sole constitution of a supreme power) I should then allow, that their early rashness ought to be remembered to the last moment of their lives.

You gently reprehend me, because in holding out the picture of your disastrous situation, I suggest no plan for a remedy. Alas! Sir, the proposition of plans, without an attention to circumstances, is the very cause of all your misfortunes; and never shall you find me aggravating, by the infusion of any speculations of mine, the evils which have arisen from the speculations of others. Your malady, in this respect, is a disorder of repletion. You seem to think, that my keeping back my poor ideas, may arise from an indifference to the welfare of a foreign, and sometimes an hostile nation. No, Sir, I faithfully assure you, my reserve is owing to no such causes. Is this letter, swelled to a second book, a mark of national antipathy, or even of national indifference? I should act altogether in the spirit of the same caution, in a similar state of our own domestic affairs. If I were to venture any advice, in any case, it would be my best. The sacred duty of an adviser (one of the most inviolable that exists) would lead me, towards a real enemy, to act as if my best friend were the party concerned. But I dare not risque a speculation with no better view of your affairs than at present I can command; my caution is not from disregard, but from sollicitude for your welfare. It is suggested solely from my dread of becoming the author of inconsiderate counsel.

It is not, that as this strange series of actions has passed before my eyes, I have not indulged my mind in a great variety of political speculations concerning them. But compelled by no such positive duty as does not permit me to evade an opinion; called upon by no ruling power, without authority as I am, and without confidence, I should ill answer my own ideas of what would become myself, or what would be serviceable to others, if I were, as a volunteer, to obtrude any project of mine upon a nation, to whose circumstances I could not be sure it might be applicable.

Permit me to say, that if I were as confident, as I ought to be diffident in my own loose, general ideas, I never should venture to broach them, if but at twenty leagues distance from the centre of your affairs. I must see with my own eyes, I must, in a manner, touch with my own hands, not only the fixed, but the momentary circumstances, before I could venture to suggest any political project whatsoever. I must know the power and disposition to accept, to execute, to persevere. I must see all the

---

aids, and all the obstacles. I must see the means of correcting the plan, where correctives would be wanted. I must see the things; I must see the men. Without a concurrence and adaptation of these to the design, the very best speculative projects might become not only useless, but mischievous. Plans must be made for men. We cannot think of making men, and binding nature to our designs. People at a distance must judge ill of men. They do not always answer to their reputation when you approach them. Nay, the perspective varies, and shews them quite otherwise than you thought them. At a distance, if we judge uncertainly of men, we must judge worse of *opportunities*, which continually vary their shapes and colours, and pass away like clouds. The Eastern politicians never do any thing without the opinion of the astrologers on the *fortunate moment*. They are in the right, if they can do no better; for the opinion of fortune is something towards commanding it. Statesmen of a more judicious prescience, look for the fortunate moment too; but they seek it, not in the conjunctions and oppositions of planets, but in the conjunctions and oppositions of men and things. These form their almanack.

To illustrate the mischief of a wise plan, without any attention to means and circumstances, it is not necessary to go farther than to your recent history. In the condition in which France was found three years ago, what better system could be proposed, what less, even savouring of wild theory, what fitter to provide for all the exigencies, whilst it reformed all the abuses of government, than the convention of the States General? I think nothing better could be imagined. But I have censured, and do still presume to censure your Parliament of Paris, for not having suggested to the King, that this proper measure was of all measures the most critical and arduous; one in which the utmost circumspection, and the greatest number of precautions, were the most absolutely necessary. The very confession that a government wants either amendment in its conformation, or relief to great distress, causes it to lose half its reputation, and as great a proportion of its strength as depends upon that reputation. It was therefore necessary, first to put government out of danger, whilst at its own desire it suffered such an operation, as a general reform at the hands of those who were much more filled with a sense of the disease, than provided with rational means of a cure.

It may be said, that this care, and these precautions, were more naturally the duty of the King's ministers, than that of the Parliament. They were so; but every man must answer in his estimation for the advice he gives, when he puts the conduct of his measure into hands who he does not know will execute his plans according to his ideas. Three or four ministers were not to be trusted with the being of the French monarchy, of all the orders, and of all the distinctions, and all the property of the kingdom. What must be the prudence of those who could think, in the then known temper of the people of Paris, of assembling the states at a place situated as Versailles?

The Parliament of Paris did worse than to inspire this blind confidence into the King. For, as if names were things, they took no notice of (indeed they rather countenanced) the deviations which were manifest in the execution, from the true antient principles of the plan which they recommended. These deviations (as guardians of the antient laws, usages, and constitution of the kingdom) the Parliament of Paris ought not to have suffered, without the strongest remonstrances to the throne. It ought to have sounded the alarm to the whole nation, as it had often done on things of infinitely less importance. Under pretence of resuscitating the antient constitution, the Parliament saw one of the strongest acts of innovation, and the most leading in its consequences, carried into effect before their eyes; and an innovation through the medium of despotism; that is, they suffered the King's ministers to new model the whole representation of the *Tiers Etat*, and, in a great measure, that of the clergy too, and to destroy the antient proportions of the orders. These changes, unquestionably the King had no right to make; and here the Parliaments failed in their duty, and along with their country, have perished by this failure.

[65]

What a number of faults have led to this multitude of misfortunes, and almost all from this one source, that of considering certain general maxims, without attending to circumstances, to times, to places, to conjunctures, and to actors! If we do not attend scrupulously to all these, the medicine of to-day becomes the poison of to-morrow. If any measure was in the abstract better than another, it was to call the states—*ea visa salus morientibus una.*[20] Certainly it had the appearance. But see the consequences of not attending to critical moments, of not regarding the symptoms which discriminate diseases, and which distinguish constitutions, complexions, and humours.

> Mox fuerat hoc ipsum exitio; furiisque refecti,
> Ardebant; ipsique suos, jam morte sub aegra,
> Discissos nudis laniabant dentibus artus.[21]

Thus the potion which was given to strengthen the constitution, to heal divisions, and to compose the minds of men, became the source of debility, phrenzy, discord, and utter dissolution.

In this, perhaps, I have answered, I think, another of your questions—Whether the British constitution is adapted to your circumstances? When I praised the British constitution, and wished it to be well studied, I did not mean that its exterior form and positive arrangement should become a model for you, or for any people servilely to copy. I meant to recommend the *principles* from which it has grown, and the policy on which it has been progressively improved out of elements common to you and to us. I am sure it is no visionary theory of mine. It is not an advice that subjects you to the hazard of any experiment. I believed the antient principles to be wise in all cases of a large empire that would be free. I thought you possessed our

[20] [This appears to be the one salvation for a dying people.]

[21] ["Soon even this led to death; they burned with the fury of fresh strength, and, though now in the weakness of death . . . rent and mangled their own limbs with bared teeth." Vergil, *Georgics* 3:511–12, 514 (Loeb Classical Library).]

principles in your old forms, in as great a perfection as we did originally. If your states agreed (as I think they did) with your circumstances, they were best for you. As you had a constitution formed upon principles similar to ours, my idea was, that you might have improved them as we have done, conforming them to the state and exigencies of the times, and the condition of property in your country, having the conservation of that property, and the substantial basis of your monarchy, as principal objects in all your reforms.

I do not advise an House of Lords to you. Your antient course by representatives of the Noblesse (in your circumstances) appears to me rather a better institution. I know, that with you, a set of men of rank have betrayed their constituents, their honour, their trust, their King, and their country, and levelled themselves with their footmen, that through this degradation they might afterwards put themselves above their natural equals. Some of these persons have entertained a project, that in reward of this their black perfidy and corruption, they may be chosen to give rise to a new order, and to establish themselves into an House of Lords. Do you think that, under the name of a British constitution, I mean to recommend to you such Lords, made of such kind of stuff? I do not however include in this description all of those who are fond of this scheme.

If you were now to form such an House of Peers, it would bear, in my opinion, but little resemblance to our's in its origin, character, or the purposes which it might answer, at the same time that it would destroy your true natural nobility. But if you are not in a condition to frame an House of Lords, still less are you capable, in my opinion, of framing any thing which virtually and substantially could be answerable (for the purposes of a stable, regular government) to our House of Commons. That House is, within itself, a much more subtle and artificial combination of parts and powers, than people are generally aware of. What knits it to the other members of the constitution; what fits it to be at once the great support, and the great controul of government; what makes it of such admirable service to that monarchy which, if it limits, it secures and strengthens, would require a long discourse, belonging to the leisure of a contemplative man, not to one whose duty it is to join in communicating practically to the people the blessings of such a constitution.

Your *Tiers Etat* was not in effect and substance an House of Commons. You stood in absolute need of something else to supply the manifest defects in such a body as your Tiers Etat. On a sober and dispassionate view of your old constitution, as connected with all the present circumstances, I was fully persuaded, that the crown, standing as things have stood (and are likely to stand, if you are to have any monarchy at all) was and is incapable, alone and by itself, of holding a just balance between the two orders, and at the same time of effecting the interior and exterior purposes of a protecting government. I, whose leading principle it is, in a reformation of the state, to make use of existing materials, am of opinion, that the representation of the clergy, as a separate order, was an institution which touched all the orders more nearly than any of them touched the other; that it was well fitted to connect them; and to hold a place in any wise monarchical commonwealth. If I refer you to your original constitution, and think it, as I do, substantially a good one, I do not amuse you in this, more than in other things, with any inventions of mine. A certain intemperance of intellect is the disease of the time, and the source of all its other diseases. I will keep myself as untainted by it as I can. Your architects build without a foundation. I would readily lend an helping hand to any superstructure, when once this is effectually secured—but first I would say δός πού στῶ.[22]

You think, Sir, and you may think rightly, upon the first view of the theory, that to provide for the exigencies of an empire, so situated and so related as that of France, its King ought to be invested with powers very much superior to those which the King of England possesses under the letter of our

---

[22] [Give me a place to stand.]

constitution. Every degree of power necessary to the state, and not destructive to the rational and moral freedom of individuals, to that personal liberty, and personal security, which contribute so much to the vigour, the prosperity, the happiness, and the dignity of a nation—every degree of power which does not suppose the total absence of all control, and all responsibility on the part of ministers, a King of France, in common sense, ought to possess. But whether the exact measure of authority, assigned by the letter of the law to the King of Great Britain, can answer to the exterior or interior purposes of the French monarchy, is a point which I cannot venture to judge upon. Here, both in the power given, and its limitations, we have always cautiously felt our way. The parts of our constitution have gradually, and almost insensibly, in a long course of time, accommodated themselves to each other, and to their common, as well as to their separate purposes. But this adaptation of contending parts, as it has not been in our's, so it can never be in your's, or in any country, the effect of a single instantaneous regulation, and no sound heads could ever think of doing it in that manner.

I believe, Sir, that many on the continent altogether mistake the condition of a King of Great Britain. He is a real King, and not an executive officer. If he will not trouble himself with contemptible details, nor wish to degrade himself by becoming a party in little squabbles, I am far from sure, that a King of Great Britain, in whatever concerns him as a King, or indeed as a rational man, who combines his public interest with his personal satisfaction, does not possess a more real, solid, extensive power, than the King of France was possessed of before this miserable Revolution. The direct power of the King of England is considerable. His indirect, and far more certain power, is great indeed. He stands in need of nothing towards dignity; of nothing towards splendour; of nothing towards authority; of nothing at all towards consideration abroad. When was it that a King of England wanted wherewithal to make him respected, courted, or perhaps even feared in every state in Europe?

A LETTER TO A MEMBER OF THE NATIONAL ASSEMBLY

I am constantly of opinion, that your states, in three orders, on the footing on which they stood in 1614, were capable of being brought into a proper and harmonious combination with royal authority. This constitution by estates, was the natural, and only just representation of France. It grew out of the habitual conditions, relations, and reciprocal claims of men. It grew out of the circumstances of the country, and out of the state of property. The wretched scheme of your present masters, is not to fit the constitution to the people, but wholly to destroy conditions, to dissolve relations, to change the state of the nation, and to subvert property, in order to fit their country to their theory of a constitution.

Until you could make out practically that great work, a combination of opposing forces, "a work of labour long, and endless praise," the utmost caution ought to have been used in the reduction of the royal power, which alone was capable of holding together the comparatively heterogeneous mass of your states. But at this day, all these considerations are unseasonable. To what end should we discuss the limitations of royal power? Your king is in prison. Why speculate on the measure and standard of liberty? I doubt much, very much indeed, whether France is at all ripe for liberty on any standard. Men are qualified for civil liberty, in exact proportion to their disposition to put moral chains upon their own appetites; in proportion as their love to justice is above their rapacity; in proportion as their soundness and sobriety of understanding is above their vanity and presumption; in proportion as they are more disposed to listen to the counsels of the wise and good, in preference to the flattery of knaves. Society cannot exist unless a controlling power upon will and appetite be placed somewhere, and the less of it there is within, the more there must be without. It is ordained in the eternal constitution of things, that men of intemperate minds cannot be free. Their passions forge their fetters.

This sentence the prevalent part of your countrymen execute on themselves. They possessed, not long since, what was next to freedom, a mild paternal monarchy. They despised it

for its weakness. They were offered a well-poised free constitution. It did not suit their taste or their temper. They carved
for themselves; they flew out, murdered, robbed, and rebelled. They have succeeded, and put over their country an
insolent tyranny, made up of cruel and inexorable masters,
and that too of a description hitherto not known in the world.
The powers and policies by which they have succeeded, are
not those of great statesmen, or great military commanders,
but the practices of incendiaries, assassins, housebreakers,
robbers, spreaders of false news, forgers of false orders from
authority, and other delinquencies, of which ordinary justice
takes cognizance. Accordingly the spirit of their rule is exactly
correspondent to the means by which they obtained it. They
act more in the manner of thieves who have got possession of
an house, than of conquerors who have subdued a nation.

Opposed to these, in appearance, but in appearance only,
is another band, who call themselves the *moderate*. These, if I
conceive rightly of their conduct, are a set of men who approve heartily of the whole new constitution, but wish to lay
heavy on the most atrocious of those crimes, by which this fine
constitution of their's has been obtained. They are a sort of
people who affect to proceed as if they thought that men may
deceive without fraud, rob without injustice, and overturn
every thing without violence. They are men who would usurp
the government of their country with decency and moderation. In fact they are nothing more or better, than men engaged in desperate designs, with feeble minds. They are not
honest; they are only ineffectual and unsystematic in their
iniquity. They are persons who want not the dispositions, but
the energy and vigour, that is necessary for great evil machinations. They find that in such designs they fall at best into a
secondary rank, and others take the place and lead in usurpation, which they are not qualified to obtain or to hold. They
envy to their companions, the natural fruit of their crimes;
they join to run them down with the hue and cry of mankind,
which pursues their common offences; and then hope to
mount into their places on the credit of the sobriety with

A Letter to a Member of the National Assembly

which they shew themselves disposed to carry on what may seem most plausible in the mischievous projects they pursue in common. But these men naturally are despised by those who have heads to know, and hearts that are able to go through the necessary demands of bold, wicked enterprizes. They are naturally classed below the latter description, and will only be used by them as inferior instruments. They will be only the Fairfaxes of your Cromwells.[23] If they mean honestly, why do they not strengthen the arms of honest men, to support their antient, legal, wise, and free government, given to them in the spring of 1788, against the inventions of craft, and the theories of ignorance and folly? If they do not, they must continue the scorn of both parties; sometimes the tool, sometimes the incumbrance of that, whose views they approve, whose conduct they decry. These people are only made to be the sport of tyrants. They never can obtain, or communicate freedom.

You ask me too, whether we have a committee of research. No, Sir, God forbid! It is the necessary instrument of tyranny and usurpation; and therefore I do not wonder that it has had an early establishment under your present Lords. We do not want it.

Excuse my length. I have been somewhat occupied, since I was honoured with your letter; and I should not have been able to answer it at all, but for the holidays, which have given me means of enjoying the leisure of the country. I am called to duties which I am neither able nor willing to evade. I must soon return to my old conflict with the corruptions and oppressions which have prevailed in our eastern dominions.[24] I must turn myself wholly from those of France.

In England, we *cannot* work so hard as Frenchmen. Frequent relaxation is necessary to us. You are naturally more

[23] [Thomas Fairfax (1612–1671) was appointed commander of the parliamentary army in 1645. He disapproved of the execution of Charles I and the war against Scotland. Upon his resignation, Cromwell assumed command.]

[24] [A reference to Burke's ongoing work in the impeachment trial of Warren Hastings, Governor-General of India.]

intense in your application. I did not know this part of your national character, until I went into France in 1773. At present, this your disposition to labour is rather encreased than lessened. In your Assembly you do not allow yourselves a recess even on Sundays. We have two days in the week, besides the festivals; and besides five or six months of the summer and autumn. This continued unremitted effort of the members of your Assembly, I take to be one among the causes of the mischief they have done. They who always labour, can have no true judgment. You never give yourselves time to cool. You can never survey, from its proper point of sight, the work you have finished, before you decree its final execution. You can never plan the future by the past. You never go into the country, soberly and dispassionately to observe the effect of your measures on their objects. You cannot feel distinctly how far the people are rendered better and improved, or more miserable and depraved, by what you have done. You cannot see with your own eyes the sufferings and afflictions you cause. You know them but at a distance, on the statements of those who always flatter the reigning power, and who, amidst their representations of the grievances, inflame your minds against those who are oppressed. These are amongst the effects of unremitted labour, when men exhaust their attention, burn out their candles, and are left in the dark. *Malo meorum negligentiam, quam istorum obscuram diligentiam.*[25]

Beaconsfield,
January 19th, 1791

I have the honor, &c.

EDMUND BURKE

---

[25] [I prefer the neglect of my own people to the dubious attentions of yours.]

4

An Appeal from the New
to the Old Whigs

August 1791

*T*he events of the spring and summer of 1791 were climacteric
for Edmund Burke. His increasing alienation from his fellow Whigs
finally issued in a rupture between him and the party's leader, Charles
James Fox, during the debates on the Quebec Bill on May 6 and 11. It
gradually became apparent that Burke was not simply alienated but
isolated within the House of Commons: "not one of the party spoke one
conciliatory word," he wrote to his patron, the Earl Fitzwilliam, of the
May 11 debate. On May 21, Burke's A Letter to a Member of the
National Assembly *was published; it was dismissed by Fox as "mere
madness." During the night of June 20–21, Louis XVI and the Queen
fled Paris, only to be captured and suspended from their royal functions on June 25. Burke wrote that British sorrow for the King was
"real, and unaffected, and general"* (Corr. Copeland 6:291).

The moment had arrived for Burke to explain his actions, not just
as a political thinker, but as a member of the Whig party. In
Thoughts on the Cause of the Present Discontents *(1770) Burke
had defined a political party as* "a body of men united, for promoting
by their joint endeavours the national interest, upon some particular
principle in which they are all agreed." *How could the man who had
changed the British attitude toward parties—from viewing them as
conspiracies to considering them respectable and even necessary bodies for free governments—now act in a way that virtually guaranteed
a split in his own party? The operative word in Burke's definition is*

"*principle*," *and* An Appeal *is meant to show how the "new" Whigs under the leadership of Charles James Fox had departed from the principles of the "old" Whigs at the time of the Glorious Revolution (1688–89), the first group of men who could rightly be called Whigs.*

Since much of An Appeal *consists in Burke's extracts from and comments on the trial of Henry Sacheverell (1674?–1724), a bit of background may prove useful. Sacheverell had virulently attacked Whigs, dissenters, and low-church Anglicans in pamphlets and sermons from the early 1700s. In 1709 the House of Commons declared that two of his printed sermons were "malicious, scandalous, and seditious libels, highly reflecting upon Her Majesty [Queen Anne] and her government, and the protestant succession." The Whig ministers ordered his trial to be heard in Westminster, guaranteeing thereby that it would become a contest between Whig and Tory political principles. Sacheverell was declared guilty by the House of Lords in March 1710, but his sentence was so mild that he was felt to have won. The Whig ministry lost credit through the trial and was later replaced by the Tories.*

An Appeal, *which Burke chose to write in the third person, may be divided into seven parts: Burke's separation from his party because of the* Reflections *and his attempt to speak on the Quebec Bill; his alleged inconsistency, for he had defended democracy and attacked privilege at other times in his career; his interpretation of the Revolution of 1688 and the trial of Sacheverell; the beliefs of the "new" Whigs, as drawn from the pamphlets directed against Burke; a true political understanding of "the people" as against a majority "told by the head"; an analysis of the extremism of the revolutionary mind; and finally, Burke's own attempt to understand the development of the British constitution by eliciting political theory from political facts and human nature. This work is central to Burke's understanding that humanity realizes its true nature through "art," including such artificial institutions as historical constitutions.*

An Appeal from the New to the Old Whigs

AT Mr. Burke's time of life, and in his dispositions, *petere honestam dimissionem*[1] was all he had to do with his political associates. This boon they have not chosen to grant him. With many expressions of good-will, in effect they tell him he has loaded the stage too long. They conceive it, tho' an harsh yet a necessary office, in full parliament to declare to the present age, and to as late a posterity, as shall take any concern in the proceedings of our day, that by one book he has disgraced the whole tenour of his life. Thus they dismiss their old partner of the war. He is advised to retire, whilst they continue to serve the public upon wiser principles, and under better auspices.

Whether Diogenes the Cynic was a true philosopher, cannot easily be determined. He has written nothing. But the sayings of his which are handed down by others, are lively; and may be easily and aptly applied on many occasions by those whose wit is not so perfect as their memory. This Diogenes (as every one will recollect) was citizen of a little bleak town situated on the coast of the Euxine, and exposed to all the buffets of that unhospitable sea. He lived at a great distance from those weather-beaten walls, in ease and indolence, and in the midst of literary leisure, when he was informed that his townsmen had condemned him to be banished from

[1] [To ask for an honorable discharge.]

Sinope; he answered coolly, "And I condemn them to live in Sinope."

The gentlemen of the party in which Mr. Burke has always acted, in passing upon him the sentence of retirement,[2] have done nothing more than to confirm the sentence which he had long before passed upon himself. When that retreat was choice, which the tribunal of his peers inflict as punishment, it is plain he does not think their sentence intolerably severe. Whether they who are to continue in the Sinope which shortly he is to leave, will spend the long years which, I hope, remain to them, in a manner more to their satisfaction, than he shall slide down, in silence and obscurity, the slope of his declining days, is best known to him who measures out years, and days, and fortunes.

The quality of the sentence does not however decide on the justice of it. Angry friendship is sometimes as bad as calm enmity. For this reason the cold neutrality of abstract justice, is, to a good and clear cause, a more desirable thing than an affection liable to be any way disturbed. When the trial is by friends, if the decision should happen to be favorable, the honor of the acquittal is lessened; if adverse, the condemnation is exceedingly embittered. It is aggravated by coming from lips professing friendship, and pronouncing judgment

---

[2] News-paper intelligence ought always to be received with some degree of caution. I do not know that the following paragraph is founded on any authority; but it comes with an air of authority. The paper is professedly in the interest of the modern Whigs, and under their direction. The paragraph is not disclaimed on their part. It professes to be the decision of those whom its author calls "The great and firm body of the Whigs of England." Who are the Whigs of a different composition, which the promulgator of the sentence considers as composed of fleeting and unsettled particles, I know not, nor whether there be any of that description. The definitive sentence of "the great and firm body of the Whigs of England" (as this paper gives it out) is as follows:

> The great and firm body of the Whigs of England, true to their principles, have decided on the dispute between Mr. Fox and Mr. Burke; and the former is declared to have maintained the pure doctrines by which they are bound together, and upon which they have invariably acted. The consequence is, that Mr. Burke retires from parliament.
>
> *Morning Chronicle, May* 12, 1791

with sorrow and reluctance. Taking in the whole view of life, it is more safe to live under the jurisdiction of severe but steady reason, than under the empire of indulgent, but capricious passion. It is certainly well for Mr. Burke that there are impartial men in the world. To them I address myself, pending the appeal which on his part is made from the living to the dead, from the modern Whigs to the antient.

The gentlemen, who, in the name of the party, have passed sentence on Mr. Burke's book, in the light of literary criticism are judges above all challenge. He did not indeed flatter himself, that as a writer, he could claim the approbation of men whose talents, in his judgment and in the public judgment, approach to prodigies; if ever such persons should be disposed to estimate the merit of a composition upon the standard of their own ability.

In their critical censure, though Mr. Burke may find himself humbled by it as a writer, as a man and as an Englishman, he finds matter not only of consolation, but of pride. He proposed to convey to a foreign people, not his own ideas, but the prevalent opinions and sentiments of a nation, renowned for wisdom, and celebrated in all ages for a well understood and well regulated love of freedom. This was the avowed purpose of the greater part of his work. As that work has not been ill received, and as his critics will not only admit but contend, that this reception could not be owing to any excellence in the composition capable of perverting the public judgment, it is clear that he is not disavowed by the nation whose sentiments he had undertaken to describe. His representation is authenticated by the verdict of his country. Had his piece, as a work of skill, been thought worthy of commendation, some doubt might have been entertained of the cause of his success. But the matter stands exactly as he wishes it. He is more happy to have his fidelity in representation recognized by the body of the people, than if he were to be ranked in point of ability (and higher he could not be ranked) with those whose critical censure he has had the misfortune to incur.

AN APPEAL FROM THE NEW TO THE OLD WHIGS

It is not from this part of their decision which the author wishes an appeal. There are things which touch him more nearly. To abandon them would argue, not diffidence in his abilities, but treachery to his cause. Had his work been recognized as a pattern for dextrous argument, and powerful eloquence, yet if it tended to establish maxims, or to inspire sentiments, adverse to the wise and free constitution of this kingdom, he would only have cause to lament, that it possessed qualities fitted to perpetuate the memory of his offence. Oblivion would be the only means of his escaping the reproaches of posterity. But, after receiving the common allowance due to the common weakness of man, he wishes to owe no part of the indulgence of the world to its forgetfulness. He is at issue with the party, before the present, and if ever he can reach it, before the coming, generation.

The author, several months previous to his publication, well knew, that two gentlemen, both of them possessed of the most distinguished abilities, and of a most decisive authority in the party, had differed with him in one of the most material points relative to the French revolution; that is in their opinion of the behaviour of the French soldiery, and its revolt from its officers. At the time of their public declaration on this subject, he did not imagine the opinion of these two gentlemen had extended a great way beyond themselves. He was however well aware of the probability, that persons of their just credit and influence would at length dispose the greater number to an agreement with their sentiments; and perhaps might induce the whole body to a tacit acquiescence in their declarations, under a natural, and not always an improper dislike of shewing a difference with those who lead their party. I will not deny, that in general this conduct in parties is defensible; but within what limits the practice is to be circumscribed, and with what exceptions the doctrine which supports it is to be received, it is not my present purpose to define. The present question has nothing to do with their motives; it only regards the public expression of their sentiments.

AN APPEAL FROM THE NEW TO THE OLD WHIGS

The author is compelled, however reluctantly, to receive the sentence pronounced upon him in the House of Commons as that of the party. It proceeded from the mouth of him who must be regarded as its authentic organ. In a discussion which continued for two days, no one gentleman of the opposition interposed a negative, or even a doubt, in favour of him or of his opinions.[3] If an idea consonant to the doctrine of his book, or favourable to his conduct, lurks in the minds of any persons in that description, it is to be considered only as a peculiarity which they indulge to their own private liberty of thinking. The author cannot reckon upon it. It has nothing to do with them as members of a party. In their public capacity, in every thing that meets the public ear, or public eye, the body must be considered as unanimous.

They must have been animated with a very warm zeal against those opinions, because they were under no *necessity* of acting as they did, from any just cause of apprehension that the errors of this writer should be taken for theirs. They might disapprove; it was not necessary they should *disavow* him, as they have done in the whole, and in all the parts of his book; because neither in the whole nor in any of the parts, were they, directly, or by any implication, involved. The author was known indeed to have been warmly, strenuously, and affectionately, against all allurements of ambition, and all possibility of alienation from pride, or personal picque, or peevish jealousy, attached to the Whig party. With one of them he has had a long friendship, which he must ever remember with a melancholy pleasure. To the great, real, and amiable virtues, and to the unequalled abilities of that gentleman, he shall always join with his country in paying a just tribute of applause. There are others in that party for whom, without any shade of sorrow, he bears as high a degree of love as can enter into the human heart; and as much veneration as ought to be paid to human creatures; because he firmly believes, that they are endowed with as many and as great vir-

---

[3] [A reference to Charles James Fox and Burke's split with him during the debates on May 6 and May 11, 1791.]

tues, as the nature of man is capable of producing, joined to great clearness of intellect, to a just judgment, to a wonderful temper, and to true wisdom. His sentiments with regard to them can never vary, without subjecting him to the just indignation of mankind, who are bound, and are generally disposed, to look up with reverence to the best patterns of their species, and such as give a dignity to the nature of which we all participate. For the whole of the party he has high respect. Upon a view indeed of the composition of all parties, he finds great satisfaction. It is, that in leaving the service of his country, he leaves parliament without all comparison richer in abilities than he found it. Very solid and very brilliant talents distinguish the ministerial benches. The opposite rows are a sort of seminary of genius, and have brought forth such and so great talents as never before (amongst us at least) have appeared together. If their owners are disposed to serve their country (he trusts they are), they are in a condition to render it services of the highest importance. If, through mistake or passion, they are led to contribute to its ruin, we shall at least have a consolation denied to the ruined country that adjoins us—we shall not be destroyed by men of mean or secondary capacities.

All these considerations of party attachment, of personal regard, and of personal admiration, rendered the author of the Reflections extremely cautious, lest the slightest suspicion should arise of his having undertaken to express the sentiments even of a single man of that description. His words at the outset of his Reflections are these:

"In the first letter I had the honour to write to you, and which at length I send, I wrote neither *for*, nor *from* any description of men; nor shall I in this. My errors, if any, are *my own*. My reputation *alone* is to answer for them."[4] In another place, he says (p. 126) "I have *no man's* proxy. I speak *only* from *myself*; when I disclaim, as I do, with all possible earnestness, all communion with the actors in that triumph, or with the

---

[4] [*Reflections*, p. 85.]

admirers of it. When I assert any thing else, as concerning the people of England, I speak from observation, *not from authority*."[5]

To say then, that the book did not contain the sentiments of their party, is not to contradict the author, or to clear themselves. If the party had denied his doctrines to be the current opinions of the majority in the nation, they would have put the question on its true issue. There, I hope and believe, his censurers will find on the trial, that the author is as faithful a representative of the general sentiment of the people of England, as any person amongst them can be of the ideas of his own party.

The French Revolution can have no connexion with the objects of any parties in England formed before the period of that event, unless they choose to imitate any of its acts, or to consolidate any principles of that revolution with their own opinions. The French revolution is no part of their original contract. The matter, standing by itself, is an open subject of political discussion, like all the other revolutions (and there are many) which have been attempted or accomplished in our age. But if any considerable number of British subjects, taking a factious interest in the proceedings of France, begin publicly to incorporate themselves for the subversion of nothing short of the *whole* constitution of this kingdom; to incorporate themselves for the utter overthrow of the body of its laws, civil and ecclesiastical, and with them of the whole system of its manners, in favour of the new constitution, and of the modern usages of the French nation, I think no party principle could bind the author not to express his sentiments strongly against such a faction. On the contrary, he was perhaps bound to mark his dissent, when the leaders of the party were daily going out of their way to make public declarations in parliament, which, notwithstanding the purity of their intentions, had a tendency to encourage ill-designing men in their practices against our constitution.

[5] [*Reflections*, p. 180.]

AN APPEAL FROM THE NEW TO THE OLD WHIGS

The members of this faction leave no doubt of the nature and the extent of the mischief they mean to produce. They declare it openly and decisively. Their intentions are not left equivocal. They are put out of all dispute by the thanks which, formally and as it were officially, they issue, in order to recommend, and to promote the circulation of the most atrocious and treasonable libels, against all the hitherto cherished objects of the love and veneration of this people. Is it contrary to the duty of a good subject, to reprobate such proceedings? Is it alien to the office of a good member of parliament, when such practices encrease, and when the audacity of the conspirators grows with their impunity, to point out in his place their evil tendency to the happy constitution which he is chosen to guard? Is it wrong in any sense, to render the people of England sensible how much they must suffer if unfortunately such a wicked faction should become possessed in this country of the same power which their allies in the very next to us have so perfidiously usurped, and so outrageously abused? Is it inhuman to prevent, if possible, the spilling of *their* blood, or imprudent to guard against the effusion of *our own*? Is it contrary to any of the honest principles of party, or repugnant to any of the known duties of friendship for any senator, respectfully, and amicably, to caution his brother members against countenancing by inconsiderate expressions a sort of proceeding which it is impossible they should deliberately approve?

He had undertaken to demonstrate, by arguments which he thought could not be refuted, and by documents, which he was sure could not be denied, that no comparison was to be made between the British government, and the French usurpation. That they who endeavoured madly to compare them, were by no means making the comparison of one good system with another good system, which varied only in local and circumstantial differences; much less, that they were holding out to us a superior pattern of legal liberty, which we might substitute in the place of our old, and, as they describe it, superannuated constitution. He meant to demonstrate, that the French scheme was not a comparative good, but a positive evil. That the question did not at all turn, as it had been stated, on a parallel between a monarchy and a republic. He denied that the present scheme of things in France, did at all deserve the respectable name of a republic: he had therefore no comparison between monarchies and republics to make. That what was done in France was a wild attempt to methodize anarchy; to perpetuate and fix disorder. That it was a foul, impious, monstrous thing, wholly out of the course of moral nature. He undertook to prove, that it was generated in treachery, fraud, falsehood, hypocrisy, and unprovoked murder. He offered to make out, that those who have led in that business, had conducted themselves with the utmost perfidy to their colleagues in function, and with the most flagrant perjury both towards their king and their constituents; to the one of whom the assembly had sworn fealty, and to the other, when under no sort of violence or constraint, they had sworn a full obedience to instructions. That by the terror of assassination they had driven away a very great number of the members, so as to produce a false appearance of a majority. That this fictitious majority had fabricated a constitution, which as now it stands, is a tyranny far beyond any example that can be found in the civilized European world of our age; that therefore the lovers of it must be lovers, not of liberty, but, if they really understand its nature, of the lowest and basest of all servitude.

He proposed to prove, that the present state of things in France is not a transient evil, productive, as some have too favourably represented it, of a lasting good; but that the present evil is only the means of producing future, and (if that were possible) worse evils. That it is not, an undigested, imperfect, and crude scheme of liberty, which may gradually be mellowed and ripened into an orderly and social freedom; but that it is so fundamentally wrong, as to be utterly incapable of correcting itself by any length of time, or of being formed into any mode of polity, of which a member of the house of commons could publicly declare his approbation.

An Appeal from the New to the Old Whigs

If it had been permitted to Mr. Burke, he would have shewn distinctly, and in detail, that what the assembly calling itself national, had held out as a large and liberal toleration, is in reality a cruel and insidious religious persecution; infinitely more bitter than any which had been heard of within this century. That it had a feature in it worse than the old persecutions. That the old persecutors acted, or pretended to act, from zeal towards some system of piety and virtue: they gave strong preferences to their own; and if they drove people from one religion, they provided for them another, in which men might take refuge, and expect consolation. That their new persecution is not against a variety in conscience, but against all conscience. That it professes contempt towards its object; and whilst it treats all religion with scorn, is not so much as neutral about the modes: It unites the opposite evils of intolerance and of indifference.

He could have proved, that it is so far from rejecting tests (as unaccountably had been asserted) that the assembly had imposed tests of a peculiar hardship, arising from a cruel and premeditated pecuniary fraud: tests against old principles, sanctioned by the laws, and binding upon the conscience. That these tests were not imposed as titles to some new honour or some new benefit, but to enable men to hold a poor compensation for their legal estates, of which they had been unjustly deprived; and, as they had before been reduced from affluence to indigence, so on refusal to swear against their conscience, they are now driven from indigence to famine, and treated with every possible degree of outrage, insult, and inhumanity. That these tests, which their imposers well knew would not be taken, were intended for the very purpose of cheating their miserable victims out of the compensation which the tyrannic impostors of the assembly had previously and purposely rendered the public unable to pay. That thus their ultimate violence arose from their original fraud.

He would have shewn that the universal peace and concord amongst nations, which these common enemies to mankind had held out with the same fraudulent ends and pretences with which they had uniformly conducted every part of their proceeding, was a coarse and clumsy deception, unworthy to be proposed as an example, by an informed and sagacious British senator, to any other country. That far from peace and good-will to men, they meditated war against all other governments; and proposed systematically to excite in them all the very worst kind of seditions, in order to lead to their common destruction. That they had discovered, in the few instances in which they have hitherto had the power of discovering it (as at Avignon, and in the Comtat, at Cavailhon and at Carpentras),[6] in what a savage manner they mean to conduct the seditions and wars they have planned against their neighbours for the sake of putting themselves at the head of a confederation of republics as wild and as mischievous as their own. He would have shewn in what manner that wicked scheme was carried on in those places, without being directly either owned or disclaimed, in hopes that the undone people should at length be obliged to fly to their tyrannic protection, as some sort of refuge from their barbarous and treacherous hostility. He would have shewn from those examples, that neither this nor any other society could be in safety as long as such a public enemy was in a condition to continue directly or indirectly such practices against its peace. That Great Britain was a principal object of their machinations; and that they had begun by establishing correspondences, communications, and a sort of federal union with the factious here. That no practical enjoyment of a thing so imperfect and precarious, as human happiness must be, even under the very best of governments, could be a security for the existence of these governments, during the prevalence of the principles of France, propagated from that grand school of every disorder, and every vice.

[6] [The French government conducted questionable plebiscites in these papal enclaves and annexed them in September 1791, a month after the publication of *An Appeal*.]

He was prepared to shew the madness of their declaration of the pretended rights of man; the childish futility of some of their maxims; the gross and stupid absurdity, and the palpable falsity of others; and the mischievous tendency of all such declarations to the wellbeing of men and of citizens, and to the safety and prosperity of every just commonwealth. He was prepared to shew that, in their conduct, the assembly had directly violated not only every sound principle of government, but every one, without exception, of their own false or futile maxims; and indeed every rule they had pretended to lay down for their own direction.

In a word, he was ready to shew, that those who could, after such a full and fair exposure, continue to countenance the French insanity, were not mistaken politicians, but bad men; but he thought that in this case, as in many others, ignorance had been the cause of admiration.

These are strong assertions. They required strong proofs. The member who laid down these positions was and is ready to give, in his place, to each position decisive evidence, correspondent to the nature and quality of the several allegations.

In order to judge on the propriety of the interruption given to Mr. Burke,[7] in his speech in the committee of the Quebec bill, it is necessary to enquire, first, whether, on general principles, he ought to have been suffered to prove his allegations? Secondly, whether the time he had chosen was so very unseasonable as to make his exercise of a parliamentary right productive of ill effects on his friends or his country? Thirdly, whether the opinions delivered in his book, and which he had begun to expatiate upon that day, were in contradiction to his former principles, and inconsistent with the general tenor of his publick conduct?

---

[7] [During the debates on the Quebec Bill, members of Burke's own Whig party interrupted him numerous times on the grounds that a discussion of the French constitution was out of order. The account of the debate may be found in *Parliamentary History* 29:364–430.]

AN APPEAL FROM THE NEW TO THE OLD WHIGS

They who have made eloquent panegyrics on the French Revolution, and who think a free discussion so very advantageous in every case, and under every circumstance, ought not, in my opinion, to have prevented their eulogies from being tried on the test of facts. If their panegyric had been answered with an invective (bating the difference in point of eloquence) the one would have been as good as the other: that is, they would both of them have been good for nothing. The panegyric and the satire ought to be suffered to go to trial; and that which shrinks from it, must be contented to stand at best as a mere declamation.

I do not think Mr. Burke was wrong in the course he took. That which seemed to be recommended to him by Mr. Pitt, was rather to extol the English constitution, than to attack the French. I do not determine what would be best for Mr. Pitt to do in his situation. I do not deny that *he* may have good reasons for his reserve. Perhaps they might have been as good for a similar reserve on the part of Mr. Fox, if his zeal had suffered him to listen to them. But there were no motives of ministerial prudence, or of that prudence which ought to guide a man perhaps on the eve of being minister, to restrain the author of the Reflections. He is in no office under the crown; he is not the organ of any party.

The excellencies of the British constitution had already exercised and exhausted the talents of the best thinkers, and the most eloquent writers and speakers, that the world ever saw. But in the present case, a system declared to be far better, and which certainly is much newer (to restless and unstable minds no small recommendation) was held out to the admiration of the good people of England. In that case, it was surely proper for those, who had far other thoughts of the French constitution, to scrutinize that plan which has been recommended to our imitation by active and zealous factions, at home and abroad. Our complexion is such, that we are palled with enjoyment, and stimulated with hope; that we become less sensible to a long-possessed benefit, from the very circumstance that it is become habitual. Specious, untried, ambiguous prospects of new advantage recommend themselves to the spirit of adventure, which more or less prevails in every mind. From this temper, men, and factions, and nations too, have sacrificed the good, of which they had been in assured possession, in favour of wild and irrational expectations. What should hinder Mr. Burke, if he thought this temper likely, at one time or other, to prevail in our country, from exposing to a multitude, eager to game, the false calculations of this lottery of fraud?

I allow, as I ought to do, for the effusions which come from a *general* zeal for liberty. This is to be indulged, and even to be encouraged, as long as the *question is general*. An orator, above all men, ought to be allowed a full and free use of the praise of liberty. A common place in favour of slavery and tyranny delivered to a popular assembly, would indeed be a bold defiance to all the principles of rhetoric. But in a question whether any particular constitution is or is not a plan of rational liberty, this kind of rhetorical flourish in favour of freedom in general, is surely a little out of its place. It is virtually a begging of the question. It is a song of triumph, before the battle.

"But Mr. Fox does not make the panegyric of the new constitution; it is the destruction only of the absolute monarchy he commends." When that nameless thing which has been lately set up in France was described as "the most stupendous and glorious edifice of liberty, which had been erected on the foundation of human integrity in any time or country," it might at first, have led the hearer into an opinion, that the construction of the new fabric was an object of admiration, as well as the demolition of the old. Mr. Fox, however, has explained himself; and it would be too like that captious and cavilling spirit, which I so perfectly detest, if I were to pin down the language of an eloquent and ardent mind, to the punctilious exactness of a pleader. Then Mr. Fox did not mean to applaud that monstrous thing, which, by the courtesy of France, they call a constitution. I easily believe it. Far from meriting the praises of a great genius like Mr. Fox, it

AN APPEAL FROM THE NEW TO THE OLD WHIGS

cannot be approved by any man of common sense, or common information. He cannot admire the change of one piece of barbarism for another, and a worse. He cannot rejoice at the destruction of a monarchy, mitigated by manners, respectful to laws and usages, and attentive, perhaps but too attentive to public opinion, in favour of the tyranny of a licentious, ferocious, and savage multitude, without laws, manners, or morals, and which so far from respecting the general sense of mankind, insolently endeavours to alter all the principles and opinions, which have hitherto guided and contained the world, and to force them into a conformity to their views and actions. His mind is made to better things.

That a man should rejoice and triumph in the destruction of an absolute monarchy; that in such an event he should overlook the captivity, disgrace, and degradation of an unfortunate prince, and the continual danger to a life which exists only to be endangered; that he should overlook the utter ruin of whole orders and classes of men, extending itself directly, or in its nearest consequences, to at least a million of our kind, and to at least the temporary wretchedness of an whole community, I do not deny to be in some sort natural: Because, when people see a political object, which they ardently desire, but in one point of view, they are apt extremely to palliate, or underrate the evils which may arise in obtaining it. This is no reflection on the humanity of those persons. Their good-nature I am the last man in the world to dispute. It only shews that they are not sufficiently informed, or sufficiently considerate. When they come to reflect seriously on the transaction, they will think themselves bound to examine what the object is that has been acquired by all this havock. They will hardly assert that the destruction of an absolute monarchy, is a thing good in itself, without any sort of reference to the antecedent state of things, or to consequences which result from the change; without any consideration whether under its ancient rule a country was, to a considerable degree, flourishing and populous, highly cultivated, and highly commercial; and whether, under that domination, though personal liberty had been precarious and insecure, property at least was ever violated. They cannot take the moral sympathies of the human mind along with them, in abstractions separated from the good or evil condition of the state, from the quality of actions, and the character of the actors. None of us love absolute and uncontrolled monarchy; but we could not rejoice at the sufferings of a Marcus Aurelius, or a Trajan, who were absolute monarchs, as we do when Nero is condemned by the senate to be punished *more majorum*:[8] Nor when that monster was obliged to fly with his wife Sporus, and to drink puddle, were men affected in the same manner, as when the venerable Galba, with all his faults and errors, was murdered by a revolted mercenary soldiery.[9] With such things before our eyes our feelings contradict our theories; and when this is the case, the feelings are true, and the theory is false. What I contend for is, that in commending the destruction of an absolute monarchy, *all the circumstances* ought not to be wholly overlooked, as considerations fit only for shallow and superficial minds.

The subversion of a government, to deserve any praise, must be considered but as a step preparatory to the formation of something better, either in the scheme of the government itself, or in the persons who administer in it, or in both. These events cannot in reason be separated. For instance, when we praise our revolution of 1688, though the nation, in that act, was on the defensive, and was justified in incurring all the evils of a defensive war, we do not rest there. We always combine with the subversion of the old government the happy settlement which followed. When we estimate that revolution, we mean to comprehend in our calculation both the value of the thing parted with, and the value of the thing received in exchange.

The burthen of proof lies heavily on those who tear to pieces the whole frame and contexture of their country, that

---

[8] [According to ancestral customs.]

[9] [Galba had succeeded Nero as emperor in late A.D. 68 and was murdered early the next year.]

AN APPEAL FROM THE NEW TO THE OLD WHIGS

they could find no other way of settling a government fit to obtain its rational ends, except that which they have pursued by means unfavourable to all the present happiness of millions of people, and to the utter ruin of several hundreds of thousands. In their political arrangements, men have no right to put the well-being of the present generation wholly out of the question. Perhaps the only moral trust with any certainty in our hands, is the care of our own time. With regard to futurity, we are to treat it like a ward. We are not so to attempt an improvement of his fortune, as to put the capital of his estate to any hazard.

It is not worth our while to discuss, like sophisters, whether, in no case, some evil, for the sake of some benefit is to be tolerated. Nothing universal can be rationally affirmed on any moral, or any political subject. Pure metaphysical abstraction does not belong to these matters. The lines of morality are not like the ideal lines of mathematics. They are broad and deep as well as long. They admit of exceptions; they demand modifications. These exceptions and modifications are not made by the process of logic, but by the rules of prudence. Prudence is not only the first in rank of the virtues political and moral, but she is the director, the regulator, the standard of them all. Metaphysics cannot live without definition; but prudence is cautious how she defines. Our courts cannot be more fearful in suffering fictitious cases to be brought before them for eliciting their determination on a point of law, than prudent moralists are in putting extreme and hazardous cases of conscience upon emergencies not existing. Without attempting therefore to define, what never can be defined, the case of a revolution in government, this, I think, may be safely affirmed, that a sore and pressing evil is to be removed, and that a good, great in its amount, and unequivocal in its nature, must be probable almost to certainty, before the inestimable price of our own morals, and the well-being of a number of our fellow-citizens, is paid for a revolution. If ever we ought to be oeconomists even to parsimony, it is in the voluntary production of evil. Every revolution contains in it something of evil.

It must always be, to those who are the greatest amateurs, or even professors of revolutions, a matter very hard to prove, that the late French government was so bad, that nothing worse, in the infinite devices of men, could come in its place. They who have brought France to its present condition ought to prove also, by something better than prattling about the Bastile, that their subverted government was as incapable, as the present certainly is, of all improvement and correction. How dare they to say so who have never made that experiment? They are experimentors by their trade. They have made an hundred others, infinitely more hazardous.

The English admirers of the forty-eight thousand republics which form the French federation, praise them not for what they are, but for what they are to become. They do not talk as politicians but as prophets. But in whatever character they choose to found panegyric on prediction, it will be thought a little singular to praise any work, not for its own merits, but for the merits of something else which may succeed to it. When any political institution is praised, in spite of great and prominent faults of every kind, and in all its parts, it must be supposed to have something excellent in its fundamental principles. It must be shewn that it is right though imperfect; that it is not only by possibility susceptible of improvement, but that it contains in it a principle tending to its melioration.

Before they attempt to shew this progression of their favourite work, from absolute pravity to finished perfection, they will find themselves engaged in a civil war with those whose cause they maintain. What! alter our sublime constitution, the glory of France, the envy of the world, the pattern for mankind, the master-piece of legislation, the collected and concentrated glory of this enlightened age! Have we not produced it ready made and ready armed, mature in its birth, a perfect goddess of wisdom and of war, hammered by our blacksmith midwives out of the brain of Jupiter himself?

AN APPEAL FROM THE NEW TO THE OLD WHIGS

Have we not sworn our devout, profane, believing, infidel people, to an allegiance to this goddess, even before she had burst the *dura mater*,[10] and as yet existed only in embryo? Have we not solemnly declared this constitution unalterable by any future legislature? Have we not bound it on posterity for ever, though our abettors have declared that no one generation is competent to bind another? Have we not obliged the members of every future assembly to qualify themselves for their seats by swearing to its conservation?

Indeed the French constitution always must be (if a change is not made in all their principles and fundamental arrangements) a government wholly by popular representation. It must be this or nothing. The French faction considers as an usurpation, as an atrocious violation of the indefeasible rights of man, every other description of government. Take it or leave it; there is no medium. Let the irrefragable doctors fight out their own controversy in their own way, and with their own weapons; and when they are tired let them commence a treaty of peace. Let the plenipotentiary sophisters of England settle with the diplomatic sophisters of France in what manner right is to be corrected by an infusion of wrong, and how truth may be rendered more true by a due intermixture of falshood.

Having sufficiently proved, that nothing could make it *generally* improper for Mr. Burke to prove what he had alledged concerning the object of this dispute, I pass to the second question, that is, whether he was justified in choosing the committee on the Quebec bill as the field for this discussion? If it were necessary, it might be shewn, that he was not the first to bring these discussions into parliament, nor the first to renew them in this session. The fact is notorious. As to the Quebec bill, they were introduced into the debate upon that subject for two plain reasons; first, that as he thought it *then* not adviseable to make the proceedings of the factious

---

[10] ["The dense, tough, outermost membranous envelope of the brain and spinal cord."—*Oxford English Dictionary*. Burke is alluding to the birth of Athena, who sprang from the head of Jupiter.]

societies the subject of a direct motion, he had no other way open to him. Nobody has attempted to shew, that it was at all admissible into any other business before the house. Here every thing was favourable. Here was a bill to form a new constitution for a French province under English dominion. The question naturally arose, whether we should settle that constitution upon English ideas, or upon French. This furnished an opportunity for examining into the value of the French constitution, either considered as applicable to colonial government, or in its own nature. The bill too was in a committee. By the privilege of speaking as often as he pleased, he hoped in some measure to supply the want of support, which he had but too much reason to apprehend. In a committee it was always in his power to bring the questions from generalities to facts; from declamation to discussion. Some benefit he actually received from this privilege. These are plain, obvious, natural reasons for his conduct. I believe they are the true, and the only true ones.

They who justify the frequent interruptions, which at length wholly disabled him from proceeding, attribute their conduct to a very different interpretation of his motives. They say, that through corruption, or malice, or folly, he was acting his part in a plot to make his friend Mr. Fox pass for a republican; and thereby to prevent the gracious intentions of his sovereign from taking effect, which at that time had began to disclose themselves in his favour.[11] This is a pretty serious

[11] To explain this, it will be necessary to advert to a paragraph which appeared in a paper in the minority interest some time before this debate.

> A very dark intrigue has lately been discovered, the authors of which are well known to us; but until the glorious day shall come, when it will not be a *libel* to tell the *truth*, we must not be so regardless of our own safety, as to publish their names. We will, however, state the fact, leaving it to the ingenuity of our readers to discover what we dare not publish.
>
> Since the business of the armament against Russia has been under discussion, a great personage has been heard to say, "that he was not so wedded to Mr. Pitt, as not to be very willing to give his confidence to Mr. Fox, if the latter should be able, in a crisis like the present, to conduct the government of the country with greater advantage to the public."

charge. This, on Mr. Burke's part, would be something more than mistake; something worse than formal irregularity. Any contumely, any outrage is readily passed over, by the indulgence which we all owe to sudden passion. These things are soon forgot upon occasions in which all men are so apt to forget themselves. Deliberate injuries, to a degree must be remembered, because they require deliberate precautions to be secured against their return.

I am authorized to say for Mr. Burke, that he considers that cause assigned for the outrage offered to him, as ten times worse than the outrage itself. There is such a strange confusion of ideas on this subject, that it is far more difficult to

---

This patriotic declaration immediately alarmed the swarm of courtly insects that live only in the sunshine of ministerial favour. It was thought to be the forerunner of the dismission of Mr. Pitt, and every engine was set at work for the purpose of preventing such an event. The principal engine employed on this occasion was *calumny*. It was whispered in the ear of a great personage, that Mr. Fox was the last man in England to be trusted by a *king*, because he was by *principle* a *republican*, and consequently an enemy to *monarchy*.

In the discussion of the Quebec bill which stood for yesterday, it was the intention of some persons to connect with this subject the French Revolution, in hopes that Mr. Fox would be warmed by a collision with Mr. Burke, and induced to defend that revolution in which so much power was taken from, and so little left in, the crown.

Had Mr. Fox fallen into the snare, his speech on the occasion would have been laid before a great personage, as a proof that a man who could defend such a revolution, might be a very good republican, but could not possibly be a friend to monarchy.

But those who laid the snare was disappointed; for Mr. Fox, in the short conversation which took place yesterday in the house of commons said, that he confessedly had thought favorably of the French revolution; but that most certainly he never had, either in parliament or out of parliament, professed or defended republican principles.

Argus, April 22d, 1791

Mr. Burke cannot answer for the truth, nor prove the falsehood of the story given by the friends of the party in this paper. He only knows that an opinion of its being well or ill authenticated had no influence on his conduct. He meant only, to the best of his power, to guard the public against the ill designs of factions out of doors. What Mr. Burke did in parliament could hardly have been intended to draw Mr. Fox into any declarations unfavourable to his principles, since (by the account of those who are his friends) he had long before effectually prevented the success of any such scandalous designs. Mr. Fox's friends have themselves done away that imputation on Mr. Burke.

understand the nature of the charge, than to refute it when understood. Mr. Fox's friends were, it seems, seized with a sudden panic terror lest he should pass for a republican. I do not think they had any ground for this apprehension. But let us admit they had. What was there in the Quebec bill, rather than in any other, which could subject him or them to that imputation? Nothing in a discussion of the French constitution, which might arise on the Quebec bill, could tend to make Mr. Fox pass for a republican; except he should take occasion to extol that state of things in France, which affects to be a republic or a confederacy of republics. If such an encomium could make any unfavourable impression on the king's mind, surely his voluntary panegyrics on that event, not so much introduced as intruded into other debates, with which they had little relation, must have produced that effect with much more certainty, and much greater force. The Quebec bill, at worst, was only one of those opportunities, carefully sought, and industriously improved by himself. Mr. Sheridan had already brought forth a panegyric on the French system in a still higher strain, with full as little demand from the nature of the business before the house, in a speech too good to be speedily forgotten. Mr. Fox followed him without any direct call from the subject matter, and upon the same ground. To canvass the merits of the French constitution on the Quebec bill could not draw forth any opinions which were not brought forward before, with no small ostentation, and with very little of necessity, or perhaps of propriety. What mode, or what time of discussing the conduct of the French faction in England would not equally tend to kindle this enthusiasm, and afford those occasions for panegyric, which, far from shunning, Mr. Fox has always industriously sought? He himself said very truly, in the debate, that no artifices were necessary to draw from him his opinions upon that subject. But to fall upon Mr. Burke for making an use, at worst not more irregular, of the same liberty, is tantamount to a plain declaration, that the topic of France is *tabooed* or forbidden ground to Mr. Burke, and to Mr. Burke alone. But surely Mr. Fox is not a republican; and what should hinder him, when such a discussion came on, from clearing himself unequivocally (as his friends say he had done near a fortnight before) of all such imputations? Instead of being a disadvantage to him, he would have defeated all his enemies, and Mr. Burke, since he has thought proper to reckon him amongst them.

But it seems, some news-paper or other had imputed to him republican principles, on occasion of his conduct upon the Quebec bill. Supposing Mr. Burke to have seen these news-papers (which is to suppose more than I believe to be true) I would ask, when did the news-papers forbear to charge Mr. Fox, or Mr. Burke himself, with republican principles, or any other principles which they thought could render both of them odious, sometimes to one description of people, sometimes to another? Mr. Burke, since the publication of his pamphlet, has been a thousand times charged in the news-papers with holding despotic principles. He could not enjoy one moment of domestic quiet, he could not perform the least particle of public duty, if he did not altogether disregard the language of those libels. But however his sensibility might be affected by such abuse, it would in *him* have been thought a most ridiculous reason for shutting up the mouths of Mr. Fox, or Mr. Sheridan, so as to prevent their delivering their sentiments of the French revolution, that forsooth, "the news-papers had lately charged Mr. Burke with being an enemy to liberty."

I allow that those gentlemen have privileges to which Mr. Burke has no claim. But their friends ought to plead those privileges; and not to assign bad reasons, on the principle of what is fair between man and man, and thereby to put themselves on a level with those who can so easily refute them. Let them say at once that his reputation is of no value, and that he has no call to assert it; but that theirs is of infinite concern to the party and the public; and to that consideration he ought to sacrifice all his opinions, and all his feelings.

In that language I should hear a style correspondent to the proceeding; lofty, indeed, but plain and consistent. Admit, however, for a moment, and merely for argument, that this gentleman had as good a right to continue as they had to begin these discussions, in candour and equity they must allow that their voluntary descant in praise of the French constitution was as much an oblique attack on Mr. Burke, as Mr. Burke's enquiry into the foundation of this encomium could possibly be construed into an imputation upon them. They well knew, that he felt like other men; and of course he would think it mean and unworthy, to decline asserting in his place, and in the front of able adversaries, the principles of what he had penned in his closet, and without an opponent before him. They could not but be convinced, that declamations of this kind would rouze him; that he must think, coming from men of their *calibre*, they were highly mischievous; that they gave countenance to bad men, and bad designs; and, though he was aware that the handling such matters in parliament was delicate, yet he was a man very likely, whenever, much against his will, they were brought there, to resolve, that there they should be thoroughly sifted. Mr. Fox, early in the preceding session, had public notice from Mr. Burke of the light in which he considered every attempt to introduce the example of France into the politics of this country; and of his resolution to break with his best friends, and to join with his worst enemies to prevent it. He hoped, that no such necessity would ever exist. But in case it should, his determination was made. The party knew perfectly that he would at least defend himself. He never intended to attack Mr. Fox, nor did he attack him directly or indirectly. His speech kept to its matter. No personality was employed even in the remotest allusion. He never did impute to that gentleman any republican principles, or any other bad principles or bad conduct whatsoever. It was far from his words; it was far from his heart. It must be remembered, that notwithstanding the attempt of Mr. Fox, to fix on Mr. Burke an unjustifiable change of opinion, and the foul crime of teaching a set of maxims to a boy, and afterwards, when these maxims became adult in his mature age, of abandoning both the disciple and the doctrine, Mr. Burke never attempted, in any one particular, either to criminate or to recriminate. It may be said, that he had nothing of the kind in his power. This he does not controvert. He certainly had it not in his inclination. That gentleman had as little ground for the charges which he was so easily provoked to make upon him.

The gentlemen of the party (I include Mr. Fox) have been kind enough to consider the dispute brought on by this business, and the consequent separation of Mr. Burke from their corps, as a matter of regret and uneasiness. I cannot be of opinion, that by his exclusion they have had any loss at all. A man whose opinions are so very adverse to theirs, adverse, as it was expressed, "as pole to pole," so mischievously as well as so directly adverse, that they found themselves under the necessity of solemnly disclaiming them in full parliament, such a man must ever be to them a most unseemly and unprofitable incumbrance. A co-operation with him could only serve to embarrass them in all their councils. They have besides publickly represented him as a man capable of abusing the docility and confidence of ingenuous youth; and, for a bad reason, or for no reason, of disgracing his whole public life by a scandalous contradiction of every one of his own acts, writings, and declarations. If these charges be true, their exclusion of such a person from their body is a circumstance which does equal honour to their justice and their prudence. If they express a degree of sensibility in being obliged to execute this wise and just sentence, from a consideration of some amiable or some pleasant qualities which in his private life their former friend may happen to possess, they add, to the praise of their wisdom and firmness, the merit of great tenderness of heart, and humanity of disposition.

On their ideas, the new Whig party have, in my opinion, acted as became them. The author of the Reflections, however, on his part, cannot, without great shame to himself, and without entailing everlasting disgrace on his posterity, admit the truth or justice of the charges which have been made upon him; or allow that he has in those Reflections discovered any principles to which honest men are bound to declare, not a shade or two of dissent, but a total fundamental opposition. He must believe, if he does not mean wilfully to abandon his cause and his reputation, that principles fundamentally at variance with those of his book, are fundamentally false. What those principles, the antipodes to his, really are, he can only discover from that contrariety. He is very unwilling to suppose, that the doctrines of some books lately circulated are the principles of the party; though, from the vehement declarations against his opinions, he is at some loss how to judge otherwise.

For the present, my plan does not render it necessary to say any thing further concerning the merits either of the one set of opinions or the other. The author would have discussed the merits of both in his place, but he was not permitted to do so.

I pass to the next head of charge, Mr. Burke's inconsistency. It is certainly a great aggravation of his fault in embracing false opinions, that in doing so he is not supposed to fill up a void, but that he is guilty of a dereliction of opinions that are true and laudable. This is the great gist of the charge against him. It is not so much that he is wrong in his book (that however is alledged also) as that he has therein belyed his whole life. I believe, if he could venture to value himself upon any thing, it is on the virtue of consistency that he would value himself the most. Strip him of this, and you leave him naked indeed.

In the case of any man who had written something, and spoken a great deal, upon very multifarious matter[s], during upwards of twenty-five years public service, and in as great a variety of important events as perhaps have ever happened in the same number of years, it would appear a little hard, in-order to charge such a man with inconsistency, to see collected by his friend, a sort of digest of his sayings, even to such as were merely sportive and jocular. This digest, however, has been made, with equal pains and partiality, and without bringing out those passages of his writings which might tend to shew with what restrictions any expressions, quoted from him, ought to have been understood. From a great statesman he did not quite expect this mode of inquisition. If it only appeared in the works of common pamphleteers, Mr. Burke might safely trust to his reputation. When thus urged, he ought, perhaps, to do a little more. It shall be as little as possible, for I hope not much is wanting. To be totally silent on his charges would not be respectful to Mr. Fox. Accusations sometimes derive a weight from the persons who make them, to which they are not entitled from their matter.

He who thinks, that the British constitution ought to consist of the three members, of three very different natures, of which it does actually consist, and thinks it his duty to preserve each of those members in its proper place, and with its proper proportion of power, must (as each shall happen to be attacked) vindicate the three several parts on the several principles peculiarly belonging to them. He cannot assert the democratic part on the principles on which monarchy is supported; nor can he support monarchy on the principles of democracy; nor can he maintain aristocracy on the grounds of the one or of the other, or of both. All these he must support on grounds that are totally different, though practically they may be, and happily with us they are, brought into one harmonious body. A man could not be consistent in defending such various, and, at first view, discordant parts of a mixed constitution, without that sort of inconsistency with which Mr. Burke stands charged.

As any one of the great members of this constitution happens to be endangered, he that is a friend to all of them chooses and presses the topics necessary for the support of the part attacked, with all the strength, the earnestness, the vehemence, with all the power of stating, of argument, and of colouring, which he happens to possess, and which the case demands. He is not to embarrass the minds of his hearers, or to encumber, or overlay his speech, by bringing into view at once (as if he were reading an academic lecture) all that may and ought, when a just occasion presents itself, to be said in favour of the other members. At that time they are out of the court; there is no question concerning them. Whilst he opposes his defence on the part where the attack is made, he presumes, that for his regard to the just rights of all the rest, he has credit in every candid mind. He ought not to apprehend, that his raising fences about popular privileges this day, will infer that he ought, on the next, to concur with those who would pull down the throne: because on the next he defends the throne, it ought not to be supposed that he has abandoned the rights of the people.

A man who, among various objects of his equal regard, is secure of some, and full of anxiety for the fate of others, is apt to go to much greater lengths in his preference of the objects of his immediate solicitude than Mr. Burke has ever done. A man so circumstanced often seems to undervalue, to vilify, almost to reprobate and disown, those that are out of danger. This is the voice of nature and truth, and not of inconsistency and false pretence. The danger of any thing very dear to us, removes, for the moment, every other affection from the mind. When Priam had his whole thoughts employed on the body of his Hector, he repels with indignation, and drives from him with a thousand reproaches, his surviving sons, who with an officious piety crouded about him to offer their assistance. A good critic (there is no better than Mr. Fox) would say, that this is a master-stroke, and marks a deep understanding of nature in the father of poetry. He would despise a Zoilus, who would conclude from this passage that Homer meant to represent this man of affliction as hating or being indifferent and cold in his affections to the poor reliques of his house, or that he preferred a dead carcase to his living children.[12]

Mr. Burke does not stand in need of an allowance of this kind, which, if he did, by candid critics ought to be granted to him. If the principles of a mixed constitution be admitted, he

[12] [*Iliad* 24:245ff. Zoilus (fl. 4th c. B.C.) was a bitter critic of Homer and a byword in eighteenth-century letters for the reader who neglected the whole for the parts.]

wants no more to justify to consistency every thing he has said and done during the course of a political life just touching to its close. I believe that gentleman has kept himself more clear of running into the fashion of wild visionary theories, or of seeking popularity through every means, than any man perhaps ever did in the same situation.

He was the first man who, on the hustings, at a popular election, rejected the authority of instructions from constituents; or who, in any place, has argued so fully against it. Perhaps the discredit into which that doctrine of compulsive instructions under our constitution is since fallen, may be due, in a great degree, to his opposing himself to it in that manner, and on that occasion.

The reforms in representation, and the bills for shortening the duration of parliaments, he uniformly and steadily opposed for many years together, in contradiction to many of his best friends. These friends, however, in his better days, when they had more to hope from his service and more to fear from his loss than now they have, never chose to find any inconsistency between his acts and expressions in favour of liberty, and his votes on those questions. But there is a time for all things.

Against the opinion of many friends, even against the solicitation of some of them, he opposed those of the church clergy, who had petitioned the House of Commons to be discharged from the subscription.[13] Although he supported the dissenters in their petition for the indulgence which he had refused to the clergy of the established church, in this, as he was not guilty of it, so he was not reproached with inconsistency. At the same time he promoted, and against the wish of several, the clause that gave the dissenting teachers another subscription in the place of that which was then taken away. Neither at that time was the reproach of inconsistency

---

[13] [Anglican clergy had to give formal assent (subscription) to the Thirty-Nine Articles. In the Parliamentary debates of 1772–74, Burke spoke in favor of maintaining subscription for Anglicans but advocated greater latitude for Dissenters. See *Writings and Speeches*, vol. 2.]

brought against him. People could then distinguish between a difference in conduct, under a variation of circumstances, and an inconsistency in principle. It was not then thought necessary to be freed of him as of an incumbrance.

These instances, a few among many, are produced as an answer to the insinuation of his having pursued high popular courses, which in his late book he has abandoned. Perhaps in his whole life he has never omitted a fair occasion, with whatever risque to him of obloquy as an individual, with whatever detriment to his interest as a member of opposition, to assert the very same doctrines which appear in that book. He told the House, upon an important occasion, and pretty early in his service, that "being warned by the ill effect of a contrary procedure in great examples, he had taken his ideas of liberty very low; in order that they should stick to him, and that he might stick to them to the end of his life."

At popular elections the most rigorous casuists will remit a little of their severity. They will allow to a candidate some unqualified effusions in favour of freedom, without binding him to adhere to them in their utmost extent. But Mr. Burke put a more strict rule upon himself than most moralists would put upon others. At his first offering himself to Bristol, where he was almost sure he should not obtain, on that or any occasion, a single Tory vote (in fact he did obtain but one), and rested wholly on the Whig interest, he thought himself bound to tell to the electors, both before and after his election, exactly what a representative they had to expect in him.

> The *distinguishing* part of our constitution (he said) is its liberty. To preserve that liberty inviolate, is the *peculiar* duty and *proper* trust of a member of the house of commons. But the liberty, the *only* liberty I mean, is a liberty connected with *order*, and that not only exists *with* order and virtue, but cannot exist at all *without* them. It inheres in good and steady government, as in *its substance and vital principle*.[14]

[14] [From Burke's speech "At His Arrival at Bristol" (1774), *Works* Bohn 1:441.]

AN APPEAL FROM THE NEW TO THE OLD WHIGS

The liberty to which Mr. Burke declared himself attached, is not French liberty. That liberty is nothing but the rein given to vice and confusion. Mr. Burke was then, as he was at the writing of his Reflections, awfully impressed with the difficulties arising from the complex state of our constitution and our empire, and that it might require, in different emergencies different sorts of exertions, and the successive call upon all the various principles which uphold and justify it. This will appear from what he said at the close of the poll.

> To be a good member of parliament is, let me tell you, no easy task; especially at this time, when there is so strong a disposition to run into the perilous extremes of *servile* compliance, *or wild popularity*. To unite circumspection with vigour, is absolutely necessary; but it is extremely difficult. We are now members for a rich commercial *city*; this city, however, is but a part of a rich commercial *nation*, the interests of which are *various, multiform, and intricate*. We are members for that great *nation* which, however, is itself but part of a great *empire*, extended by our virtue and our fortune to the farthest limits of the east and of the west. *All* these wide-spread interests must be *considered*; must be *compared*; must be *reconciled*, if possible. We are members for a *free* country; and surely we all know that the machine of a free constitution is no *simple* thing; but as *intricate* and as *delicate*, as it is valuable. We are members in a *great and antient monarchy; and we must preserve religiously the true legal rights of the sovereign, which form the key-stone that binds together the noble and well-constructed arch of our empire and our constitution.* A constitution made up of *balanced powers*, must ever be a critical thing. As such I mean to touch that part of it which comes within my reach.[15]

In this manner Mr. Burke spoke to his constituents seventeen years ago. He spoke, not like a partizan of one particular member of our constitution, but as a person strongly, and on principle, attached to them all. He thought these great and essential members ought to be preserved, and preserved each in its place; and that the monarchy ought not only to be secured in its peculiar existence, but in its pre-eminence too, as

[15] [*Works* Bohn 1:448.]

the presiding and connecting principle of the whole. Let it be considered, whether the language of his book, printed in 1790, differs from his speech at Bristol in 1774.

With equal justice his opinions on the American war are introduced, as if in his late work he had belied his conduct and opinions in the debates which arose upon that great event. On the American war he never had any opinions which he has seen occasion to retract, or which he has ever retracted. He indeed differs essentially from Mr. Fox as to the cause of that war. Mr. Fox has been pleased to say, that the Americans rebelled, "because they thought they had not enjoyed liberty enough." This cause of the war *from him* I have heard of for the first time. It is true that those who stimulated the nation to that measure, did frequently urge this topic. They contended, that the Americans had from the beginning aimed at independence; that from the beginning they meant wholly to throw off the authority of the crown, and to break their connection with the parent country. This Mr. Burke never believed. When he moved his second conciliatory proposition in the year 1776, he entered into the discussion of this point at very great length; and from nine several heads of presumption, endeavored to prove the charge upon that people not to be true.

If the principles of all he has said and wrote on the occasion, be viewed with common temper, the gentlemen of the party will perceive, that on a supposition that the Americans had rebelled merely in order to enlarge their liberty, Mr. Burke would have thought very differently of the American cause. What might have been in the secret thoughts of some of their leaders it is impossible to say. As far as a man, so locked up as Dr. Franklin, could be expected to communicate his ideas, I believe he opened them to Mr. Burke. It was, I think, the very day before he set out for America, that a very long conversation passed between them, and with a greater air of openness on the Doctor's side, than Mr. Burke had observed in him before. In this discourse Dr. Franklin lamented, and with apparent sincerity, the separation which he feared was inevitable between Great Britain and her colonies. He certainly spoke of it as an event which gave him the greatest concern. America, he said, would never again see such happy days as she had passed under the protection of England. He observed, that ours was the only instance of a great empire, in which the most distant parts and members had been as well governed as the metropolis and its vicinage: But that the Americans were going to lose the means which secured to them this rare and precious advantage. The question with them was not whether they were to remain as they had been before the troubles, for better, he allowed they could not hope to be; but whether they were to give up so happy a situation without a struggle? Mr. Burke had several other conversations with him about that time, in none of which, soured and exasperated as his mind certainly was, did he discover any other wish in favour of America than for a security to its *ancient* condition. Mr. Burke's conversation with other Americans was large indeed, and his enquiries extensive and diligent. Trusting to the result of all these means of information, but trusting much more in the public presumptive indications I have just referred to, and to the reiterated solemn declarations of their assemblies, he always firmly believed that they were purely on the defensive in that rebellion. He considered the Americans as standing at that time, and in that controversy, in the same relation to England, as England did to king James the Second, in 1688. He believed, that they had taken up arms from one motive only; that is our attempting to tax them without their consent; to tax them for the purposes of maintaining civil and military establishments. If this attempt of ours could have been practically established, he thought with them, that their assemblies would become totally useless; that under the system of policy which was then pursued, the Americans could have no sort of security for their laws or liberties, or for any part of them; and, that the very circumstance of *our* freedom would have augmented the weight of *their* slavery.

Considering the Americans on that defensive footing, he thought Great Britain ought instantly to have closed with them by the repeal of the taxing act. He was of opinion that our general rights over that country would have been preserved by this timely concession.[16] When, instead of this, a Boston port bill, a Massachuset's charter bill, a Fishery bill, an Intercourse bill, I know not how many hostile bills rushed out like so many tempests from all points of the compass, and were accompanied first with great fleets and armies of English, and followed afterwards with great bodies of foreign troops, he thought that their cause grew daily better, because daily more defensive; and that ours, because daily more offensive, grew daily worse. He therefore in two motions, in two successive years, proposed in parliament many concessions beyond what he had reason to think in the beginning of the troubles would ever be seriously demanded.

So circumstanced, he certainly never could and never did wish the colonists to be subdued by arms. He was fully persuaded, that if such should be the event, they must be held in that subdued state by a great body of standing forces, and perhaps of foreign forces. He was strongly of opinion, that such armies, first victorious over Englishmen, in a conflict for English constitutional rights and privileges, and afterwards habituated (though in America) to keep an English people in a state of abject subjection, would prove fatal in the end to the liberties of England itself; that in the mean time this military system would lie as an oppressive burthen upon the national finances; that it would constantly breed and feed new discussions, full of heat and acrimony, leading possibly to a new series of wars; and that foreign powers, whilst we continued in a state at once burthened and distracted, must at length obtain a decided superiority over us. On what part of his late publication, or on what expression that might have escaped him in that work, is any man authorized to charge Mr. Burke with a contradiction to the line of his conduct, and to the

[16] See his speech on American taxation, the 19th of April, 1774.

current of his doctrines on the American war? The pamphlet is in the hands of his accusers, let them point out the passage if they can.

Indeed, the author has been well sifted and scrutinized by his friends. He is even called to an account for every jocular and light expression. A ludicrous picture which he made with regard to a passage in the speech of a late minister,[17] has been brought up against him. That passage contained a lamentation for the loss of monarchy to the Americans, after they had separated from Great Britain. He thought it to be unseasonable, ill judged, and ill sorted with the circumstances of all the parties. Mr. Burke, it seems, considered it ridiculous to lament the loss of some monarch or other, to a rebel people, at the moment they had for ever quitted their allegiance to theirs and our sovereign; at the time when they had broken off all connexion with this nation, and had allied themselves with its enemies. He certainly must have thought it open to ridicule: and, now that it is recalled to his memory (he had, I believe, wholly forgotten the circumstance), he recollects that he did treat it with some levity. But is it a fair inference from a jest on this unseasonable lamentation, that he was then an enemy to monarchy either in this or in any other country? The contrary perhaps ought to be inferred, if any thing at all can be argued from pleasantries good or bad. Is it for this reason, or for any thing he has said or done relative to the American war, that he is to enter into an alliance offensive and defensive with every rebellion, in every country, under every circumstance, and raised upon whatever pretence? Is it because he did not wish the Americans to be subdued by arms, that he must be inconsistent with himself, if he reprobates the conduct of those societies in England, who alledging no one act of tyranny or oppression, and complaining of no hostile attempt against our antient laws, rights, and usages, are now endeavouring to work the destruction of the crown of this kingdom, and the whole of its constitution? Is he

[17] Lord Lansdown.

obliged, from the concessions he wished to be made to the colonies, to keep any terms with those clubs and federations, who hold out to us as a pattern for imitation, the proceedings in France, in which a king, who had voluntarily and formally divested himself of the right of taxation, and of all other species of arbitrary power, has been dethroned? Is it because Mr. Burke wished to have America rather conciliated than vanquished, that he must wish well to the army of republics which are set up in France; a country wherein not the people, but the monarch was wholly on the defensive (a poor, indeed, and feeble defensive) to preserve *some fragments* of the royal authority against a determined and desperate body of conspirators, whose object it was, with whatever certainty of crimes, with whatever hazard of war and every other species of calamity, to annihilate the *whole* of that authority; to level all ranks, orders, and distinctions in the state; and utterly to destroy property, not more by their acts than in their principles?

Mr. Burke has been also reproached with an inconsistency between his late writings and his former conduct, because he had proposed in parliament several oeconomical, leading to several constitutional reforms. Mr. Burke thought, with a majority of the House of Commons, that the influence of the crown at one time was too great; but after his Majesty had by a gracious message, and several subsequent acts of parliament, reduced it to a standard which satisfied Mr. Fox himself, and, apparently at least, contented whoever wished to go farthest in that reduction, is Mr. Burke to allow that it would be right for us to proceed to indefinite lengths upon that subject? that it would therefore be justifiable in a people owing allegiance to a monarchy, and professing to maintain it, not to *reduce*, but wholly to *take away all* prerogative, and *all* influence whatsoever? Must his having made, in virtue of a plan of oeconomical regulation, a reduction of the influence of the crown, compel him to allow, that it would be right in the French or in us to bring a king to so abject a state, as in function not to be so respectable as an under sheriff, but in person not to differ from the condition of a mere prisoner? One would think that such a thing as a medium had never been heard of in the moral world.

This mode of arguing from your having done *any* thing in a certain line, to the necessity of doing *every* thing, has political consequences of other moment than those of a logical fallacy. If no man can propose any diminution or modification of an invidious or dangerous power or influence in government, without entitling friends turned into adversaries, to argue him into the destruction of all prerogative, to a spoliation of the whole patronage of royalty, I do not know what can more effectually deter persons of sober minds from engaging in any reform; nor how the worst enemies to the liberty of the subject could contrive any method more fit to bring all correctives on the power of the crown into suspicion and disrepute.

If, say his accusers, the dread of too great influence in the crown of Great Britain could justify the degree of reform which he adopted, the dread of a return under the despotism of a monarchy might justify the people of France in going much further, and reducing monarchy to its present nothing. Mr. Burke does not allow, that a sufficient argument *ad hominem* is inferable from these premises. If the horror of the excesses of an absolute monarchy furnishes a reason for abolishing it, no monarchy once absolute (all have been so at one period or other) could ever be limited. It must be destroyed; otherwise no way could be found to quiet the fears of those who were formerly subjected to that sway. But the principle of Mr. Burke's proceeding ought to lead him to a very different conclusion; to this conclusion, that a monarchy is a thing perfectly susceptible of reform; perfectly susceptible of a balance of power; and that, when reformed and balanced, for a great country, it is the best of all governments. The example of our country might have led France, as it has led him, to perceive that monarchy is not only reconcilable to liberty, but that it may be rendered a great and stable security to its perpetual enjoyment. No correctives which he proposed to the power of the crown could lead him to approve of a plan of a republic (if so it may be reputed) which has no correctives, and which he believes to be incapable of admitting any. No principle of Mr. Burke's conduct or writings obliged him, from consistency, to become an advocate for an exchange of mischiefs; no principle of his could compel him to justify the setting up in the place of a mitigated monarchy, a new and far more despotic power, under which there is no trace of liberty, except what appears in confusion and in crime.

Mr. Burke does not admit that the faction predominant in France have abolished their monarchy and the orders of their state, from any dread of arbitrary power that lay heavy on the minds of the people. It is not very long since he has been in that country. Whilst there he conversed with many descriptions of its inhabitants. A few persons of rank did, he allows, discover strong and manifest tokens of such a spirit of liberty, as might be expected one day to break all bounds. Such gentlemen have since had more reason to repent of their want of foresight than I hope any of the same class will ever have in this country. But this spirit was far from general even amongst the gentlemen. As to the lower orders and those a little above them, in whose name the present powers domineer, they were far from discovering any sort of dissatisfaction with the power and prerogatives of the crown. That vain people were rather proud of them: they rather despised the English for not having a monarch possessed of such high and perfect authority. *They* had felt nothing from *Lettres de Cachet*.[18] The Bastile could inspire no horrors into *them*. This was a treat for their betters. It was by art and impulse; it was by the sinister use made of a season of scarcity; it was under an infinitely diversified succession of wicked pretences, wholly foreign to the question of monarchy or aristocracy, that this light people were inspired with their present spirit of levelling. Their old vanity was led by art to take another turn: It was dazzled and seduced by military liveries, cockades, and epaulets, until the French populace was led to become the willing, but still the proud and thoughtless instrument and

[18] [A sealed letter containing a royal decree by which a person could be imprisoned without trial or explanation.]

victim of another domination. Neither did that people despise, or hate, or fear their nobility. On the contrary, they valued themselves on the generous qualities which distinguished the chiefs of their nation.

So far as to the attack on Mr. Burke, in consequence of his reforms.

To shew that he has in his last publication abandoned those principles of liberty which have given energy to his youth, and in spite of his censors will afford repose and consolation to his declining age, those who have thought proper in parliament to declare against his book, ought to have produced something in it, which directly or indirectly militates with any rational plan of free government. It is something extraordinary, that they whose memories have so well served them with regard to light and ludicrous expressions which years had consigned to oblivion, should not have been able to quote a single passage in a piece so lately published, which contradicts any thing he has formerly ever said in a style either ludicrous or serious. They quote his former speeches, and his former votes, but not one syllable from the book. It is only by a collation of the one with the other that the alledged inconsistency can be established. But as they are unable to cite any such contradictory passage, so neither can they shew any thing in the general tendency and spirit of the whole work unfavourable to a rational and generous spirit of liberty; unless a warm opposition to the spirit of levelling, to the spirit of impiety, to the spirit of proscription, plunder, murder, and cannibalism, be adverse to the true principles of freedom.

The author of that book is supposed to have passed from extreme to extreme; but he has always kept himself in a medium. This charge is not so wonderful. It is in the nature of things, that they who are in the centre of a circle should appear directly opposed to those who view them from any part of the circumference. In that middle point, however, he will still remain, though he may hear people who themselves run beyond Aurora and the Ganges, cry out, that he is at the extremity of the west.

In the same debate Mr. Burke was represented as arguing in a manner which implied that the British constitution could not be defended, but by abusing all republics antient and modern. He said nothing to give the least ground for such a censure. He never abused all republics. He has never professed himself a friend or an enemy to republics or to monarchies in the abstract. He thought that the circumstances and habits of every country, which it is always perilous and productive of the greatest calamities to force, are to decide upon the form of its government. There is nothing in his nature, his temper, or his faculties, which should make him an enemy to any republic modern or antient. Far from it. He has studied the form and spirit of republics very early in life; he has studied them with great attention; and with a mind undisturbed by affection or prejudice. He is indeed convinced that the science of government would be poorly cultivated without that study. But the result in his mind from that investigation has been, and is, that neither England nor France, without infinite detriment to them, as well in the event as in the experiment, could be brought into a republican form; but that every thing republican which can be introduced with safety into either of them, must be built upon a monarchy; built upon a real, not a nominal monarchy, *as its essential basis*; that all such institutions, whether aristocratic or democratic, must originate from their crown, and in all their proceedings must refer to it; that by the energy of that main spring alone those republican parts must be set in action, and from thence must derive their whole legal effect (as amongst us they actually do), or the whole will fall into confusion. These republican members have no other point but the crown in which they can possibly unite.

This is the opinion expressed in Mr. Burke's book. He has never varied in that opinion since he came to years of discretion. But surely, if at any time of his life he had entertained other notions (which however he has never held or professed to hold), the horrible calamities brought upon a great people, by the wild attempt to force their country into a republick, might be more than sufficient to undeceive his understanding, and to free it for ever from such destructive fancies. He is certain, that many, even in France, have been made sick of their theories by their very success in realizing them.

To fortify the imputation of a desertion from his principles, his constant attempts to reform abuses, have been brought forward. It is true, it has been the business of his strength to reform abuses in government; and his last feeble efforts are employed in a struggle against them. Politically he has lived in that element; politically he will die in it. Before he departs, I will admit for him that he deserves to have all his titles of merit brought forth, as they have been, for grounds of condemnation, if one word, justifying or supporting abuses of any sort, is to be found in that book which has kindled so much indignation in the mind of a great man. On the contrary, it spares no existing abuse. Its very purpose is to make war with abuses; not, indeed, to make war with the dead, but with those which live, and flourish, and reign.

The *purpose* for which the abuses of government are brought into view, forms a very material consideration in the mode of treating them. The complaints of a friend are things very different from the invectives of an enemy. The charge of abuses on the late monarchy of France, was not intended to lead to its reformation, but to justify its destruction. They who have raked into all history for the faults of kings, and who have aggravated every fault they have found, have acted consistently; because they acted as enemies. No man can be a friend to a tempered monarchy who bears a decided hatred to monarchy itself. He who, at the present time, is favourable, or even fair to that system, must act towards it as towards a friend with frailties, who is under the prosecution of implacable foes. I think it a duty in that case, not to inflame the public mind against the obnoxious person, by any exaggeration of his faults. It is our duty rather to palliate his errors and defects, or to cast them into the shade, and industriously to bring forward any good qualities that he may happen to possess. But when the man is to be amended, and by amendment to be preserved, then the line of duty takes another direction. When his safety is effectually provided for, it then becomes the office of a friend to urge his faults and vices with all the energy of enlightened affection, to paint them in their most vivid colours, and to bring the moral patient to a better habit. Thus I think with regard to individuals; thus I think with regard to antient and respected governments and orders of men. A spirit of reformation is never more consistent with itself, than when it refuses to be rendered the means of destruction.

I suppose that enough is said upon these heads of accusation. One more I had nearly forgotten, but I shall soon dispatch it. The author of the Reflections, in the opening of the last parliament, entered on the Journals of the House of Commons a motion for a remonstrance to the crown, which is substantially a defence of the preceding parliament, that had been dissolved under displeasure. It is a defence of Mr. Fox. It is a defence of the Whigs. By what connection of argument, by what association of ideas, this apology for Mr. Fox and his party is, by him and them, brought to criminate his and their apologist, I cannot easily divine. It is true, that Mr. Burke received no previous encouragement from Mr. Fox, nor any the least countenance or support at the time when the motion was made, from him or from any gentleman of the party, one only excepted, from whose friendship, on that and on other occasions, he derives an honour to which he must be dull indeed to be insensible.[19] If that remonstrance therefore was a false or feeble defence of the measures of the party, they were in no wise affected by it. It stands on the Journals. This secures to it a permanence which the author cannot expect to any other work of his. Let it speak for itself to the present age, and to all posterity. The party had no concern in it; and it can never be quoted against them. But in the late debate it was produced, not to clear the party from an improper defence in which they had no share, but for the kind purpose of insinuat-

[19] Mr. Windham.

ing an inconsistency between the principles of Mr. Burke's defence of the dissolved parliament, and those on which he proceeded in his late Reflections on France.

It requires great ingenuity to make out such a parallel between the two cases, as to sound a charge of inconsistency in the principles assumed in arguing the one and the other. What relation had Mr. Fox's India bill to the constitution of France? What relation had that constitution to the question of right, in an house of commons, to give or to withhold its confidence from ministers, and to state that opinion to the crown? What had this discussion to do with Mr. Burke's idea in 1784, of the ill consequences which must in the end arise to the crown from setting up the commons at large as an opposite interest to the commons in parliament? What has this discussion to do with a recorded warning to the people, of their rashly forming a precipitate judgment against their representatives? What had Mr. Burke's opinion of the danger of introducing new theoretic language unknown to the records of the kingdom, and calculated to excite vexatious questions, into a parliamentary proceeding, to do with the French assembly, which defies all precedent, and places its whole glory in realizing what had been thought the most visionary theories? What had this in common with the abolition of the French monarchy, or with the principles upon which the English revolution was justified; a revolution in which parliament, in all its acts and all its declarations, religiously adheres to 'the form of sound words,'[20] without excluding from private discussions, such terms of art as may serve to conduct an inquiry for which none but private persons are responsible? These were the topics of Mr. Burke's proposed remonstrance; all of which topics suppose the existence and mutual relation of our three estates; as well as the relation of the East India Company to the crown, to parliament, and to the peculiar laws, rights, and usages of the people of Hindostan? What reference, I say, had these topics to the constitution of

[20] [II Timothy 1:13.]

France, in which there is no king, no lords, no commons, no India company to injure or support, no Indian empire to govern or oppress? What relation had all or any of these, or any question which could arise between the prerogatives of the crown and the privileges of parliament, with the censure of those factious persons in Great Britain, whom Mr. Burke states to be engaged, not in favour of privilege against prerogative, or of prerogative against privilege, but in an open attempt against our crown and our parliament; against our constitution in church and state; against all the parts and orders which compose the one and the other?

No persons were more fiercely active against Mr. Fox, and against the measures of the house of commons dissolved in 1784, which Mr. Burke defends in that remonstrance, than several of those revolution-makers, whom Mr. Burke condemns alike in his remonstrance, and in his book. These revolutionists indeed may be well thought to vary in their conduct. He is, however, far from accusing them, in this variation, of the smallest degree of inconsistency. He is persuaded, that they are totally indifferent at which end they begin the demolition of the constitution. Some are for commencing their operations with the destruction of the civil powers, in order the better to pull down the ecclesiastical; some wish to begin with the ecclesiastical, in order to facilitate the ruin of the civil; some would destroy the house of commons through the crown; some the crown through the house of commons; and some would overturn both the one and the other through what they call the people. But I believe that this injured writer will think it not at all inconsistent with his present duty, or with his former life, strenuously to oppose all the various partizans of destruction, let them begin where, or when, or how they will. No man would set his face more determinedly against those who should attempt to deprive them, or any description of men, of the rights they possess. No man would be more steady in preventing them from abusing those rights to the destruction of that happy order under which they enjoy them. As to their title to any thing further, it ought to be grounded on the proof they give of the safety with which power may be trusted in their hands. When they attempt without disguise, not to win it from our affections, but to force it from our fears, they shew, in the character of their means of obtaining it, the use they would make of their dominion. That writer is too well read in men, not to know how often the desire and design of a tyrannic domination lurks in the claim of an extravagant liberty. Perhaps in the beginning it *always* displays itself in that manner. No man has ever affected power which he did not hope from the favour of the existing government, in any other mode.

The attacks on the author's consistency relative to France, are (however grievous they may be to his feelings) in a great degree external to him and to us, and comparatively of little moment to the people of England. The substantial charge upon him is concerning his doctrines relative to the Revolution of 1688. Here it is, that they who speak in the name of the party have thought proper to censure him the most loudly, and with the greatest asperity. Here they fasten; and, if they are right in their fact, with sufficient judgment in their selection. If he be guilty in this point he is equally blameable, whether he is consistent or not. If he endeavours to delude his countrymen by a false representation of the spirit of that leading event, and of the true nature and tenure of the government formed in consequence of it, he is deeply responsible; he is an enemy to the free constitution of the kingdom. But he is not guilty in any sense. I maintain that in his Reflections he has stated the Revolution and the settlement upon their true principles of legal reason and constitutional policy.

His authorities are the acts and declarations of parliament given in their proper words. So far as these go, nothing can be added to what he has quoted. The question is, whether he has understood them rightly. I think they speak plain enough. But we must now see whether he proceeds with other authority than his own constructions; and if he does, on what sort of authority he proceeds. In this part, his defence will not be made by argument, but by wager of law. He takes his compurgators, his vouchers, his guarantees, along with him. I know, that he will not be satisfied with a justification proceeding on general reasons of policy. He must be defended on party grounds too; or his cause is not so tenable as I wish it to appear. It must be made out for him, not only, that in his construction of these public acts and monuments he conforms himself to the rules of fair, legal, and logical interpretation; but it must be proved that his construction is in perfect harmony with that of the ancient Whigs, to whom, against the sentence of the modern, on his part, I here appeal.

This July, it will be twenty-six years[21] since he became connected with a man whose memory will ever be precious to Englishmen of all parties, as long as the ideas of honour and virtue, public and private, are understood and cherished in this nation.[22] That memory will be kept alive with particular veneration by all rational and honourable Whigs. Mr. Burke entered into a connexion with that party, through that man, at an age, far from raw and immature; at those years when men are all they are ever likely to become; when he was in the prime and vigour of his life; when the powers of his understanding, according to their standard, were at the best; his memory exercised; his judgment formed; and his reading, much fresher in the recollection, and much readier in the application, than now it is. He was at that time as likely as most men to know what were Whig and what were Tory principles. He was in a situation to discern what sort of Whig principles they entertained, with whom it was his wish to form an eternal connexion. Foolish he would have been at that time of life (more foolish than any man who undertakes a public trust would be thought) to adhere to a cause, which he, amongst all those who were engaged in it, had the least sanguine hopes of, as a road to power.

[21] July 17th, 1765.

[22] [Charles Watson-Wentworth, 2nd Marquis of Rockingham. He was the Whig leader to whom Burke attached himself at age 36, finding his true party and vocation.]

An Appeal from the New to the Old Whigs

There are who remember, that on the removal of the
Whigs in the year 1766, he was as free to choose another connexion as any man in the kingdom. To put himself out of the
way of the negociations which were then carrying on very
eagerly, and through many channels, with the Earl of Chat-
ham, he went to Ireland very soon after the change of ministry, and did not return until the meeting of parliament. He
was at that time free from any thing which looked like an
engagement. He was further free at the desire of his friends;
for the very day of his return, the Marquis of Rockingham
wished him to accept an employment under the new system.
He believes he might have had such a situation; but again he
cheerfully took his fate with the party.

It would be a serious imputation upon the prudence of
my friend, to have made even such trivial sacrifices as it was in
his power to make, for principles which he did not truly embrace, or did not perfectly understand. In either case the folly
would have been great. The question now is, whether, when
he first practically professed Whig principles, he understood
what principles he professed; and whether, in his book, he
has faithfully expressed them.

When he entered into the Whig party, he did not conceive
that they pretended to any discoveries. They did not affect to
be better Whigs, than those were who lived in the days in
which principle was put to the test. Some of the Whigs of
those days were then living. They were what the Whigs had
been at the Revolution;[23] what they had been during the
reign of queen Anne; what they had been at the accession of
the present royal family.

What they were at those periods is to be seen. It rarely
happens to a party to have the opportunity of a clear, authentic, recorded, declaration of their political tenets upon

---

[23] ["The Revolution" for Burke is the Glorious Revolution of 1688–89,
which deposed James II and brought to the throne William III (1650–1702)
and Mary II (1662–1694), eldest daughter of James. Mary's sister, Queen
Anne, reigned from 1702 to 1714, after which "the present royal family" of
Hanover assumed the throne.]

the subject of a great constitutional event like that of the Revolution. The Whigs had that opportunity, or, to speak more properly, they made it. The impeachment of Dr. Sacheverel was undertaken by a Whig Ministry and a Whig House of Commons, and carried on before a prevalent and steady majority of Whig Peers. It was carried on for the express purpose of stating the true grounds and principles of the Revolution; what the Commons emphatically called their *foundation*. It was carried on for the purpose of condemning the principles on which the Revolution was first opposed, and afterwards calumniated, in order by a juridical sentence of the highest authority to confirm and fix Whig principles, as they had operated both in the resistance to King James, and in the subsequent settlement; and to fix them in the extent and with the limitations with which it was meant they should be understood by posterity. The ministers and managers for the Commons were persons who had, many of them, an active share in the Revolution. Most of them had seen it at an age capable of reflection. The grand event, and all the discussions which led to it, and followed it, were then alive in the memory and conversation of all men. The managers for the Commons must be supposed to have spoken on that subject the prevalent ideas of the leading party in the Commons, and of the Whig ministry. Undoubtedly they spoke also their own private opinions; and the private opinions of such men are not without weight. They were not *umbratiles doctores*,[24] men who had studied a free constitution only in its anatomy, and upon dead systems. They knew it alive and in action.

In this proceeding, the Whig principles, as applied to the Revolution and settlement, are to be found, or they are to be found no where. I wish the Whig readers of this appeal first to turn to Mr. Burke's Reflections from p. 20 to p. 50; and then to attend to the following extracts from the trial of Dr. Sacheverel. After this, they will consider two

[24] ["Ivory-tower" scholars.]

things; first, whether the doctrine in Mr. Burke's Reflections be consonant to that of the Whigs of that period; and secondly, whether they choose to abandon the principles which belonged to the progenitors of some of them, and to the predecessors of them all, and to learn new principles of Whiggism, imported from France, and disseminated in this country from dissenting pulpits, from federation societies, and from the pamphlets, which (as containing the political creed of those synods) are industriously circulated in all parts of the two kingdoms. This is their affair, and they will make their option.

These new Whigs hold, that the sovereignty, whether exercised by one or many, did not only originate *from* the people (a position not denied, nor worth denying or assenting to) but that, in the people the same sovereignty constantly and unalienably resides; that the people may lawfully depose kings, not only for misconduct, but without any misconduct at all; that they may set up any new fashion of government for themselves, or continue without any government at their pleasure; that the people are essentially their own rule, and their will the measure of their conduct; that the tenure of magistracy is not a proper subject of contract; because magistrates have duties, but no rights: and that if a contract *de facto* is made with them in one age, allowing that it binds at all, it only binds those who were immediately concerned in it, but does not pass to posterity. These doctrines concerning the *people* (a term which they are far from accurately defining, but by which, from many circumstances, it is plain enough they mean their own faction, if they should grow by early arming, by treachery, or violence, into the prevailing force) tend, in my opinion, to the utter subversion, not only of all government, in all modes, and to all stable securities to rational freedom, but to all the rules and principles of morality itself.

I assert, that the ancient Whigs held doctrines, totally different from those I have last mentioned. I assert, that the foundations laid down by the Commons, on the trial of Doctor Sacheverel, for justifying the revolution of 1688, are the very same laid down in Mr. Burke's Reflections; that is to say, a breach of the *original contract*, implied and expressed in the constitution of this country, as a scheme of government fundamentally and inviolably fixed in King, Lords, and Commons. That the fundamental subversion of this antient constitution, by one of its parts, having been attempted, and in effect accomplished, justified the Revolution. That it was justified *only* upon the *necessity* of the case; as the *only* means left for the recovery of that *antient* constitution, formed by the *original contract* of the British state; as well as for the future preservation of the *same* government. These are the points to be proved.

A general opening to the charge against Dr. Sacheverel was made by the Attorney General, Sir John Montagu; but as there is nothing in that opening speech which tends very accurately to settle the principle upon which the Whigs proceeded in the prosecution (the plan of the speech not requiring it) I proceed to that of Mr. Lechmere, the manager who spoke next after him. The following are extracts, given, not in the exact order in which they stand in the printed trial, but in that which is thought most fit to bring the ideas of the Whig Commons distinctly under our view.

MR. LECHMERE

"It becomes an *indispensable duty* upon us, who appear in the name and on the behalf of all the Commons of Great Britain, not only to demand your lordships justice on such a criminal [Dr. Sacheverel] *but clearly and openly to assert our foundations.* . . .

"The nature of our constitution is that of a *limited monarchy*; wherein the supreme power is communicated and divided between Queen, Lords, and Commons; though the executive power and administration be wholly in the crown. The terms of such a constitution do not only suppose, but express, an original contract between the crown and the people; by which that supreme power was (by mutual consent, and not

That the terms of our constitution imply and express an original contract.

by accident) limited, and lodged in more hands than one. And *the uniform preservation of such a constitution for so many ages, without any fundamental change, demonstrates to your lordships the continuance of the same contract.* . . .

"The consequences of such a frame of government are obvious. That the *laws* are the rule to both; the common measure of the power of the crown, and of the obedience of the subject; and if the executive part endeavours the *subversion and total destruction of the government*, the original contract is thereby broke, and the right of allegiance ceases; that part of the government, thus *fundamentally* injured, hath a right to save or recover *that* constitution, in which it had an original interest. . . .

"The *necessary* means (which is the phrase used by the Commons in their first article) are words made choice of by them *with the greatest caution*. Those means are described (in the preamble to their charge) to be, that glorious enterprize, which his late majesty undertook, with an armed force, to deliver this kingdom from popery and arbitrary power; the concurrence of many subjects of the realm, who came over with him in that enterprize, and of many others of *all ranks and orders*, who appeared in arms in many parts of the kingdom in aid of that enterprize.

"These were the *means* that brought about the Revolution; and which the act that passed soon after, *declaring the rights and liberties of the subject, and settling the succession of the crown*, intends, when his late majesty is therein called the *glorious instrument of delivering the kingdom*; and which the Commons, in the last part of their first article, express by the word *resistance*.

"But the Commons, who will never be unmindful of the *allegiance* of the subjects to the *crown* of this realm, judged it highly incumbent upon them, out of regard to the *safety of her majesty's person and government, and the antient and legal constitution of this kingdom*, to call that resistance the *necessary* means; thereby plainly founding that power, right, and resistance, which was exercised by the people at the time of the happy

That the contract is by mutual consent, and binding at all times upon the parties.

The mixed constitution uniformly preserved for many ages, and is a proof of the contract.

Laws the common measure to king and subject.

Case of fundamental injury, and breach of original contract.

Words necessary means selected with caution.

Regard of the Commons to their allegiance to the crown, and to the antient constitution.

Revolution, and which the duties of *self-preservation* and religion called them to, *upon the* NECESSITY *of the case, and at the same time effectually securing her majesty's government, and the due allegiance of all her subjects.* . . .

"The nature of such an *original contract* of government proves, that there is not only a power in the people, who have *inherited this freedom*, to assert their own title to it; but they are bound in duty to transmit the *same* constitution to their posterity also."[25]

All ages have the same interest in preservation of the contract, and the same constitution.

———————◆———————

Mr. Lechmere made a second speech. Notwithstanding the clear and satisfactory manner in which he delivered himself in his first upon this arduous question, he thinks himself bound again distinctly to assert the same foundation; and to justify the Revolution on the *case of necessity only*, upon principles perfectly coinciding with those laid down in Mr. Burke's Letter on the French affairs.

MR. LECHMERE

"Your lordships were acquainted, in opening the charge, with how *great caution*, and with what unfeigned regard to her majesty and her government, and the *duty and allegiance* of her subjects, the commons made use of the words *necessary means*, to express the resistance that was made use of to bring about the Revolution, and with the condemning of which the Doctor is charged by this article; not doubting but that the honour and justice of that resistance, *from the necessity of that case, and to which alone we have strictly confined ourselves*, when duly considered, would confirm and strengthen,† and be understood to be an effectual security for an allegiance of the subject to the crown of this realm, *in every other case where there is not the same necessity*; and that the right of the people to *self-defence, and preservation of their liberties, by resistance, as their last*

The commons strictly confine their ideas of a Revolution to necessity alone and self-defence.

† N.B. The remark implies that allegiance would be insecure without this restriction.

[25] State Trials, vol. v, p. 651.

remedy, is the result of a case of such necessity only, *and by which the* original contract *between king and people, is broke. This was the principle laid down and carried through all that was said with respect to* allegiance; *and on* which foundation, *in the name and on the behalf of all the commons of Great Britain, we assert and justify that resistance by which the late happy revolution was brought about.* . . . .

"It appears to your lordships and the world, that *breaking the original contract between king and people*, were the words made choice of by that House of Commons [the House of Commons which had originated the declaration of right], with the *greatest deliberation and judgment*, and approved of by your lordships, in that first and fundamental step towards the *re-establishment of the government*, which had received so great a shock from the evil counsels which had been given to that unfortunate prince."

———————

Sir John Hawles, another of the managers, follows the steps of his brethren, positively affirming the doctrine of non-resistance to government to be the general, moral, religious, and political rule for the subject; and justifying the Revolution on the same principle with Mr. Burke, that is, *as an exception from necessity.* Indeed he carries the doctrine on the general idea of non-resistance much further than Mr. Burke has done; and full as far as it can perhaps be supported by any duty of *perfect obligation*; however noble and heroic it may be, in many cases, to suffer death rather than disturb the tranquillity of our country.

Sir John Hawles

"Certainly it must be granted, that the doctrine that commands obedience to the supreme power, *though in things contrary to nature*, even to suffer death, which is the highest injustice that can be done a man, rather than make an opposition to the supreme power [is reasonable[26]]; because the death of

[26] The words necessary to the completion of the sentence are wanted in the printed trial—but the construction of the sentence, as well as the foregoing

one, or some few private persons, is a less evil than *disturbing the whole government*; that law must needs be understood to forbid the doing or saying any thing to disturb the government; the rather because the obeying that law cannot be pretended to be against nature: and the Doctor's refusing to obey that implicit law, is the reason for which he is now prosecuted; though he would have it believed, that the reason he is now prosecuted, was for the doctrine he asserted of obedience to the supreme power; which he might have preached as long as he had pleased, and the Commons would have taken no offence at it, if he had stopped there, and not have taken upon him, on that pretence or occasion, to have cast odious colours upon the Revolution."[27]

———————————————

General Stanhope was among the managers: He begins his speech by a reference to the opinion of his fellow managers, which he hoped had put beyond all doubt the limits and qualifications that the Commons had placed to their doctrines concerning the Revolution; yet not satisfied with this general reference, after condemning the principle of non-resistance, which is asserted in the sermon *without any exception*, and stating, that under the specious pretence of preaching a peaceable doctrine, Sacheverel and the Jacobites meant in reality to excite a rebellion in favour of the Pretender,[28] he explicitly limits his ideas of resistance with the boundaries laid down by his colleagues and by Mr. Burke.

part of the speech, justify the insertion of some such supplemental words as the above.

[27] P. 676.

[28] [The doctrine of "non-resistance," as used in the seventeenth and eighteenth centuries, refers to the principled refusal to resist any authority, regardless of how unjust. The doctrine was upheld by Sacheverell and the Jacobites in the early eighteenth century; they wished to bring the Pretender (James Francis Edward Stuart or Charles Edward Stuart, son and grandson of James II) to the throne. Burke here distinguishes this doctrine from Whig principles.]

An Appeal from the New to the Old Whigs

General Stanhope

"The constitution of England is founded upon *compact*; and the subjects of this kingdom have, in their several public and private capacities, *as* legal a title to what are their rights by law, *as* a prince to the possession of his crown.

Rights of the subject and the crown equally legal.

"Your lordships, and most that hear me, are witnesses, and must remember the *necessities* of those times which brought about the Revolution: that *no other* remedy was left to preserve our religion and liberties; *that resistance was* necessary *and consequently just.* . . .

Justice of resistance founded on necessity.

"Had the Doctor, in the remaining part of his sermon, preached up peace, quietness, and the like, and shewn how happy we are under her majesty's administration, and exhorted obedience to it, he had never been called to answer a charge at your lordships bar. But the tenor of all his subsequent discourse is one continued invective against the government."

Mr. Walpole (afterwards Sir Robert) was one of the managers on this occasion. He was an honourable man and a sound Whig. He was not, as the Jacobites and discontented Whigs of his time have represented him, and as ill-informed people still represent him, a prodigal and corrupt minister. They charged him in their libels and seditious conversations as having first reduced corruption to a system. Such was their cant. But he was far from governing by corruption. He governed by party attachments. The charge of systematic corruption is less applicable to him, perhaps, than to any minister who ever served the crown for so great a length of time. He gained over very few from the Opposition. Without being a genius of the first class, he was an intelligent, prudent, and safe minister. He loved peace; and he helped to communicate the same disposition to nations at least as warlike and restless as that in which he had the chief direction of affairs. Though he served a master who was fond of martial fame, he kept all the establishments very low. The land tax continued at two shillings in the pound

for the greater part of his administration. The other imposi-
tions were moderate. The profound repose, the equal liberty,
the firm protection of just laws during the long period of his
power, were the principal causes of that prosperity which afterwards took such rapid strides towards perfection; and
which furnished to this nation ability to acquire the military
glory which it has since obtained, as well as to bear the
burthens, the cause and consequence of that warlike reputation. With many virtues, public and private, he had his faults;
but his faults were superficial. A careless, coarse, and over fa-
miliar style of discourse, without sufficient regard to persons
or occasions, and an almost total want of political decorum,
were the errours by which he was most hurt in the public opinion: and those through which his enemies obtained the greatest advantage over him. But justice must be done. The prudence, steadiness, and vigilance of that man, joined to the
greatest possible lenity in his character and his politics, preserved the crown to this royal family; and with it, their laws and
liberties to this country. Walpole had no other plan of defence
for the Revolution, than that of the other managers, and of
Mr. Burke; and he gives full as little countenance to any arbitrary attempts, on the part of restless and factious men, for
framing new governments according to their fancies.

MR. WALPOLE

"Resistance is no where enacted to be legal, but subjected,
by all the laws now in being, to the greatest penalties. It is what
is not, cannot, nor ought ever to be described, or affirmed, in
any positive law, to be excusable: when, and upon what *never-
to-be-expected* occasions, it may be exercised, no man can foresee; *and it ought never to be thought of, but when an utter subversion
of the laws of the realm threatens the whole frame of our constitution,
and no redress can otherwise be hoped for.* It therefore does, and
ought for ever, to stand, in the eye and letter of the law, as the
highest offence. But because any man, or party of men, may not,
out of folly or wantonness, commit treason, or make their
own discontents, ill principles, or disguised affections to an-

*Case of resis-
tance out of
the law; and
the highest
offence.*

other interest, a pretence to resist the supreme power, will it follow from thence that the *utmost necessity* ought not to engage a nation, *in its own defence, for the preservation of the whole?*"

Utmost necessity justifies it.

Sir Joseph Jekyl was, as I have always heard and believed, as nearly as any individual could be, the very standard of Whig principles in his age. He was a learned, and an able man; full of honour, integrity, and public spirit; no lover of innovation; nor disposed to change his solid principles for the giddy fashion of the hour. Let us hear this Whig.

SIR JOSEPH JEKYL

"In clearing up and vindicating the justice of the Revolution, which was the second thing proposed, it is far from the intent of the Commons to state the *limits and bounds* of the subject's submission to the sovereign. That which the law hath been wisely silent in, the Commons desire to be silent in too; nor will they put *any* case of a justifiable resistance, but that of the Revolution only; and *they persuade themselves that the doing right to that resistance will be so far from promoting popular licence or confusion, that it will have a contrary effect, and be a means of settling men's minds in the love of, and veneration for the laws*; to rescue and secure which, was the ONLY *aim and intention of those concerned in resistance.*"

Commons do not state the limits of submission.

To secure the laws, the only aim of the Revolution.

Dr. Sacheverel's counsel defended him on this principle, namely—that whilst he enforced from the pulpit the general doctrine of non-resistance, he was not obliged to take notice of the theoretic limits which ought to modify that doctrine. Sir Joseph Jekyl, in his reply, whilst he controverts its application to the Doctor's defence, fully admits and even enforces the principle itself, and supports the Revolution of 1688, as he and all the managers had done before, exactly upon the same grounds on which Mr. Burke has built, in his Reflections on the French Revolution.

SIR JOSEPH JEKYL

"If the Doctor had pretended to have stated the particular bounds and limits of non-resistance, and told the people in what cases they might, or might not resist, *he would have been much to blame*; nor was one word said in the articles, or by the managers, as if that was expected from him: but, *on the contrary, we have insisted, that in* NO *case can resistance be lawful, but in case of* extreme necessity, *and where the constitution cannot otherwise be preserved; and such necessity ought to be plain and obvious to the sense and judgment of the whole nation; and this was the case at the Revolution.*"

Blameable to state the bounds of non-resistance.

Resistance lawful only in case of extreme and obvious necessity.

The counsel for Doctor Sacheverel, in defending their client, were driven in reality to abandon the fundamental principles of his doctrine, and to confess, that an exception to the general doctrine of passive obedience and non-resistance did exist in the case of the Revolution. This the managers for the Commons considered as having gained their cause; as their having obtained *the whole* of what they contended for. They congratulated themselves and the nation on a civil victory, as glorious and as honourable as any that had obtained in arms during that reign of triumphs.

Sir Joseph Jekyl, in his reply to Harcourt, and the other great men who conducted the cause for the Tory side, spoke in the following memorable terms, distinctly stating the whole of what the Whig House of Commons contended for, in the name of all their constituents:

SIR JOSEPH JEKYL

"My lords, the concessions [the concessions of Sacheverel's counsel] are these: That *necessity* creates an *exception* to the general rule of submission to the prince; that such exception is understood or implied in the laws that require such submission; and that *the case of the Revolution was a case of necessity.*

"These are concessions *so ample*, and do so *fully* answer the drift of the Commons in this article, and are to *the utmost extent of their meaning in it,* that I can't forbear congratulating them upon this success of their impeachment; that in full parliament, this erroneous doctrine of *unlimited* non-resistance is given up, and disclaimed. And may it not, in after ages, be an addition to the glories of this bright reign, that so many of those who are honoured with being in her majesty's service have been at your lordships bar, thus successfully contending for the *national* rights of her people, and proving they are not precarious or remediless?

"But to return to these concessions; I must appeal to your lordships, whether they are not a *total departure* from the Doctor's answer."

Necessity creates an exception, and the Revolution a case of necessity, the utmost extent of the demand of the Commons.

———————◆———————

I now proceed to shew that the Whig managers for the Commons meant to preserve the government on a firm foundation, by asserting the perpetual validity of the settlement then made, and its coercive power upon posterity. I mean to shew that they gave no sort of countenance to any doctrine tending to impress the *people*, taken separately from the legislature which includes the crown, with an idea that *they* had acquired a moral or civil competence to alter (without breach of the original compact on the part of the king) the succession to the crown, at their pleasure; much less that they had acquired any right, in the case of such an event as caused the Revolution, to set up any new form of government. The author of the Reflections, I believe, thought that no man of common understanding could oppose to this doctrine, the ordinary sovereign power, as declared in the act of queen Anne. That is, that the kings or queens of the realm, with the consent of parliament, are competent to regulate and to settle the succession of the crown. This power is and ever was inherent in the supreme sovereignty; and was not, as the political divines vainly talk, acquired by the revolution. It is declared in the old statute of Queen Elizabeth. Such a power must reside in the complete sovereignty of every kingdom; and it is in fact exercised in all of them. But this right of *competence* in the legislature, not in the people, is by the legislature itself to be exercised with *sound discretion*; that is to say, it is to be exercised or not, in conformity to the fundamental principles of this government; to the rules of moral obligation; and to the faith of pacts, either contained in the nature of the transaction, or entered into by the body corporate of the kingdom; which body, in juridical construction, never dies; and in fact never loses its members at once by death.

Whether this doctrine is reconcileable to the modern philosophy of government, I believe the author neither knows nor cares; as he has little respect for any of that sort of philosophy. This may be because his capacity and knowledge do not reach to it. If such be the case, he cannot be blamed, if he acts on the sense of that incapacity; he cannot be blamed, if in the most arduous and critical questions which can possibly arise, and which affect to the quick the vital parts of our constitution, he takes the side which leans most to safety and settlement; that he is resolved not "to be wise beyond what is written" in the legislative record and practice; that when doubts arise on them, he endeavours to interpret one statute by another; and to reconcile them all to established recognized morals, and to the general antient known policy of the laws of England. Two things are equally evident, the first is, that the legislature possesses the power of regulating the succession of the crown, the second, that in the exercise of that right it has uniformly acted as if under the *restraints* which the author has stated. That author makes what the antients call *mos majorum*,[29] not indeed his sole, but certainly his principal rule of policy, to guide his judgment in whatever regards our laws. Uniformity and analogy can be preserved in them by this

[29] [Ancestral custom.]

process only. That point being fixed, and laying fast hold of a strong bottom, our speculations may swing in all directions, without public detriment; because they will ride with sure anchorage.

In this manner these things have been always considered by our ancestors. There are some indeed who have the art of turning the very acts of parliament which were made for securing the hereditary succession in the present royal family by rendering it penal to doubt of the validity of those acts of parliament, into an instrument for defeating all their ends and purposes: but upon grounds so very foolish, that it is not worth while to take further notice of such sophistry.

To prevent any unnecessary subdivision, I shall here put together what may be necessary to shew the perfect agreement of the Whigs with Mr. Burke, in his assertions, that the Revolution made no

> essential change in the constitution of the monarchy, or in any of its ancient, sound, and legal principles; that the succession was settled in the Hanover family, upon the idea, and in the mode of an hereditary succession qualified with Protestantism; that it was not settled upon *elective* principles, in any sense of the word *elective*, or under any modification or description of *election* whatsoever; but, on the contrary, that the nation, after the Revolution, renewed by a fresh compact the spirit of the original compact of the state, binding itself, *both in its existing members and all its posterity*, to adhere to the settlement of an hereditary succession in the Protestant line, drawn from James the First, as the stock of inheritance.[30]

Sir John Hawles

"If he [Dr. Sacheverel] is of the opinion he pretends, I cannot imagine how it comes to pass, that he that pays that deference to the supreme power has preached so directly contrary to the determinations of the supreme power in this government; he very well knowing that the lawfulness of the

Necessity of settling the right of the crown, and submission to the settlement.

---

[30] [This is Burke's argument in the *Reflections*, pp. 108–110.]

Revolution, and of the means whereby it was brought about, has already been determined by the aforesaid acts of parliament: and do it in the worst manner he could invent. *For questioning the right to the crown here in England, has procured the shedding of more blood, and caused more slaughter, than all the other matters tending to disturbances in the government, put together.* If, therefore, the doctrine which the apostles had laid down, was only to continue the peace of the world, as thinking the death of some few particular persons better to be borne with than a civil war; sure it is the highest breach of that law to question the first principles of this government.

"If the Doctor had been contented with the liberty he took of preaching up the duty of passive obedience, in the most extensive manner he had thought fit, and would have stopped there, your lordships would not have had the trouble, in relation to him, that you now have; but it is plain, that he preached up his absolute and unconditional obedience, not *to continue the peace and tranquillity of this nation, but to set the subjects at strife, and to raise a war in the bowels of this nation;* and it is for *this* that he is now prosecuted; though he would fain have it believed that the prosecution was for preaching the peaceable doctrine of absolute obedience."

SIR JOSEPH JEKYL

"The whole tenor of the administration, then in being, was agreed by all to be *a total departure from the constitution.* The nation was at that time united in that opinion, all but the criminal part of it. And as the nation joined in the judgment of their disease, so they did in the remedy. *They saw there was no remedy left, but the last;* and when that remedy took place, *the whole frame of the government was restored entire and unhurt.*[31]

Whole frame of government restored unhurt on the Revolution.

[31] "What we did was, in truth and substance and in a constitutional light, a revolution, not made, but prevented. We took solid securities; we settled doubtful questions; we corrected anomalies in our law. In the stable funda-

An Appeal from the New to the Old Whigs

This shewed the excellent temper the nation was in at that time, that, after such provocations from an abuse of the regal power, and such a convulsion, *no one part of the constitution was altered, or suffered the least damage; but, on the contrary, the whole received new life and vigour.*"

The Tory council for Dr. Sacheverel having insinuated, that a great and essential alteration in the constitution had been wrought by the Revolution, Sir Joseph Jekyl is so strong on this point, that he takes fire even at the insinuation of his being of such an opinion.

Sir Joseph Jekyl

"If the Doctor instructed his counsel to insinuate that there was *any innovation in the constitution wrought by the Revolution, it is an addition to his crime. The Revolution did not introduce any innovation; it was a restoration of the antient fundamental constitution of the kingdom,* and giving it its proper force and energy."

No innovation at the Revolution.

The Solicitor General, Sir Robert Eyre, distinguishes expressly the case of the Revolution, and its principles, from a proceeding at pleasure, on the part of the people, to change their antient constitution, and to frame a new government for themselves. He distinguishes it with the same care from the principles of regicide, and republicanism, and the sorts of

mental parts of our constitution we made no revolution; no, nor any alteration at all. We did not impair the monarchy. Perhaps it might be shewn that we strengthened it very considerably. The nation kept the same ranks, the same orders, the same privileges, the same franchises, the same rules for property, the same subordinations, the same order in the law, in the revenue, and in the magistracy; the same lords, the same commons, the same corporations, the same electors." *Mr. Burke's speech in the House of Commons, 9th February 1790.* It appears how exactly he coincides in every thing with Sir Joseph Jekyl.

resistance condemned by the doctrines of the church of England, and, which ought to be condemned, by the doctrines of all churches professing Christianity.

MR. SOLICITOR GENERAL, SIR ROBERT EYRE

"The resistance at the Revolution, which was founded in *unavoidable necessity,* could be no defence to a man that was attacked *for asserting that the people might cancel their allegiance at pleasure, or dethrone and murder their sovereign by a judiciary sentence.* For it can never be inferred from the lawfulness of resistance, at a time when *a total subversion of the government both in church and state was intended,* that a people may take up arms, and *call their sovereign to account at pleasure;* and, therefore, since *the Revolution could be of no service in giving the least colour for asserting any such wicked principle,* the Doctor could never intend to put it into the mouths of those new preachers, and new politicians, for a defence; unless it be his opinion, that the resistance at the Revolution can bear any parallel with the *execrable murder of the royal martyr, so justly detested by the whole nation.*

Revolution no precedent for voluntary cancelling allegiance.

Revolution not like the case of Charles the First.

"It is plain that the Doctor is not impeached for preaching a general doctrine, and enforcing the general duty of obedience, but for preaching against an *excepted case, after he has stated the exception.* He is not impeached for preaching the general doctrine of obedience, and the utter illegality of resistance upon any pretence whatsoever; but because, having first laid down the general doctrine as true, without any exception, *he states the excepted case,* the Revolution, in express terms, as an objection; and then assuming the consideration of that excepted case, denies there was any resistance in the Revolution; and asserts, that to impute resistance to the Revolution, would cast black and odious colours upon it. This is not preaching the doctrine of non-resistance, in the *general* terms used by the homilies, and the fathers of the church, where cases of necessity may be *understood to be excepted by a tacit implication, as the counsel have allowed;* but is preaching directly against the resistance at the Revolution, which, in the course of this debate, has been all along admitted to *be necessary and just,* and can have no other meaning than to bring a dishonour upon the Revolution, and an odium upon those great and illustrious persons, *those friends to the monarchy and the church, that assisted in bringing it about.* For had the Doctor intended any thing else, he would have treated the case of the Revolution in a different manner, and have given *it the true and fair answer*; he would have said, that the resistance at the Revolution was *of absolute necessity, and the only means left to revive the constitution; and must therefore be taken as an excepted case,* and could never come within the reach and intention of the general doctrine of the church.

Sacheverel's doctrine intended to bring an odium on the Revolution.

True defence of the Revolution an absolute necessity.

"Your lordships take notice on what grounds the Doctor continues to assert the same position in his answer. But is it not most evident, that the general exhortations to be met with in the homilies of the church of England, and such like declarations in the statutes of the kingdom, are meant only as rules for the civil obedience of the subject to the legal administration of the supreme power in *ordinary cases?* And it is equally absurd, to construe any words in a positive law to authorize the destruction of the whole, as to expect that king, lords, and commons should, in express terms of law, declare *such an ultimate resort as the right of resistance, at a time when the case supposes that the force of all law is ceased.*[32]

"The Commons must always resent, with the utmost detestation and abhorrence, every position that may shake the authority of that act of parliament, whereby the crown is settled upon her majesty, *and whereby the lords spiritual and temporal and commons do, in the name of all the people of England, most humbly and faithfully submit themselves, their heirs and posterities, to her majesty,* which this general principle of absolute non-resistance must certainly shake.

Commons abhor whatever shakes the submission of posterity to the settlement of the crown.

"For, if the resistance at the Revolution was illegal, the Revolution settled in usurpation, and this act can have no greater force and authority than an act passed under an usurper.

[32] See Reflections [pp. 115–116.]

"And the Commons take leave to observe, that the authority of the parliamentary settlement is a matter of the greatest consequence to maintain, in a case where the hereditary right to the crown is contested.

"It appears by the several instances mentioned in the act declaring the rights and liberties of the subject, and settling the succession of the crown, that at the time of the Revolution there was *a total subversion of the constitution of government both in church and state, which is a case that the laws of England could never suppose, provide for, or have in view.*"

Sir Joseph Jekyl, so often quoted, considered the preservation of the monarchy, and of the rights and prerogatives of the crown, as essential objects with all sound Whigs; and that they were bound, not only to maintain them when injured or invaded, but to exert themselves as much for their re-establishment, if they should happen to be over thrown by popular fury, as any of their own more immediate and popular rights and privileges, if the latter should be at any time subverted by the crown. For this reason he puts the cases of the *Revolution* and the *Restoration*,[33] exactly upon the same footing. He plainly marks, that it was the object of all honest men, not to sacrifice one part of the constitution to another; and much more, not to sacrifice any of them to visionary theories of the rights of man; but to preserve our whole inheritance in the constitution, in all its members and all its relations, entire, and unimpaired, from generation to generation. In this Mr. Burke exactly agrees with him.

SIR JOSEPH JEKYL

"Nothing is plainer than that the people have a right to the laws and the constitution. This right the nation hath as-

[33] [The Restoration of the monarchy of Charles II, in 1660, succeeded the death of Cromwell (1658) and the loss of confidence in the government of the Commonwealth.]

serted, and recovered out of the hands of those who had dis-possessed them of it at several times. There are of this *two famous instances* in the knowledge of the present age; I mean that of the *Restauration*, and that of the *Revolution*; in both of these great events were the *regal power*, and the *rights of the people* recovered. And it is *hard to say in which the people have the greatest interest; for the commons are sensible that there is not one legal power belonging to the crown, but they have an interest in it; and I doubt not but they will always be as careful to support the rights of the crown, as their own privileges."

What are the rights of the people.

Restoration and Revolution. People have an equal interest in the legal rights of the crown and of their own.

———————

The other Whig managers regarded (as he did) the overturn-ing of the monarchy by a republican faction with the very same horror and detestation with which they regarded the destruction of the privileges of the people by an arbitrary monarch.

Mr. Lechmere

Speaking of our constitution, states it as "a constitution which happily recovered itself, at the Restoration, from the confusions and disorders which *the horrid and detestable pro-ceedings of faction and usurpation had thrown it into*, and which, after many convulsions and struggles, was providentially saved at the late happy Revolution; and, by the many good laws passed since that time, stands now upon a firmer founda-tion: together with the most comfortable prospect of *security to all posterity,* by the settlement of the crown in the Protestant line."

Constitution recovered at the restoration and revolution.

———————

I mean now to shew that the Whigs (if Sir Joseph Jekyl was one), and if he spoke in conformity to the sense of the Whig house of commons and the Whig ministry who employed him, did carefully guard against any presumption that might arise from the repeal of the non-resistance oath of Charles the second, as if, at the Revolution, the antient principles of our government were at all changed—or that republican doctrines were countenanced, or any sanction given to seditious proceedings upon general undefined ideas of misconduct—or for changing the form of government—or for resistance upon any other ground than the *necessity* so often mentioned for the purpose of self-preservation. It will shew still more clearly the equal care of the then Whigs, to prevent either the regal power from being swallowed up on pretence of popular rights, or the popular rights from being destroyed on pretence of regal prerogatives.

SIR JOSEPH JEKYL

"Further, I desire it may be considered, that these legislators [the legislators who framed the non-resistance oath of Charles the Second] were guarding against the consequences of those *pernicious and antimonarchical principles, which had been broached a little before in this nation*; and those large declarations in favour of *non-resistance* were made to encounter or obviate the *mischief* of those principles; as appears by the preamble to the fullest of those acts, which is the *militia act*, in the 13th and 14th of King Charles the Second. The words of that act are these: *And, during the late usurped governments, many evil and rebellious principles have been instilled into the minds of the people of this kingdom, which may break forth, unless prevented, to the disturbance of the peace and quiet thereof: Be it therefore enacted, &c.* Here your lordships may see the reason that inclined those legislators to express themselves in such a manner against resistance. *They had seen the regal rights swallowed up, under the pretence of popular ones;* and it is no imputation on them that they did not then forsee a *quite different case*, as was that of the Revolution; where, under the pretence of regal authority, a total subversion of the rights of the subject was advanced, and in a manner effected. And this may serve to shew, that it was not the design of those legislators to condemn resistance, in a case *of absolute necessity, for preserving the constitution*, when they were guarding against principles which had so lately destroyed it.

"As to the truth of the doctrine in this declaration which was repealed, *I will admit it to be as true as the Doctor's counsel assert it; that is, with an exception of cases of necessity;* and it was not repealed because it was false, *understanding it with that restriction;* but it was repealed because it might be interpreted in *an unconfined sense, and exclusive of that restriction;* and being so understood, would reflect on the justice of the Revolution: and this the legislature had at heart, and were very jealous of; and by this repeal of that declaration, gave a parliamentary or legislative admonition, against asserting this doctrine of non-resistance *in an unlimited sense.* . . .

> Non-resistance oath not repealed, because (with the restriction of necessity) it was false, but to prevent false interpretations.

"Though the general doctrine of non-resistance, the doctrine of the church of England, as stated in her homilies, or elsewhere delivered, by which the general duty of subjects to the higher powers is taught, be owned to be, as unquestionably it is, *a godly and wholesome doctrine;* though this general doctrine has been constantly inculcated by the reverend fathers of the church, dead and living, and preached by them as a preservative against the popish doctrine of deposing princes, and as the ordinary rule of obedience; and though the same doctrine has been preached, maintained, and avowed by our most orthodox and able divines from the time of the Reformation; and how *innocent a man* Dr. Sacheverel had been, if, *with an honest and well-meant* zeal, he had preached the same doctrine in the same general terms in which he found it delivered by the apostles of Christ, as taught by the homilies, and the reverend fathers of our church, and, in imitation of those great examples, had only pressed the general duty of obedience, and the illegality of resistance, without taking notice of any exception."

> General doctrine of non-resistance godly and wholesome; not bound to state *explicitly* the exceptions.

Another of the managers for the house of commons, Sir John Holland, was not less careful in guarding against a confusion of the principles of the revolution, with any loose general doctrines of a right in the individual, or even in the people, to undertake for themselves, on any prevalent temporary opinions of convenience or improvement, any fundamental change in the constitution, or to fabricate a new government for themselves, and thereby to disturb the public peace, and to unsettle the antient constitution of this kingdom.

Sir John Holland

Submission to the sovereign a conscientious duty, except in cases of necessity.

"The commons would not be understood, as if they were pleading for a licentious resistance; as if *subjects* were left to *their* good-will and pleasure, when they are to *obey*, and when to *resist*. No, my lords, they know they are *obliged by all the ties of social creatures and Christians, for wrath and conscience sake, to submit to their sovereign*. The commons do not abet *humoursome factious arms*: they aver them to be *rebellious*. But yet they maintain, that that resistance at the Revolution, which was so *necessary, was lawful and just from that necessity*.

"These general rules of obedience may, upon a *real necessity*, admit a lawful *exception*; and such a *necessary exception* we assert the revolution to be.

Right of resistance how to be understood.

" 'Tis with this view of *necessity* only, *absolute necessity* of preserving our laws, liberties, and religion; 'tis with *this limitation* that we desire to be understood, when any of us speak of resistance in general. The *necessity* of the resistance at the Revolution, was at that time obvious to every man."

I shall conclude these extracts with a reference to the prince of Orange's declaration, in which he gives the nation the fullest assurance that in his enterprize he was far from the intention of introducing any change whatever in the fundamental law and constitution of the state. He considered the object of his enterprize, not to be a precedent for further revolutions, but that it was the great end of his expedition to make such revolutions so far as human power and wisdom could provide, unnecessary.

Extracts from the Prince of Orange's Declaration

"*All magistrates, who have been* unjustly turned out, shall *forthwith resume their former* employments, as well as all the boroughs of England shall return again to *their antient prescriptions and charters*: and more particularly, that *the antient* charter of the great and famous city of London shall be again in force. And that the writs for the members of parliament shall be addressed to the *proper officers, according to law and custom*. . . .

"And for the doing of all other things, which the two houses of parliament shall find necessary for the peace, honour, and safety of the nation, so that there may *be no danger of the nation's falling, at any time hereafter, under arbitrary government.*"

Extract from the Prince of Orange's additional Declaration

"We are confident that no persons can have *such hard thoughts of us,* as to imagine that we have any other design in this undertaking, than to procure a settlement of the *religion, and of the liberties and properties of the subjects, upon so sure a foundation, that there may be no danger of the nation's relapsing into the like miseries at any time hereafter*. And, as the forces that we have brought along with us are utterly disproportioned to that wicked design of conquering the nation, if we were capable of intending it; *so the great numbers of the principal nobility and gentry, that are men of eminent quality and estates, and persons of known integrity and zeal, both for the religion and government of England, many of them also being distinguished by their constant fidelity to the crown*, who do both accompany us in this expedition, and have earnestly solicited us to it, will cover us from all such malicious insinuations."

Principal nobility and gentry well affected to the church and crown security against the design of innovation.

In the spirit, and upon one occasion in the words,[34] of this declaration, the statutes passed in that reign made such provisions for preventing these dangers, that scarcely any thing short of combination of king, lords, and commons for the destruction of the liberties of the nation, can in any probability make us liable to similar perils. In that dreadful, and, I hope, not to be looked for case, any opinion of a right to make revolutions, grounded on this precedent, would be but a poor resource. Dreadful indeed would be our situation.

These are the doctrines held by *the Whigs of the Revolution*, delivered with as much solemnity, and as authentically at least, as any political dogmas were ever promulgated from the beginning of the world. If there be any difference between their tenets and those of Mr. Burke it is, that the old Whigs oppose themselves still more strongly than he does against the doctrines which are now propagated with so much industry by those who would be thought their successors.

It will be said perhaps, that the old Whigs, in order to guard themselves against popular odium, pretended to assert tenets contrary to those which they secretly held. This, if true, would prove, what Mr. Burke has uniformly asserted, that the extravagant doctrines which he meant to expose, were disagreeable to the body of the people; who, though they perfectly abhor a despotic government, certainly approach more nearly to the love of mitigated monarchy, than to any thing which bears the appearance even of the best republic. But if these old Whigs deceived the people, their conduct was unaccountable indeed. They exposed their power, as every one conversant in history knows, to the greatest peril, for the propagation of opinions which, on this hypothesis, they did not hold. It is a new kind of martyrdom. This supposition does as little credit to their integrity as their wisdom: It makes

[34] Declaration of Right.

An Appeal from the New to the Old Whigs

them at once hypocrites and fools. I think of those great men very differently. I hold them to have been, what the world thought them, men of deep understanding, open sincerity, and clear honour. However, be that matter as it may; what these old Whigs pretended to be, Mr. Burke is. This is enough for him.

I do indeed admit, that though Mr. Burke has proved that his opinions were those of the old Whig party, solemnly declared by one house, in effect and substance by both houses of parliament, this testimony standing by itself will form no proper defence for his opinions, if he and the old Whigs were both of them in the wrong. But it is his present concern, not to vindicate these old Whigs, but to shew his agreement with them. He appeals to them as judges: he does not vindicate them as culprits. It is current that these old politicians knew little of the rights of men; that they lost their way by groping about in the dark, and fumbling among rotten parchments and musty records. Great lights they say are lately obtained in the world; and Mr. Burke, instead of shrowding himself in exploded ignorance, ought to have taken advantage of the blaze of illumination which has been spread about him. It may be so. The enthusiasts of this time, it seems, like their predecessors in another faction of fanaticism, deal in lights. Hudibras pleasantly says of them, they

Have *lights*, where better eyes are blind,
As pigs are said to see the wind.[35]

The author of the Reflections has *heard* a great deal concerning the modern lights; but he has not yet had the good fortune to *see* much of them. He has read more than he can justify to any thing but the spirit of curiosity, of the works of these illuminators of the world. He has learned nothing from the far greater number of them, than a full certainty of their shallowness, levity, pride, petulance, presumption and igno-

---

[35] [Samuel Butler, *Hudibras* 3.2.1107-08 (altered).]

rance. Where the old authors whom he has read, and the old men whom he has conversed with, have left him in the dark, he is in the dark still. If others, however, have obtained any of this extraordinary light, they will use it to guide them in their researches and their conduct. I have only to wish, that the nation may be as happy and as prosperous under the influence of the new light, as it has been in the sober shade of the old obscurity. As to the rest, it will be difficult for the author of the Reflections to conform to the principles of the avowed leaders of the party, until they appear otherwise than negatively. All we can gather from them is this, that their principles are diametrically opposite to his. This is all that we know from authority. Their negative declaration obliges me to have recourse to the books which contain positive doctrines. They are indeed, to those Mr. Burke holds, diametrically opposite; and if it be true (as the oracles of the party have said, I hope hastily), that their opinions differ so widely, it should seem they are the most likely to form the creed of the modern Whigs.

I have stated what were the avowed sentiments of the old Whigs, not in the way of argument, but narratively. It is but fair to set before the reader, in the same simple manner, the sentiments of the modern, to which they spare neither pains nor expence to make proselytes. I choose them from the books upon which most of that industry and expenditure in circulation have been employed;[36] I choose them not from those who speak with a politic obscurity; not from those who only controvert the opinions of the old Whigs, without advancing any of their own, but from those who speak plainly and affirmatively. The Whig reader may make his choice between the two doctrines.

[36] [Burke's *Reflections* began a pamphlet war whose magnitude is only now being understood. His most famous antagonists included Sir James Mackintosh, Mary Wollstonecraft, and Thomas Paine, whose *Rights of Man* is quoted below. See Gayle Trusdel Pendleton, "Towards a Bibliography of the *Reflections* and *The Rights of Man* Controversy," *Bulletin of Research in the Humanities* 85 (1982): 65–103.]

AN APPEAL FROM THE NEW TO THE OLD WHIGS

The doctrine then propagated by these societies, which gentlemen think they ought to be very tender in discouraging, as nearly as possible in their own words, is as follows: that in Great Britain we are not only without a good constitution, but that we have "no constitution." That, "tho' it is much talked about, no such thing as a constitution exists, or ever did exist; and consequently that *the people have a constitution yet to form*; that since William the Conqueror, the country has never yet *regenerated itself*, and is therefore without a constitution. That where it cannot be produced in a visible form, there is none. That a constitution is a thing antecedent to government; and that the constitution of a country is not the act of its government, but of a people constituting a government. That *every thing* in the English government is the reverse of what it ought to be, and what it is said to be in England. That the right of war and peace resides in a metaphor shewn at the Tower, for six pence or a shilling a-piece. That it signifies not where the right resides, whether in the crown or in parliament. War is the common harvest of those who participate in the division and expenditure of public money. That the portion of liberty enjoyed in England is just enough to enslave a country more productively than by despotism."

So far as to the general state of the British constitution. As to our house of lords, the chief virtual representative of our aristocracy, the great ground and pillar of security to the landed interest, and that main link by which it is connected with the law and the crown, these worthy societies are pleased to tell us, that, "whether we view aristocracy before, or behind, or side-ways, or any way else, domestically or publicly, it is still a *monster*. That aristocracy in France had one feature less in its countenance than what it has in some other countries; it did not compose a body of hereditary legislators. It was not a corporation of aristocracy"; for such it seems that profound legislator Mr. De la Fayette describes the house of peers. "That it is kept up by family tyranny and injustice— that there is an unnatural unfitness in aristocracy to be legislators for a nation—that their ideas of distributive justice are corrupted at the very source; they begin life by trampling on all their younger brothers, and sisters, and relations of every kind, and are taught and educated so to do. That the idea of an hereditary legislator is as absurd as an hereditary mathematician. That a body holding themselves unaccountable to any body, ought to be trusted by no body—that it is continuing the uncivilized principles of governments founded in conquest, and the base idea of man having a property in man, and governing him by a personal right—that aristocracy has a tendency to degenerate the human species," &c. &c.

As to our law of primogeniture, which with few and inconsiderable exceptions is the standing law of all our landed inheritance, and which without question has a tendency, and I think a most happy tendency, to preserve a character of consequence, weight, and prevalent influence over others in the whole body of the landed interest, they call loudly for its destruction. They do this for political reasons that are very manifest. They have the confidence to say, "that it is a law against every law of nature, and nature herself calls for its destruction. Establish family justice, and aristocracy falls. By the aristocratical law of primogenitureship, in a family of six children, five are exposed. Aristocracy has never but *one* child. The rest are begotten to be devoured. They are thrown to the cannibal for prey, and the natural parent prepares the unnatural repast."

As to the house of commons, they treat it far worse than the house of lords or the crown have been ever treated. Perhaps they thought they had a greater right to take this amicable freedom with those of their own family. For many years it has been the perpetual theme of their invectives. "Mockery, insult, usurpation," are amongst the best names they bestow upon it. They damn it in the mass, by declaring "that it does not arise out of the inherent rights of the people, as the national assembly does in France, and whose name designates its original."

Of the charters and corporations, to whose rights, a few years ago, these gentlemen were so tremblingly alive, they say, "that when the people of England come to reflect upon them, they will, like France, annihilate those badges of oppression, those traces of a conquered nation."

As to our monarchy, they had formerly been more tender of that branch of the constitution, and for a good reason. The laws had guarded against all seditious attacks upon it, with a greater degree of strictness and severity. The tone of these gentlemen is totally altered since the French Revolution. They now declaim as vehemently against the monarchy, as in former occasions they treacherously flattered and soothed it.

"When we survey the wretched condition of man under the monarchical and hereditary systems of government, dragged from his home by one power, or driven by another, and impoverished by taxes more than by enemies, it becomes evident that those systems are bad, and that a general revolution in the principle and construction of governments is necessary.

"What is government more than the management of the affairs of a nation? It is not, and from its nature cannot be, the property of any particular man or family, but of the whole community, at whose expence it is supported; and though by force or contrivance it has been usurped into an inheritance, the usurpation cannot alter the right of things. Sovereignty, as a matter of right, appertains to the nation only, and not to any individual; and a nation has at all times an inherent indefeasible right to abolish any form of government it finds inconvenient, and establish such as accords with its interest, disposition, and happiness. The romantic and barbarous distinction of men into kings and subjects, though it may suit the condition of courtiers, cannot that of citizens; and is exploded by the principle upon which governments are now founded. Every citizen is a member of the sovereignty, and, as such, can acknowledge no personal subjection; and his obedience can be only to the laws."

Warmly recommending to us the example of France, where they have destroyed monarchy, they say—

"Monarchical sovereignty, the enemy of mankind, and the source of misery, is abolished; and sovereignty itself is restored to its natural and original place, the nation. Were this the case throughout Europe, the cause of wars would be taken away."

"But, after all, what is this metaphor called a crown, or rather what is monarchy? Is it a thing, or is it a name, or is it a fraud? Is it 'a contrivance of human wisdom,' or of human craft to obtain money from a nation under specious pretences? Is it a thing necessary to a nation? If it is, in what does that necessity consist, what services does it perform, what is its business, and what are its merits? Doth the virtue consist in the metaphor, or in the man? Doth the goldsmith that makes the crown make the virtue also? Doth it operate like Fortunatus's wishing-cap, or Harlequin's wooden sword? Doth it make a man a conjuror? In fine, what is it? It appears to be a something going much out of fashion, falling into ridicule, and rejected in some countries both as unnecessary and expensive. In America it is considered as an absurdity; and in France it has so far declined, that the goodness of the man, and the respect for his personal character, are the only things that preserve the appearance of its existence."

"Mr. Burke talks about what he calls an hereditary crown, as if it were some production of Nature; or as if, like Time, it had a power to operate, not only independently, but in spite of man; or as if it were a thing or a subject universally consented to. Alas! it has none of those properties, but is the reverse of them all. It is a thing in imagination, the propriety of which is more than doubted, and the legality of which in a few years will be denied."

"If I ask the farmer, the manufacturer, the merchant, the tradesman, and down through all the occupations of life to the common labourer, what service monarchy is to him? he can give me no answer. If I ask him what monarchy is, he believes it is something like a sinecure."

———

"The French constitution says, That the right of war and peace is in the nation. Where else should it reside, but in those who are to pay the expence?

"In England, this right is said to reside in a *metaphor*, shewn at the Tower for sixpence or a shilling a-piece: So are the lions; and it would be a step nearer to reason to say it resided in them, for any inanimate metaphor is no more than a hat or a cap. We can all see the absurdity of worshipping Aaron's molten calf, or Nebuchadnezzar's golden image; but why do men continue to practice themselves the absurdities they despise in others?"

———

The Revolution and Hanover succession had been objects of the highest veneration to the old Whigs. They thought them not only proofs of the sober and steady spirit of liberty which guided their ancestors; but of their wisdom and provident care of posterity. The modern Whigs have quite other notions of these events and actions. They do not deny that Mr. Burke has given truly the words of the acts of parliament which secured the succession, and the just sense of them. They attack not him but the law.

"Mr. Burke (say they) has done some service, not to his cause, but to his country, by bringing those clauses into public view. They serve to demonstrate how necessary it is at all times to watch against the attempted encroachment of power, and to prevent its running to excess. It is somewhat extraordinary, that the offence for which James II was expelled, that of setting up power by *assumption*, should be re-acted, under another shape and form, by the parliament that expelled him. It shews that the rights of man were but imperfectly understood at the Revolution; for, certain it is, that the right which that parliament set up by *assumption* (for by delegation it had it not, and could not have it, because none could give it) over the persons and freedom of posterity for ever, was of the same tyrannical unfounded kind which James attempted to set up over the parliament and the nation, and for which he was expelled. The only difference is (for in principle they differ not), that the one was an usurper over the living, and the other over the unborn; and as the one has no better authority to stand upon than the other, both of them must be equally null and void, and of no effect."

_____

"As the estimation of all things is by comparison, the Revolution of 1688, however from circumstances it may have been exalted beyond its value, will find its level. It is already on the wane; eclipsed by the enlarging orb of reason, and the luminous revolutions of America and France. In less than another century, it will go, as well as Mr. Burke's labours, 'to the family vault of all the Capulets.' *Mankind will then scarcely believe that a country calling itself free, would send to Holland for a man, and clothe him with power, on purpose to put themselves in fear of him, and give him almost a million sterling a-year for leave to submit themselves and their posterity, like bond-men and bond-women, for ever.*
"Mr. Burke having said that the king holds his crown in contempt of the choice of the Revolution society, who individually or collectively have not" (as most certainly they have not) "a vote for a king amongst them, they take occasion from thence to infer, that a king who does not hold his crown by election, despises the people."

_____

"The King of England," says he, "holds *his* crown (for it does not belong to the nation, according to Mr. Burke) in *contempt* of the choice of the Revolution Society." &c.

_____

"As to who is King in England or elsewhere, or whether there is any King at all, or whether the people chuse a Cherokee Chief, or a Hessian Hussar for a King, it is not a matter that I trouble myself about—be that to themselves; but with respect to the doctrine, so far as it relates to the Rights of Men and Nations, it is as abominable as any thing ever uttered in the most enslaved country under heaven. Whether it sounds worse to my ear, by not being accustomed to hear such despotism, than what it does to the ear of another person, I am not so well a judge of; but of its abominable principle I am at no loss to judge."

These societies of modern Whigs push their insolence as far as it can go. In order to prepare the minds of the people for treason and rebellion, they represent the king as tainted with principles of despotism, from the circumstance of his having dominions in Germany. In direct defiance of the most notorious truth, they describe his government there to be a despotism; whereas it is a free constitution, in which the states of the electorate have their part in the government; and this privilege has never been infringed by the king, or, that I have heard of, by any of his predecessors. The constitution of the electoral dominions has indeed a double control, both from the laws of the empire, and from the privileges of the country. Whatever rights the king enjoys as elector, have been always parentally exercised, and the calumnies of these scandalous societies have not been authorized by a single complaint of oppression.

"When Mr. Burke says that 'his majesty's heirs and successors, each in their time and order, will come to the crown with the *same contempt* of their choice with which his majesty has succeeded to that he wears,' it is saying too much even to the humblest individual in the country; part of whose daily labour goes towards making up the million sterling a year, which the country gives the person it stiles a king. Government with insolence, is despotism; but when contempt is added, it becomes worse; and to pay for contempt, is the excess of slavery. This species of government comes from Germany; and reminds me of what one of the Brunswick soldiers told me, who was taken prisoner by the Americans in the late war: 'Ah!' said he, 'America is a fine free country, it is worth the people's fighting for; I know the difference by knowing my own: in my country, *if the prince says, Eat straw, we eat straw.*'

AN APPEAL FROM THE NEW TO THE OLD WHIGS

God help that country, thought I, be it England or elsewhere, whose liberties are to be protected by *German principles of government, and princes of Brunswick!"*

"It is somewhat curious to observe, that although the people of England have been in the habit of talking about kings, it is always a Foreign House of kings; hating Foreigners, yet governed by them. It is now the House of Brunswick, one of the petty tribes of Germany."

"If Government be what Mr. Burke describes it, 'a contrivance of human wisdom,' I might ask him, if wisdom was at such a low ebb in England, that it was become necessary to import it from Holland and from Hanover? But I will do the country the justice to say, that was not the case; and even if it was, it mistook the cargo. The wisdom of every country, when properly exerted, is sufficient for all its purposes; *and there could exist no more real occasion in England to have sent for a Dutch Stadtholder, or a German Elector, than* there was in America to have done a similar thing. If a country does not understand its own affairs, how is a foreigner to understand them, who knows neither its laws, its manners, nor its language? If there existed a man so transcendantly wise above all others, that his wisdom was necessary to instruct a nation, some reason might be offered for monarchy; but when we cast our eyes about a country, and observe how every part understands its own affairs; and when we look around the world, and see that of all men in it, the race of kings are the most insignificant in capacity, our reason cannot fail to ask us—What are those men kept for?"[37]

These are the notions which, under the idea of Whig principles, several persons, and among them persons of no mean mark, have associated themselves to propagate. I will not attempt in the smallest degree to refute them. This will

[37] Vindication of the Rights of Man, recommended by the several societies. [Mary Wollstonecraft, *Vindication of the Rights of Men* (1790)]

probably be done (if such writings shall be thought to deserve any other than the refutation of criminal justice) by others, who may think with Mr. Burke. He has performed his part.

I do not wish to enter very much at large into the discussions which diverge and ramify in all ways from this productive subject. But there is one topic upon which I hope I shall be excused in going a little beyond my design. The factions, now so busy amongst us, in order to divest men of all love for their country, and to remove from their minds all duty with regard to the state, endeavour to propagate an opinion, that the *people*, in forming their commonwealth, have by no means parted with their power over it. This is an impregnable citadel, to which these gentlemen retreat whenever they are pushed by the battery of laws, and usages, and positive conventions. Indeed it is such and of so great force, that all they have done in defending their outworks is so much time and labour thrown away. Discuss any of their schemes—their answer is—It is the act of the *people*, and that is sufficient. Are we to deny to a *majority* of the people the right of altering even the whole frame of their society, if such should be their pleasure? They may change it, say they, from a monarchy to a republic to-day, and to-morrow back again from a republic to a monarchy; and so backward and forward as often as they like. They are masters of the commonwealth; because in substance they are themselves the commonwealth. The French revolution, say they, was the act of the majority of the people; and if the majority of any other people, the people of England for instance, wish to make the same change, they have the same right.

Just the same undoubtedly. That is, none at all. Neither the few nor the many have a right to act merely by their will, in any matter connected with duty, trust, engagement, or obligation. The constitution of a country being once settled upon some compact, tacit or expressed, there is no power existing of force to alter it, without the breach of the covenant, or the consent of all the parties. Such is the nature of a contract. And the votes of a majority of the people, whatever their infamous flatterers may teach in order to corrupt their minds, cannot alter the moral any more than they can alter the physical essence of things. The people are not to be taught to think lightly of their engagements to their governors; else they teach governors to think lightly of their engagements towards them. In that kind of game in the end the people are sure to be losers. To flatter them into a contempt of faith, truth, and justice, is to ruin them; for in these virtues consists their whole safety. To flatter any man, or any part of mankind, in any description, by asserting, that in engagements he or they are free whilst any other human creature is bound, is ultimately to vest the rule of morality in the pleasure of those who ought to be rigidly submitted to it; to subject the sovereign reason of the world to the caprices of weak and giddy men.

But, as no one of us men can dispense with public or private faith, or with any other tie of moral obligation, so neither can any number of us. The number engaged in crimes, instead of turning them into laudable acts, only augments the quantity and the intensity of the guilt. I am well aware, that men love to hear of their power, but have an extreme disrelish to be told of their duty. This is of course; because every duty is a limitation of some power. Indeed arbitrary power is so much to the depraved taste of the vulgar, of the vulgar of every description, that almost all the dissensions which lacerate the commonwealth, are not concerning the manner in which it is to be exercised, but concerning the hands in which it is to be placed. Somewhere they are resolved to have it. Whether they desire it to be vested in the many or the few, depends with most men upon the chance which they imagine they themselves may have of partaking in the exercise of that arbitrary sway, in the one mode or in the other.

It is not necessary to teach men to thirst after power. But it is very expedient that, by moral instruction, they should be taught, and by their civil constitutions they should be compelled, to put many restrictions upon the immoderate exercise of it, and the inordinate desire. The best method of obtaining these two great points forms the important, but at the same time the difficult problem to the true statesman. He thinks of the place in which political power is to be lodged, with no other attention, than as it may render the more or the less practicable, its salutary restraint, and its prudent direction. For this reason no legislator, at any period of the world, has willingly placed the seat of active power in the hands of the multitude: Because there it admits of no control, no regulation, no steady direction whatsoever. The people are the natural control on authority; but to exercise and to control together is contradictory and impossible.

As the exorbitant exercise of power cannot, under popular sway, be effectually restrained, the other great object of political arrangement, the means of abating an excessive desire of it, is in such a state still worse provided for. The democratick commonwealth is the foodful nurse of ambition. Under the other forms it meets with many restraints. Whenever, in states which have had a democratick basis, the legislators have endeavoured to put restraints upon ambition, their methods were as violent, as in the end they were ineffectual; as violent indeed as any the most jealous despotism could invent. The ostracism could not very long save itself, and much less the state which it was meant to guard, from the attempts of ambition, one of the natural inbred incurable distempers of a powerful democracy.

But to return from this short digression, which however is not wholly foreign to the question of the effect of the will of the majority upon the form or the existence of their society. I cannot too often recommend it to the serious consideration of all men, who think civil society to be within the province of moral jurisdiction, that if we owe to it any duty, it is not subject to our will. Duties are not voluntary. Duty and will are even contradictory terms. Now though civil society might be at first a voluntary act (which in many cases it undoubtedly was) its continuance is under a permanent standing covenant, coexisting with the society; and it attaches upon every individual of that society, without any formal act of his own. This is warranted by the general practice, arising out of the general sense of mankind. Men without their choice derive benefits from that association; without their choice they are subjected to duties in consequence of these benefits; and without their choice they enter into a virtual obligation as binding as any that is actual. Look through the whole of life and the whole system of duties. Much the strongest moral obligations are such as were never the results of our option. I allow, that if no supreme ruler exists, wise to form, and potent to enforce, the moral law, there is no sanction to any contract, virtual or even actual, against the will of prevalent power. On that hypothesis, let any set of men be strong enough to set their duties at defiance, and they cease to be duties any longer. We have but this one appeal against irresistible power—

Si genus humanum et mortalia temnitis arma,
At sperate Deos memores fandi atque nefandi.[38]

Taking it for granted that I do not write to the disciples of the Parisian philosophy, I may assume, that the awful author of our being is the author of our place in the order of existence; and that having disposed and marshalled us by a divine tactick, not according to our will, but according to his, he has, in and by that disposition, virtually subjected us to act the part which belongs to the place assigned us. We have obligations to mankind at large, which are not in consequence of any special voluntary pact. They arise from the relation of man to man, and the relation of man to God, which relations are not matters of choice. On the contrary, the force of all the pacts which we enter into with any particular person or number of persons amongst mankind, depends upon those prior obligations. In some cases the subordinate relations are voluntary, in others they are necessary—but the duties are all compulsive. When we marry, the choice is voluntary, but the duties

[38] ["If you have no respect for the human race and mortal arms,
Yet beware the gods who remember right and wrong."
Vergil, *Aeneid*, 1.542–43]

are not matter of choice. They are dictated by the nature of the situation. Dark and inscrutable are the ways by which we come into the world. The instincts which give rise to this mysterious process of nature are not of our making. But out of physical causes, unknown to us, perhaps unknowable, arise moral duties, which, as we are able perfectly to comprehend, we are bound indispensably to perform. Parents may not be consenting to their moral relation; but consenting or not, they are bound to a long train of burthensome duties towards those with whom they have never made a convention of any sort. Children are not consenting to their relation, but their relation, without their actual consent, binds them to its duties; or rather it implies their consent because the presumed consent of every rational creature is in unison with the predisposed order of things. Men come in that manner into a community with the social state of their parents, endowed with all the benefits, loaded with all the duties of their situation. If the social ties and ligaments, spun out of those physical relations which are the elements of the commonwealth, in most cases begin, and always continue, independently of our will, so without any stipulation, on our part, are we bound by that relation called our country, which comprehends (as it has been well said) "all the charities of all."[39] Nor are we left without powerful instincts to make this duty as dear and grateful to us, as it is awful and coercive. Our country is not a thing of mere physical locality. It consists, in a great measure, in the antient order into which we are born. We may have the same geographical situation, but another country; as we may have the same country in another soil. The place that determines our duty to our country is a social, civil relation.

These are the opinions of the author whose cause I defend. I lay them down not to enforce them upon others by disputation, but as an account of his proceedings. On them he acts; and from them he is convinced that neither he, nor any man, or number of men, have a right (except what necessity,

[39] Omnes omnium charitates patria una complectitur. Cic[ero]

which is out of and above all rule, rather imposes than bestows) to free themselves from that primary engagement into
which every man born into a community as much contracts by
his being born into it, as he contracts an obligation to certain
parents by his having been derived from their bodies. The
place of every man determines his duty. If you ask, *Quem te
Deus esse jussit?* You will be answered when you resolve this
other question, *Humana qua parte locatus es in re?*[40]

I admit, indeed, that in morals, as in all things else, difficulties will sometimes occur. Duties will sometimes cross one
another. Then questions will arise, which of them is to be
placed in subordination; which of them may be entirely su-
perseded? These doubts give rise to that part of moral science
called *casuistry;* which, though necessary to be well studied by
those who would become expert in that learning, who aim at
becoming what, I think Cicero somewhere calls, *artifices offici-
orum*; it requires a very solid and discriminating judgment,
great modesty and caution, and much sobriety of mind in the
handling; else there is a danger that it may totally subvert
those offices which it is its object only to methodize and reconcile. Duties, at their extreme bounds, are drawn very fine, so
as to become almost evanescent. In that state, some shade of
doubt will always rest on these questions, when they are pur-

---

[40] A few lines in Persius contain a good summary of all the objects of moral
investigation, and hint the result of our enquiry: There human will has no
place.

> Quid *sumus?* et quidnam *victuri gignimur?* ordo
> Quis *datus?* et *metae* quis mollis flexus et unde?
> Quis modus argento? Quid *fas optare?* Quid asper
> Utile nummus habet? *Patriae charisque propinquis*
> Quantum elargiri *debeat?*—Quem te Deus esse
> *Jussit?*—et humana qua parte *locatus es* in re?

["[L]earn what we are, and for what sort of lives we were born; what place
was assigned to us at the start; how to round the turning-post gently, and
from what point to begin the turn; what limit should be placed on wealth;
what prayers may rightfully be offered; what good there is in fresh-minted
coin; how much should be spent on country and on your dear kin; what
part God has ordered you to play, and at what point of the human commonwealth you have been stationed." Persius, *Satires* 3.67–72 (Loeb Classical Library)]

sued with great subtilty. But the very habit of stating these extreme cases is not very laudable or safe: because, in general, it is not right to turn our duties into doubts. They are imposed to govern our conduct, not to exercise our ingenuity; and therefore, our opinions about them ought not to be in a state of fluctuation, but steady, sure, and resolved.

Amongst these nice, and therefore dangerous, points of casuistry may be reckoned the question so much agitated in the present hour—Whether, after the people have discharged themselves of their original power by an habitual delegation, no occasion can possibly occur which may justify their resumption of it? This question, in this latitude, is very hard to affirm or deny: but I am satisfied that no occasion can justify such a resumption, which would not equally authorize a dispensation with any other moral duty, perhaps with all of them together. However, if in general it be not easy to determine concerning the lawfulness of such devious proceedings, which must be ever on the edge of crimes, it is far from difficult to foresee the perilous consequences of the resuscitation of such a power in the people. The practical consequences of any political tenet go a great way in deciding upon its value. Political problems do not primarily concern truth or falsehood. They relate to good or evil. What in the result is likely to produce evil, is politically false: that which is productive of good, politically is true.

Believing it therefore a question at least arduous in the theory, and in the practice very critical, it would become us to ascertain, as well as we can, what form it is that our incantations are about to call up from darkness and the sleep of ages. When the supreme authority of the people is in question, before we attempt to extend or to confine it, we ought to fix in our minds, with some degree of distinctness, an idea of what it is we mean when we say the PEOPLE.

In a state of *rude* nature there is no such thing as a people. A number of men in themselves have no collective capacity. The idea of a people is the idea of a corporation. It is wholly artificial; and made like all other legal fictions by common agreement. What the particular nature of that agreement was, is collected from the form into which the particular society has been cast. Any other is not *their* covenant. When men, therefore, break up the original compact or agreement which gives its corporate form and capacity to a state, they are no longer a people; they have no longer a corporate existence; they have no longer a legal coactive force to bind within, nor a claim to be recognized abroad. They are a number of vague loose individuals, and nothing more. With them all is to begin again. Alas! they little know how many a weary step is to be taken before they can form themselves into a mass, which has a true politic personality.

We hear much from men, who have not acquired their hardiness of assertion from the profundity of their thinking, about the omnipotence of a *majority*, in such a dissolution of an ancient society as hath taken place in France. But amongst men so disbanded, there can be no such thing as majority or minority; or power in any one person to bind another. The power of acting by a majority, which the gentlemen theorists seem to assume so readily, after they have violated the contract out of which it has arisen (if at all it existed), must be grounded on two assumptions; first, that of an incorporation produced by unanimity; and secondly, an unanimous agreement, that the act of a mere majority (say of one) shall pass with them and with others as the act of the whole.

We are so little affected by things which are habitual, that we consider this idea of the decision of a *majority* as if it were a law of our original nature: But such constructive whole, residing in a part only, is one of the most violent fictions of positive law, that ever has been or can be made on the principles of artificial incorporation. Out of civil society nature knows nothing of it; nor are men, even when arranged according to civil order, otherwise than by very long training, brought at all to submit to it. The mind is brought far more easily to acquiesce in the proceedings of one man, or a few, who act under a general procuration for the state, than in the vote of a victorious majority in councils in which every man has his share in the deliberation. For there the beaten party are exasperated and soured by the previous contention, and mortified by the conclusive defeat. This mode of decision, where wills may be so nearly equal, where, according to circumstances, the smaller number may be the stronger force, and where apparent reason may be all upon one side, and on the other little else than impetuous appetite; all this must be the result of a very particular and special convention, confirmed afterwards by long habits of obedience, by a sort of discipline in society, and by a strong hand, vested with stationary permanent power, to enforce this sort of constructive general will. What organ it is that shall declare the corporate mind is so much a matter of positive arrangement, that several states, for the validity of several of their acts, have required a proportion of voices much greater than that of a mere majority. These proportions are so entirely governed by convention, that in some cases the minority decides. The laws in many countries to *condemn* require more than a mere majority; less than an equal number to *acquit*. In our judicial trials we require unanimity either to condemn or to absolve. In some incorporations one man speaks for the whole; in others, a few. Until the other day, in the constitution of Poland, unanimity was required to give validity to any act of their great national council or diet. This approaches much more nearly to rude nature than the institutions of any other country. Such, indeed, every commonwealth must be, without a positive law to recognize in a certain number the will of the entire body.

If men dissolve their antient incorporation, in order to regenerate their community, in that state of things each man has a right, if he pleases, to remain an individual. Any number of individuals, who can agree upon it, have an undoubted right to form themselves into a state apart and wholly independent. If any of these is forced into the fellowship of another, this is conquest and not compact. On every principle, which supposes society to be in virtue of a free covenant, this compulsive incorporation must be null and void.

AN APPEAL FROM THE NEW TO THE OLD WHIGS

As a people can have no right to a corporate capacity without universal consent, so neither have they a right to hold exclusively any lands in the name and title of a corporation. On the scheme of the present rulers in our neighbouring country, regenerated as they are, they have no more right to the territory called France than I have. I have a right to pitch my tent in any unoccupied place I can find for it; and I may apply to my own maintenance any part of their unoccupied soil. I may purchase the house or vineyard of any individual proprietor who refuses his consent (and most proprietors have, as far as they dared, refused it) to the new incorporation. I stand in his independent place. Who are these insolent men calling themselves the French nation, that would monopolize this fair domain of nature? Is it because they speak a certain jargon? Is it their mode of chattering, to me unintelligible, that forms their title to my land? Who are they who claim by prescription and descent from certain gangs of banditti called Franks, and Burgundians, and Visigoths, of whom I may have never heard, and ninety-nine out of an hundred of themselves certainly never have heard; whilst at the very time they tell me, that prescription and long possession form no title to property? Who are they that presume to assert that the land which I purchased of the individual, a natural person, and not a fiction of state, belongs to them, who in the very capacity in which they make their claim can exist only as an imaginary being, and in virtue of the very prescription which they reject and disown? This mode of arguing might be pushed into all the detail, so as to leave no sort of doubt, that on their principles, and on the sort of footing on which they have thought proper to place themselves, the crowd of men on the other side of the channel, who have the impudence to call themselves a people, can never be the lawful exclusive possessors of the soil. By what they call reasoning without prejudice, they leave not one stone upon another in the fabric of human society. They subvert all the authority which they hold, as well as all that which they have destroyed.

AN APPEAL FROM THE NEW TO THE OLD WHIGS

As in the abstract, it is perfectly clear, that, out of a state of civil society, majority and minority are relations which can have no existence; and that in civil society, its own specific conventions in each incorporation, determine what it is that constitutes the people, so as to make their act the signification of the general will; to come to particulars, it is equally clear, that neither in France nor in England has the original, or any subsequent compact of the state, expressed or implied, constituted *a majority of men, told by the head,* to be the acting people of their several communities. And I see as little of policy or utility, as there is of right, in laying down a principle that a majority of men told by the head are to be considered as the people, and that as such their will is to be law. What policy can there be found in arrangements made in defiance of every political principle? To enable men to act with the weight and character of a people, and to answer the ends for which they are incorporated into that capacity, we must suppose them (by means immediate or consequential) to be in that state of habitual social discipline, in which the wiser, the more expert, and the more opulent, conduct, and by conducting enlighten and protect the weaker, the less knowing, and the less provided with the goods of fortune. When the multitude are not under this discipline, they can scarcely be said to be in civil society. Give once a certain constitution of things, which produces a variety of conditions and circumstances in a state, and there is in nature and reason a principle which, for their own benefit, postpones, not the interest but the judgment, of those who are *numero plures,* to those who are *virtute et honore majores.*[41] Numbers in a state (supposing, which is not the case in France, that a state does exist) are always of consideration—but they are not the whole consideration. It is in things more serious than a play, that it may be truly said, *satis est equitem mihi plaudere.*[42]

---

[41] [The two phrases contrast "the greater number" with those who are "the greater in virtue and honor."]

[42] [It is sufficient that gentlemen applaud me. (Perhaps an adaptation from Horace, *Satires* 1.1.62– 66.)]

AN APPEAL FROM THE NEW TO THE OLD WHIGS

A true natural aristocracy is not a separate interest in the state, or separable from it. It is an essential integrant part of any large people rightly constituted. It is formed out of a class of legitimate presumptions, which, taken as generalities, must be admitted for actual truths. To be bred in a place of estimation; To see nothing low and sordid from one's infancy; To be taught to respect one's self; To be habituated to the censorial inspection of the public eye; To look early to public opinion; To stand upon such elevated ground as to be enabled to take a large view of the wide-spread and infinitely diversified combinations of men and affairs in a large society; To have leisure to read, to reflect, to converse; To be enabled to draw the court and attention of the wise and learned wherever they are to be found; To be habituated in armies to command and to obey; To be taught to despise danger in the pursuit of honour and duty; To be formed to the greatest degree of vigilance, foresight, and circumspection, in a state of things in which no fault is committed with impunity, and the slightest mistakes draw on the most ruinous consequences—To be led to a guarded and regulated conduct, from a sense that you are considered as an instructor of your fellow-citizens in their highest concerns, and that you act as a reconciler between God and man—To be employed as an administrator of law and justice, and to be thereby amongst the first benefactors to mankind—To be a professor of high science, or of liberal and ingenuous art—To be amongst rich traders, who from their success are presumed to have sharp and vigorous understandings, and to possess the virtues of diligence, order, constancy, and regularity, and to have cultivated an habitual regard to commutative justice—These are the circumstances of men, that form what I should call a *natural* aristocracy, without which there is no nation.

The state of civil society, which necessarily generates this aristocracy, is a state of nature; and much more truly so than a savage and incoherent mode of life. For man is by nature reasonable; and he is never perfectly in his natural state, but when he is placed where reason may be best cultivated, and most predominates. Art is man's nature. We are as much, at least, in a state of nature in formed manhood, as in immature and helpless infancy. Men qualified in the manner I have just described, form in nature, as she operates in the common modification of society, the leading, guiding, and governing part. It is the soul to the body, without which the man does not exist. To give therefore no more importance, in the social order, to such descriptions of men, than that of so many units, is an horrible usurpation.

When great multitudes act together, under that discipline of nature, I recognize the PEOPLE. I acknowledge something that perhaps equals, and ought always to guide, the sovereignty of convention. In all things the voice of this grand chorus of national harmony ought to have a mighty and decisive influence. But when you disturb this harmony; when you break up this beautiful order, this array of truth and nature, as well as of habit and prejudice; when you separate the common sort of men from their proper chieftains so as to form them into an adverse army, I no longer know that venerable object called the people in such a disbanded race of deserters and vagabonds. For a while they may be terrible indeed; but in such a manner as wild beasts are terrible. The mind owes to them no sort of submission. They are, as they have always been reputed, rebels. They may lawfully be fought with, and brought under, whenever an advantage offers. Those who attempt by outrage and violence to deprive men of any advantage which they hold under the laws, and to destroy the natural order of life, proclaim war against them.

We have read in history of that furious insurrection of the common people in France called the *Jacquerie*;[43] for this is not the first time that the people have been enlightened into treason, murder, and rapine. Its object was to extirpate the gentry. The *Captal de Buche*, a famous soldier of those days, dishonoured the name of a gentleman and of a man by tak-

[43] [The rising of the peasants against the nobles in northern France in 1357–1358. Burke is the first to employ the term as a more general designation of a mass peasant uprising, according to the *Oxford English Dictionary*.]

ing, for their cruelties, a cruel vengeance on these deluded wretches: It was, however, his right and his duty to make war upon them, and afterwards, in moderation, to bring them to punishment for their rebellion; though in the sense of the French revolution, and of some of our clubs, they were the *people*; and were truly so, if you will call by that appellation *any majority of men told by the head*.

At a time not very remote from the same period (for these humours never have affected one of the nations without some influence on the other) happened several risings of the lower commons in England. These insurgents were certainly the majority of the inhabitants of the counties in which they resided; and Cade, Ket, and Straw, at the head of their national guards, and fomented by certain traitors of high rank, did no more than exert, according to the doctrines of ours and the Parisian societies, the sovereign power inherent in the majority.[44]

We call the time of those events a dark age. Indeed we are too indulgent to our own proficiency. The Abbé John Ball understood the rights of man as well as the Abbé Gregoire. That reverend patriarch of sedition, and prototype of our modern preachers, was of opinion with the national assembly, that all the evils which have fallen upon men had been caused by an ignorance of their "having been born and continued equal as to their rights." Had the populace been able to repeat that profound maxim all would have gone perfectly well with them. No tyranny, no vexation, no oppression, no care, no sorrow, could have existed in the world. This would have cured them like a charm for the tooth-ach. But the lowest wretches, in their most ignorant state, were able at all times to talk such stuff; and yet at all times have they suffered many evils and many oppressions, both before and since the republication by the national assembly of this spell of healing potency and virtue. The enlightened Dr. Ball, when he

[44] [Burke is alluding to several medieval and Renaissance rebellions, the most famous of which is that of John Ball (1381).]

wished to rekindle the lights and fires of his audience on this point, chose for the text the following couplet:

When Adam delved and Eve span,
Who was then the gentleman?

Of this sapient maxim, however, I do not give him for the inventor. It seems to have been handed down by tradition, and had certainly become proverbial; but whether then composed, or only applied, thus much must be admitted, that in learning, sense, energy, and comprehensiveness, it is fully equal to all the modern dissertations on the equality of mankind; and it has one advantage over them, that it is in rhyme.[45]

[45] It is no small loss to the world, that the whole of this enlightened and philosophic sermon, preached to *two hundred thousand* national guards assembled at Blackheath (a number probably equal to the sublime and majestic *Federation* of the 14th of July 1790, in the *Champs de Mars*) is not preserved. A short abstract is, however, to be found in Walsingham. I have added it here for the edification of the modern Whigs, who may possibly except this precious little fragment from their general contempt of antient learning.

Ut suâ doctrinâ plures inficeret ad le Blackheth (ubi ducenta millia hominum communium fuêre simul congregata) hujuscemodi sermonem est exorsus.

Whan Adam dalfe, and Evé span, who was than a gentleman?

Continuansque sermonem inceptum nitebatur per verba proverbii quod pro themate sumpserat, introducere & probare, *ab initio omnes pares creatos à naturâ*, servitutem per injustam oppressionem nequam hominum introductam contra Dei voluntatem, quia si Deo placuisset servos creâsse, utique in principio mundi constituisset, quis servus, quisve dominus futurus fuisset. Considerarent igitur jam tempus à Deo datum eis, in quo (deposito servitutis jugo diutius) possent si vellent, libertate diu concupitâ gaudere. Quapropter monuit ut essent viri cordati, & amore boni patrisfamilias excolentis agrum suum & extirpantis ac resecantis noxia gramina quae fruges solent opprimere, & ipsi in praesenti facere festinarent; primò *majores regni dominos occidendo; deindè juridicos, justiciarios & juratores patriae perimendo;* postremò quoscunque scirent *in posterum communitati nocivos:* tollerent de terrâ suâ: sic demum & *pacem* sibimet *parerent & securitatem* in futurum; *si sublatis majoribus esset inter eos aequa libertas, eadem nobilitas, par dignitas, similisque potestas.* [He delivered a sermon of this sort at Blackheath (where 200,000 common men were congregated) in order to enforce his doctrine all the more.

When Adam delved, and Eve spun, who then was a "gentleman"?

AN APPEAL FROM THE NEW TO THE OLD WHIGS

There is no doubt, but that this great teacher of the rights of man decorated his discourse on this valuable text, with lemmas, theorems, scholia, corollaries, and all the apparatus of science, which was furnished in as great plenty and perfection out of the dogmatic and polemic magazines, the old horse-armory, of the schoolmen, among whom the Rev. Dr. Ball was bred, as they can be supplied from the new arsenal at

Continuing the sermon he had begun, he relied on the words of the proverb, which he had taken as his theme, to introduce and prove that *from the beginning all were created equal by nature*, that slavery had been introduced by men through unjust oppression contrary to the will of God because if to create slaves had been pleasing to God, He would have decided at the beginning of the world who was to be a slave and who a master. They thought therefore that the time had been given by God to them in which (having set aside the yoke of servitude) they could, if they wanted, enjoy freedom. Wherefore he warned that men should be united, and with the love of a good *paterfamilias*, who cultivates his own field and eradicates and prunes harmful grasses which damage his crops, they themselves should hasten at the present moment to: first, *kill the greatest lords of the kingdom; then, the judges, jurists and notaries of the counties;* finally, they should remove from their lands *whomsoever they knew to be harmful to the community in the future.* Thus finally they would win *peace for themselves and security* for the future. *Thus the great people having been liquidated, there would be among them and equitable liberty, nobility, dignity, and power.*]

Here is displayed at once the whole of the grand arcanum pretended to be found out by the national assembly, for securing future happiness, peace, and tranquillity. There seems however to be some doubt whether this venerable protomartyr of philosophy was inclined to carry his own declaration of the rights of men more rigidly into practice than the national assembly themselves. He was, like them, only preaching licentiousness to the populace to obtain power for himself, if we may believe what is subjoined by the historian.

Cumque haec *& plura alia deliramenta* [think of this old fool's calling all the wise maxims of the French academy *deliramenta*] praedicâsset, commune vulgus cum tanto favore prosequitur, ut *acclamarent eum archiepiscopum futurum, & regni cancellarium.* [When he had preached this *and much more madness* . . . , the common crowd followed him with such fervor that they *proclaimed him archbishop and chancellor of the kingdom.*] Whether he would have taken these situations under these names, or would have changed the whole nomenclature of the state and church, to be understood in the sense of the Revolution, is not so certain. It is probable that he would have changed the names and kept the substance of power.

We find too, that they had in those days their *Society for constitutional information,* of which the reverend John Ball was a conspicuous member, sometimes under his own name, sometimes under the feigned name of John Schep. Besides him it consisted (as Knyghton tells us) of persons who went by the real or fictitious names of Jack Mylner, Tom Baker, Jack Straw, Jack Trewman, Jack Carter, and probably of many more. Some of the

An Appeal from the New to the Old Whigs

Hackney. It was, no doubt, disposed with all the adjutancy of definition and division, in which (I speak it with submission) the old marshals were as able as the modern martinets. Neither can we deny, that the philosophic auditory, when they had once obtained this knowledge, could never return to their former ignorance; or after so instructive a lecture be in

---

choicest flowers of the publications, charitably written and circulated by them gratis, are upon record in Walsingham and Knyghton: and I am inclined to prefer the pithy and sententious brevity of these *bulletins* of ancient rebellion, before the loose and confused prolixity of the modern advertisements of constitutional information. They contain more good morality, and less bad politics; they had much more foundation in real oppression; and they have the recommendation of being much better adapted to the capacities of those for whose instruction they were intended. Whatever laudable pains the teachers of the present day appear to take, I cannot compliment them, so far as to allow, that they have succeeded in writing down to the level of their pupils, *the members of the sovereign*, with half the ability of Jack Carter and the reverend John Ball. That my readers may judge for themselves, I shall give them one or two specimens.

The first is an address from the reverend John Ball under his *nom de guerre* of John Schep. I know not against what particular "guyle in borough" the writer means to caution the people; it may have been only a general cry against "*rotten boroughs,*" which it was thought convenient then as now to make the first pretext, and place at the head of the list of grievances.

JOHN SCHEP

John Schep sometime Seint Mary Priest of Yorke, and now of Colchester, greeteth well John Namelesse, & John the Miller & John Carter, and *biddeth them that they beware of guyle in borough,* and stand together in God's name; and biddeth Piers Ploweman goe to his werke, and chastise well *Hob the robber* [probably the king], and take with you John Trewman, and all his fellows and no moe.

John the Miller hath yground smal, small, small:
The King's Sonne of Heaven shal pay for all.
Beware or ye be woe,
Know your frende fro your foe,
Have enough and say hoe:
And do wel and better, and flee sinne;
And seeke peace and holde you therein;

& so biddeth John Trewman, & all his fellowes.

The reader has perceived, from the last lines of this curious state paper, how well the national assembly has copied its union of the profession of universal peace, with the practice of murder and confusion, and the blast of the trumpet of sedition in all nations. He will, in the following constitutional paper, observe how well, in their enigmatical style, like the assembly and their abettors, the old philosophers proscribe all hereditary distinction, and bestow it only on virtue and wisdom, according to their estimation of

the same state of mind as if they had never heard it.[46] But these poor people, who were not to be envied for their knowledge, but pitied for their delusion, were not reasoned (that was impossible) but beaten out of their lights. With their teacher they were delivered over to the lawyers; who wrote in their blood the statutes of the land, as harshly, and in the same sort of ink, as they and their teachers had written the rights of man.

Our doctors of the day are not so fond of quoting the opinions of this antient sage as they are of imitating his conduct; First, because it might appear, that they are not as great inventors as they would be thought; and next, because, unfortunately for his fame, he was not successful. It is a remark,

---

both. Yet these people are supposed never to have heard of "the rights of man"!

JACK MYLNER
Jakke Mylner asketh help to turne his mylne aright.

He hath grounden smal, smal,
The King's Sone of Heven he shall pay for alle.

Loke thy mylne go a ryyt with the four sayles, and the post stande in steadfastnesse.

With ryyt & with myyt,
With skill & with wylle,
Lat myyt help ryyt,
And skyl go before wille,
And ryyht before myght,
Than goth our mylne aryght.
And if myght go before ryght,
And wylle before skylle;
Than is our mylne mys-a-dyght.

JACK CARTER
understood perfectly the doctrine of looking to the *end*, with an indifference to the *means*, and the probability of much good arising from great evil.

Jakke Carter prayes yowe alle that ye make a gode *ende* of that ye have begunnen, & doth wele and ay bettur & bettur, for at the even men heryth the day. *For if the ende be wele than is alle wele.* Lat Peres the plowman my brother dwelle at home and dyght us corne, & I will go with yowe & helpe, that I may, to dyghte youre mete and youre drynke, that ye none fayle. Lokke that Hobbe robbyoure be wele chastysed for lesyng of your grace; for ye have gret nede to take God with yowe in all your dedes. For now is tyme to be war.

[46] See the wise remark on this subject, in the Defence of Rights of Man, circulated by the societies.

liable to as few exceptions as any generality can be, that they who applaud prosperous folly, and adore triumphant guilt, have never been known to succour or even to pity human weakness or offence when they become subject to human vicissitude, and meet with punishment instead of obtaining power. Abating for their want of sensibility to the sufferings of their associates, they are not so much in the wrong: for madness and wickedness are things foul and deformed in themselves; and stand in need of all the coverings and trappings of fortune to recommend them to the multitude. Nothing can be more loathsome in their naked nature.

Aberrations like these, whether antient or modern, unsuccessful or prosperous, are things of passage. They furnish no argument for supposing a *multitude told by the head to be the people*. Such a multitude can have no sort of title to alter the seat of power in the society, in which it ever ought to be the obedient, and not the ruling or presiding part. What power may belong to the whole mass, in which mass, the natural *aristocracy*, or what by convention is appointed to represent and strengthen it, acts in its proper place, with its proper weight, and without being subjected to violence, is a deeper question. But in that case, and with that concurrence, I should have much doubt whether any rash or desperate changes in the state, such as we have seen in France, could ever be effected.

I have said, that in all political questions the consequences of any assumed rights are of great moment in deciding upon their validity. In this point of view let us a little scrutinize the effects of a right in the mere majority of the inhabitants of any country of superseding and altering their government *at pleasure*.

The sum total of every people is composed of its units. Every individual must have a right to originate what afterwards is to become the act of the majority. Whatever he may lawfully originate, he may lawfully endeavour to accomplish. He has a right therefore in his own particular to break the ties and engagement which bind him to the country in which he lives; and he has a right to make as many converts to his opinions, and to obtain as many associates in his designs, as he can procure: For how can you know the dispositions of the majority to destroy their government, but by tampering with some part of the body? You must begin by a secret conspiracy, that you may end with a national confederation. The mere pleasure of the beginner must be the sole guide; since the mere pleasure of others must be the sole ultimate sanction, as well as the sole actuating principle in every part of the progress. Thus arbitrary will (the last corruption of ruling power) step by step, poisons the heart of every citizen. If the undertaker fails, he has the misfortune of a rebel, but not the guilt. By such doctrines, all love to our country, all pious veneration and attachment to its laws and customs, are obliterated from our minds; and nothing can result from this opinion, when grown into a principle, and animated by discontent, ambition, or enthusiasm, but a series of conspiracies and seditions, sometimes ruinous to their authors, always noxious to the state. No sense of duty can prevent any man from being a leader or a follower in such enterprizes. Nothing restrains the tempter; nothing guards the tempted. Nor is the new state, fabricated by such arts, safer than the old. What can prevent the mere will of any person, who hopes to unite the wills of others to his own, from an attempt wholly to overturn it? It wants nothing but a disposition to trouble the established order, to give a title to the enterprize.

When you combine this principle of the right to change a fixed and tolerable constitution of things, at pleasure, with the theory and practice of the French assembly, the political, civil, and moral irregularity are if possible aggravated. The assembly have found another road, and a far more commodious, to the destruction of an old government, and the legitimate formation of a new one, than through the previous will of the majority of what they call the people. Get, say they, the possession of power by any means you can into your hands; and then a subsequent consent (what they call an *address of adhesion*) makes your authority as much the act of the people

---

as if they had conferred upon you originally that kind and degree of power, which, without their permission, you had seized upon. This is to give a direct sanction to fraud, hypocrisy, perjury, and the breach of the most sacred trusts that can exist between man and man. What can sound with such horrid discordance in the moral ear, as this position, That a delegate with limited powers may break his sworn engagements to his constituent, assume an authority, never committed to him, to alter all things at his pleasure; and then, if he can persuade a large number of men to flatter him in the power he has usurped, that he is absolved in his own conscience, and ought to stand acquitted in the eyes of mankind? On this scheme the maker of the experiment must begin with a determined perjury. That point is certain. He must take his chance for the expiatory addresses. This is to make the success of villainy the standard of innocence.

Without drawing on, therefore, very shocking consequences, neither by previous consent, nor by subsequent ratification of a *mere reckoned majority,* can any set of men attempt to dissolve the state at their pleasure. To apply this to our present subject. When the several orders, in their several bailliages, had met in the year 1789, such of them, I mean, as had met peaceably and constitutionally, to choose and to instruct their representatives, so organized, and so acting (because they were organized and were acting according to the conventions which made them a people), they were the *people* of France. They had a legal and a natural capacity to be considered as that people. But observe, whilst they were in this state, that is, whilst they were a people, in no one of their instructions did they charge or even hint at any of those things, which have drawn upon the usurping assembly, and their adherents, the detestation of the rational and thinking part of mankind. I will venture to affirm, without the least apprehension of being contradicted by any person who knows the then state of France, that if any one of the changes were proposed, which form the fundamental parts of their revolution, and compose its most distinguishing acts, it would not have had one vote in twenty thousand in any order. Their instructions purported the direct contrary to all those famous proceedings, which are defended as the acts of the people. Had such proceedings been expected, the great probability is, that the people would then have risen, as to a man, to prevent them. The whole organization of the assembly was altered, the whole frame of the kingdom was changed, before these things could be done. It is long to tell, by what evil arts of the conspirators, and by what extreme weakness and want of steadiness in the lawful government, this equal usurpation on the rights of the prince and people, having first cheated, and then offered violence to both, has been able to triumph, and to employ with success the forged signature of an imprisoned sovereign, and the spurious voice of dictated addresses, to a subsequent ratification of things that had never received any previous sanction, general or particular, expressed or implied, from the nation (in whatever sense that word is taken) or from any part of it.[47]

After the weighty and respectable part of the people had been murdered, or driven by the menaces of murder from their houses, or were dispersed in exile into every country in Europe; after the soldiery had been debauched from their officers; after property had lost its weight and consideration, along with its security; after voluntary clubs and associations of factious and unprincipled men were substituted in the place of all the legal corporations of the kingdom arbitrarily dissolved; after freedom had been banished from those popular meetings,[48] whose sole recommendation is freedom—After it had come to that pass, that no dissent dared to appear in any of them, but at the certain price of life; after even dissent had been anticipated, and assassination became as quick as suspicion; such pretended ratification by addresses could be no act of what any lover of the people would choose to call by their name. It is that voice which every successful

[47] [Louis XVI accepted the new French Constitution, then disavowed it and attempted to flee France in June 1791.]

[48] The primary assemblies.

usurpation, as well as this before us, may easily procure, even without making (as these tyrants have made) donatives from the spoil of one part of the citizens to corrupt the other.

The pretended *rights of man,* which have made this havock, cannot be the rights of the people. For to be a people, and to have these rights, are things incompatible. The one supposes the presence, the other the absence of a state of civil society. The very foundation of the French commonwealth is false and self-destructive; nor can its principles be adopted in any country, without the certainty of bringing it to the very same condition in which France is found. Attempts are made to introduce them into every nation in Europe. This nation, as possessing the greatest influence, they wish most to corrupt, as by that means they are assured the contagion must become general. I hope, therefore, I shall be excused, if I endeavour to shew, as shortly as the matter will admit, the danger of giving to them, either avowedly or tacitly, the smallest countenance.

There are times and circumstances, in which not to speak out is at least to connive. Many think it enough for them, that the principles propagated by these clubs and societies enemies to their country and its constitution, are not owned by the *modern Whigs in parliament,* who are so warm in condemnation of Mr. Burke and his book, and of course of all the principles of the ancient constitutional Whigs of this kingdom. Certainly they are not owned. But are they condemned with the same zeal as Mr. Burke and his book are condemned? Are they condemned at all? Are they rejected or discountenanced in any way whatsoever? Is any man who would fairly examine into the demeanour and principles of those societies, and that too very moderately, and in the way rather of admonition than of punishment, is such a man even decently treated? Is he not reproached, as if, in condemning such principles, he had belied the conduct of his whole life, suggesting that his life had been governed by principles similar to those which he now reprobates? The French system is in the mean time, by many active agents out of doors, rapturously praised; The

British constitution is coldly tolerated. But these constitutions are different, both in the foundation and in the whole superstructure; and it is plain, that you cannot build up the one but on the ruins of the other. After all, if the French be a superior system of liberty, why should we not adopt it? To what end are our praises? Is excellence held out to us only that we should not copy after it? And what is there in the manners of the people, or in the climate of France, which renders that species of republic fitted for them, and unsuitable to us? A strong and marked difference between the two nations ought to be shewn, before we can admit a constant affected panegyrick, a standing annual commemoration, to be without any tendency to an example.

But the leaders of party will not go the length of the doctrines taught by the seditious clubs. I am sure they do not mean to do so. God forbid! Perhaps even those who are directly carrying on the work of this pernicious foreign faction, do not all of them intend to produce all the mischiefs which must inevitably follow from their having any success in their proceedings. As to leaders in parties, nothing is more common than to see them blindly led. The world is governed by go-betweens. These go-betweens influence the persons with whom they carry on the intercourse, by stating their own sense to each of them as the sense of the other; and thus they reciprocally master both sides. It is first buzzed about the ears of leaders, "that their friends without doors are very eager for some measure, or very warm about some opinion—that you must not be too rigid with them. They are useful persons, and zealous in the cause. They may be a little wrong; but the spirit of liberty must not be damped; and by the influence you obtain from some degree of concurrence with them at present, you may be enabled to set them right hereafter."

Thus the leaders are at first drawn to a connivance with sentiments and proceedings, often totally different from their serious and deliberate notions. But their acquiescence answers every purpose.

An Appeal from the New to the Old Whigs

With no better than such powers, the go-betweens assume a new representative character. What at best was but an acquiescence, is magnified into an authority, and thence into a desire on the part of the leaders; and it is carried down as such to the subordinate members of parties. By this artifice they in their turn are led into measures which at first, perhaps, few of them wished at all, or at least did not desire vehemently or systematically.

There is in all parties, between the principal leaders in parliament, and the lowest followers out of doors, a middle sort of men; a sort of equestrian order, who, by the spirit of that middle situation, are the fittest for preventing things from running to excess. But indecision, though a vice of a totally different character, is the natural accomplice of violence. The irresolution and timidity of those who compose this middle order, often prevents the effect of their controlling situation. The fear of differing with the authority of leaders on the one hand, and of contradicting the desires of the multitude on the other, induces them to give a careless and passive assent to measures in which they never were consulted: and thus things proceed, by a sort of activity of inertness, until whole bodies, leaders, middle men, and followers, are all hurried, with every appearance, and with many of the effects, of unanimity, into schemes of politics, in the substance of which no two of them were ever fully agreed, and the origin and authors of which, in this circular mode of communication, none of them find it possible to trace. In my experience I have seen much of this in affairs, which, though trifling in comparison to the present, were yet of some importance to parties; and I have known them suffer by it. The sober part give their sanction, at first through inattention and levity; at last they give it through necessity. A violent spirit is raised, which the presiding minds, after a time, find it impracticable to stop at their pleasure, to control, to regulate, or even to direct.

This shews, in my opinion, how very quick and awakened all men ought to be, who are looked up to by the public, and who deserve that confidence, to prevent a surprise on their opinions, when dogmas are spread, and projects pursued, by which the foundations of society may be affected. Before they listen even to moderate alterations in the government of their country, they ought to take care that principles are not propagated for that purpose, which are too big for their object. Doctrines limited in their present application, and wide in their general principles, are never meant to be confined to what they at first pretend. If I were to form a prognostic of the effect of the present machinations on the people, from their sense of any grievance they suffer under this constitution, my mind would be at ease. But there is a wide difference between the multitude, when they act against their government from a sense of grievance, or from zeal for some opinions. When men are thoroughly possessed with that zeal, it is difficult to calculate its force. It is certain, that its power is by no means in exact proportion to its reasonableness. It must always have been discoverable by persons of reflection, but it is now obvious to the world, that a theory concerning government may become as much a cause of fanaticism as a *dogma* in religion. There is a boundary to men's passions when they act from feeling; none when they are under the influence of imagination. Remove a grievance, and, when men act from feeling, you go a great way towards quieting a commotion. But the good or bad conduct of a government, the protection men have enjoyed, or the oppression they have suffered under it, are of no sort of moment, when a faction proceeding upon speculative grounds, is thoroughly heated against its form. When a man is, from system, furious against monarchy or episcopacy, the good conduct of the monarch or the bishop has no other effect than further to irritate the adversary. He is provoked at it as furnishing a plea for preserving the thing which he wishes to destroy. His mind will be heated as much by the sight of a sceptre, a mace, or a verge, as if he had been daily bruised and wounded by these symbols of authority. Mere spectacles, mere names, will become sufficient causes to stimulate the people to war and tumult.

AN APPEAL FROM THE NEW TO THE OLD WHIGS

Some gentlemen are not terrified by the facility with which government has been overturned in France. The people of France, they say, had nothing to lose in the destruction of a bad constitution; but though not the best possible, we have still a good stake in ours, which will hinder us from desperate risques. Is this any security at all against those who seem to persuade themselves, and who labour to persuade others, that our constitution is an usurpation in its origin, unwise in its contrivance, mischievous in its effects, contrary to the rights of man, and in all its parts a perfect nuisance? What motive has any rational man, who thinks in that manner, to spill his blood, or even to risque a shilling of his fortune, or to waste a moment of his leisure, to preserve it? If he has any duty relative to it, his duty is to destroy it. A constitution on sufferance is a constitution condemned. Sentence is already passed upon it. The execution is only delayed. On the principles of these gentlemen it neither has, nor ought to have, any security. So far as regards them, it is left naked, without friends, partizans, assertors, or protectors.

Let us examine into the value of this security upon the principles of those who are more sober; of those who think, indeed, the French constitution better, or at least as good, as the British, without going to all the lengths of the warmer politicians in reprobating their own. Their security amounts in reality to nothing more than this; that the difference between their republican system and the British limited monarchy is not worth a civil war. This opinion, I admit, will prevent people not very enterprising in their nature, from an active undertaking against the British constitution. But it is the poorest defensive principle that ever was infused into the mind of man against the attempts of those who will enterprise. It will tend totally to remove from their minds that very terror of a civil war which is held out as our sole security. They who think so well of the French constitution, certainly will not be the persons to carry on a war to prevent their obtaining a great benefit, or at worst a fair exchange. They will not go to battle in favour of a cause in which their defeat might be more advantageous to the public than their victory. They must at least tacitly abet those who endeavour to make converts to a sound opinion; they must discountenance those who would oppose its propagation. In proportion as by these means the enterprising party is strengthened, the dread of a struggle is lessened. See what an encouragement this is to the enemies of the constitution! A few assassinations, and a very great destruction of property, we know they consider as no real obstacles in the way of a grand political change. And they will hope, that here, if antimonarchical opinions gain ground, as they have done in France, they may, as in France, accomplish a revolution without a war.

They who think so well of the French constitution cannot be seriously alarmed by any progress made by its partizans. Provisions for security are not to be received from those who think that there is no danger. No! there is no plan of security to be listened to but from those who entertain the same fears with ourselves; from those who think that the thing to be secured is a great blessing; and the thing against which we would secure it a great mischief. Every person of a different opinion must be careless about security.

I believe the author of the Reflections, whether he fears the designs of that set of people with reason or not, cannot prevail on himself to despise them. He cannot despise them for their numbers, which, though small, compared with the sound part of the community, are not inconsiderable: he cannot look with contempt on their influence, their activity, or the kind of talents and tempers which they possess, exactly calculated for the work they have in hand, and the minds they chiefly apply to. Do we not see their most considerable and accredited ministers, and several of their party of weight and importance, active in spreading mischievous opinions, in giving sanction to seditious writings, in promoting seditious anniversaries? and what part of their description has disowned them or their proceedings? When men, circumstanced as these are, publickly declare such admiration of a foreign constitution, and such contempt of our own, it would be, in the author of the Reflections, thinking as he does of the French constitution, infamously to cheat the rest of the nation to their ruin, to say there is no danger.

In estimating danger, we are obliged to take into our calculation the character and disposition of the enemy into whose hands we may chance to fall. The genius of this faction is easily discerned by observing with what a very different eye they have viewed the late foreign revolutions. Two have passed before them. That of France and that of Poland. The state of Poland was such, that there could scarcely exist two opinions, but that a reformation of its constitution, even at some expence of blood, might be seen without much disapprobation. No confusion could be feared in such an enterprize; because the establishment to be reformed was itself a state of confusion. A king without authority; nobles without union or subordination; a people without arts, industry, commerce, or liberty; no order within; no defence without; no effective publick force, but a foreign force, which entered a naked country at will, and disposed of every thing at pleasure. Here was a state of things which seemed to invite and might perhaps justify bold enterprize and desperate experiment. But in what manner was this chaos brought into order? The means were as striking to the imagination, as satisfactory to the reason, and soothing to the moral sentiments. In contemplating that change, humanity has every thing to rejoice and to glory in; nothing to be ashamed of, nothing to suffer. So far as it has gone, it probably is the most pure and defecated public good which ever has been conferred on mankind. We have seen anarchy and servitude at once removed; a throne strengthened for the protection of the people, without trenching on their liberties; all foreign cabal banished, by changing the crown from elective to hereditary; and what was a matter of pleasing wonder, we have seen a reigning king, from an heroic love to his country, exerting himself with all the toil, the dexterity, the management, the intrigue, in favour of a family of strangers, with which ambitious men labour for the aggrandisement of their own. Ten millions of men in a way of being freed gradually, and therefore safely to themselves and the state, not from civil or political chains, which, bad as they are, only fetter the mind, but from substantial personal bondage. Inhabitants of cities, before without privileges, placed in the consideration which belongs to that improved and connecting situation of social life. One of the most proud, numerous, and fierce bodies of nobility and gentry ever known in the world, arranged only in the foremost rank of free and generous citizens. Not one man incurred loss, or suffered degradation. All, from the king to the day-labourer, were improved in their condition. Every thing was kept in its place and order; but in that place and order every thing was bettered. To add to this happy wonder (this unheard-of conjunction of wisdom and fortune) not one drop of blood was spilled; no treachery; no outrage; no system of slander more cruel than the sword; no studied insults on religion, morals, or manners; no spoil; no confiscation; no citizen beggared; none imprisoned; none exiled: the whole was effected with a policy, a discretion, an unanimity and secrecy, such as have never been before known on any occasion; but such wonderful conduct was reserved for this glorious conspiracy in favour of the true and genuine rights and interests of men. Happy people, if they know to proceed as they have begun! Happy prince, worthy to begin with splendor, or to close with glory, a race of patriots and of kings: and to leave

> A name, which every wind to heav'n would bear,
> Which men to speak, and angels joy to hear.

To finish all—this great good, as in the instant it is, contains in it the seeds of all further improvement; and may be considered as in a regular progress, because founded on similar principles, towards the stable excellence of a British constitution.

Here was a matter for congratulation and for festive remembrance through ages. Here moralists and divines might indeed relax in their temperance to exhilarate their humanity. But mark the character of our faction. All their enthusiasm is kept for the French revolution. They cannot pretend that France had stood so much in need of a change as Poland. They cannot pretend that Poland has not obtained a better system of liberty or of government than it enjoyed before. They cannot assert, that the Polish revolution cost more dearly than that of France to the interests and feelings of multitudes of men. But the cold and subordinate light in which they look upon the one, and the pains they take to preach up the other of these revolutions, leave us no choice in fixing on their motives. Both revolutions profess liberty as their object; but in obtaining this object the one proceeds from anarchy to order: the other from order to anarchy. The first secures its liberty by establishing its throne; the other builds its freedom on the subversion of its monarchy. In the one their means are unstained by crimes, and their settlement favours morality. In the other, vice and confusion are in the very essence of their pursuit and of their enjoyment. The circumstances in which these two events differ, must cause the difference we make in their comparative estimation. These turn the scale with the societies in favour of France. *Ferrum est quod amant.*[49] The frauds, the violences, the sacrileges, the havock and ruin of families, the dispersion and exile of the pride and flower of a great country, the disorder, the confusion, the anarchy, the violation of property, the cruel murders, the inhuman confiscations, and in the end the insolent domination of bloody, ferocious, and senseless clubs. These are the things which they love and admire. What men admire and love, they would surely act. Let us see what is done in France; and then let us undervalue any the slightest danger of falling into the hands of such a merciless and savage faction!

"But the leaders of the factious societies are too wild to succeed in this their undertaking." I hope so. But supposing them wild and absurd, is there no danger but from wise and

---

[49] [The sword is what they love.]

reflecting men? Perhaps the greatest mischiefs that have happened in the world, have happened from persons as wild as those we think the wildest. In truth, they are the fittest beginners of all great changes. Why encourage men in a mischievous proceeding, because their absurdity may disappoint their malice? "But noticing them may give them consequence." Certainly. But they are noticed; and they are noticed, not with reproof, but with that kind of countenance which is given by an *apparent* concurrence (not a *real* one, I am convinced) of a great party, in the praises of the object which they hold out to imitation.

But I hear a language still more extraordinary, and indeed of such a nature as must suppose, or leave, us at their mercy. It is this—"You know their promptitude in writing, and their diligence in caballing; to write, speak, or act against them, will only stimulate them to new efforts." This way of considering the principle of their conduct pays but a poor compliment to these gentlemen. They pretend that their doctrines are infinitely beneficial to mankind; but it seems they would keep them to themselves, if they were not greatly provoked. They are benevolent from spite. Their oracles are like those of *Proteus* (whom some people think they resemble in many particulars) who never would give his responses unless you used him as ill as possible. These cats, it seems, would not give out their electrical light without having their backs well rubbed. But this is not to do them perfect justice. They are sufficiently communicative. Had they been quiet, the propriety of any agitation of topics on the origin and primary rights of government, in opposition to their private sentiments, might possibly be doubted. But, as it is notorious, that they were proceeding as fast, and as far, as time and circumstances would admit, both in their discussions and cabals—as it is not to be denied, that they had opened a correspondence with a foreign faction, the most wicked the world ever saw, and established anniversaries to commemorate the most monstrous, cruel, and perfidious of all the proceedings of that faction—the question is, whether their conduct was to be regarded in silence, lest our interference should render them outrageous? Then let them deal as they please with the constitution. Let the lady be passive, lest the ravisher should be driven to force. Resistance will only increase his desires. Yes, truly, if the resistance be feigned and feeble. But they who are wedded to the constitution will not act the part of wittols. They will drive such seducers from the house on the first appearance of their love-letters, and offered assignations. But if the author of the Reflections, though a vigilant, was not a discreet guardian of the constitution, let them who have the same regard to it, shew themselves as vigilant and more skilful in repelling the attacks of seduction or violence. Their freedom from jealousy is equivocal, and may arise as well from indifference to the object, as from confidence in her virtue.

On their principle, it is the resistance, and not the assault, which produces the danger. I admit, indeed, that if we estimated the danger by the value of the writings, it would be little worthy of our attention: contemptible these writings are in every sense. But they are not the cause; they are the disgusting symptoms, of a frightful distemper. They are not otherwise of consequence than as they shew the evil habit of the bodies from whence they come. In that light the meanest of them is a serious thing. If however I should under-rate them; and if the truth is, that they are not the result, but the cause of the disorders I speak of, surely those who circulate operative poisons, and give, to whatever force they have by their nature, the further operation of their authority and adoption, are to be censured, watched, and, if possible, repressed.

At what distance the direct danger from such factions may be, it is not easy to fix. An adaptation of circumstances to designs and principles is necessary. But these cannot be wanting for any long time in the ordinary course of sublunary affairs. Great discontents frequently arise in the best-constituted governments, from causes which no human wisdom can foresee, and no human power can prevent. They occur at uncertain periods, but at periods which are not commonly far asunder. Governments of all kinds are administered only by men; and great mistakes, tending to inflame these discontents, may concur. The indecision of those who happen to rule at the critical time, their supine neglect, or their precipitate and ill-judged attention, may aggravate the public misfortunes. In such a state of things, the principles, now only sown, will shoot out and vegetate in full luxuriance. In such circumstances the minds of the people become sore and ulcerated. They are put out of humour with all public men, and all public parties; they are fatigued with their dissensions; they are irritated at their coalitions; they are made easily to believe (what much pains are taken to make them believe), that all oppositions are factious, and all courtiers base and servile. From their disgust at men, they are soon led to quarrel with their frame of government, which they presume gives nourishment to the vices, real or supposed, of those who administer in it. Mistaking malignity for sagacity, they are soon led to cast off all hope from a good administration of affairs, and come to think that all reformation depends, not on a change of actors, but upon an alteration in the machinery. Then will be felt the full effect of encouraging doctrines which tend to make the citizens despise their constitution. Then will be felt the plenitude of the mischief of teaching the people to believe, that all antient institutions are the results of ignorance; and that all prescriptive government is in its nature usurpation. Then will be felt, in all its energy, the danger of encouraging a spirit of litigation in persons of that immature and imperfect state of knowledge which serves to render them susceptible of doubts but incapable of their solution. Then will be felt, in all its aggravation, the pernicious consequence of destroying all docility in the minds of those who are not formed for finding their own way in the labyrinths of political theory, and are made to reject the clue, and to disdain the guide. Then will be felt, and too late will be acknowledged, the ruin which follows the disjoining of religion from the state; the separation of morality from policy; and the giving conscience no concern and no coactive or coercive force in the most material of all the social ties, the principle of our obligations to government.

I know too, that besides this vain, contradictory, and self-destructive security, which some men derive from the habitual attachment of the people to this constitution, whilst they suffer it with a sort of sportive acquiescence to be brought into contempt before their faces, they have other grounds for removing all apprehension from their minds. They are of opinion, that there are too many men of great hereditary estates and influence in the kingdom, to suffer the establishment of the levelling system which has taken place in France. This is very true, if in order to guide the power, which now attends their property, these men possess the wisdom which is involved in early fear. But if through a supine security, to which such fortunes are peculiarly liable, they neglect the use of their influence in the season of their power, on the first derangement of society, the nerves of their strength will be cut. Their estates, instead of being the means of their security, will become the very causes of their danger. Instead of bestowing influence they will excite rapacity. They will be looked to as a prey.

Such will be the impotent condition of those men of great hereditary estates, who indeed dislike the designs that are carried on, but whose dislike is rather that of spectators, than of parties that may be concerned in the catastrophe of the piece. But riches do not in all cases secure even an inert and passive resistance. There are always, in that description, men whose fortunes, when their minds are once vitiated by passion or by evil principle, are by no means a security from their actually taking their part against the public tranquillity. We see to what low and despicable passions of all kinds many men in that class are ready to sacrifice the patrimonial estates, which might be perpetuated in their families with splendor, and with the fame of hereditary benefactors to mankind from generation to generation. Do we not see how lightly people treat their fortunes when under the influence of the passion of gaming? The game of ambition or resentment will be played by many of the rich and great, as desperately, and with as much blindness to the consequences, as any other game. Was he a man of no rank or fortune, who first set on foot the disturbances which have ruined France? Passion blinded him to the consequences, so far as they concerned himself; and as to the consequences with regard to others, they were no part of his consideration; nor ever will be with those who bear any resemblance to that virtuous patriot and lover of the rights of man.

There is also a time of insecurity, when interests of all sorts become objects of speculation. Then it is, that their very attachment to wealth and importance will induce several persons of opulence to lift themselves, and even to take a lead with the party which they think most likely to prevail, in order to obtain to themselves consideration in some new order or disorder of things. They may be led to act in this manner, that they may secure some portion of their own property; and perhaps to become partakers of the spoil of their own order. Those who speculate on change, always make a great number among people of rank and fortune, as well as amongst the low and the indigent.

What security against all this? All human securities are liable to uncertainty. But if any thing bids fair for the prevention of so great a calamity, it must consist in the use of the ordinary means of just influence in society, whilst those means continue unimpaired. The public judgment ought to receive a proper direction. All weighty men may have their share in so good a work. As yet, notwithstanding the strutting and lying independence of a braggart philosophy, nature maintains her rights, and great names have great prevalence. Two such men as Mr. Pitt and Mr. Fox, adding to their authority in a point in which they concur, even by their disunion in every thing else, might frown these wicked opinions out of the kingdom. But if the influence of either of them, or the influence of men like them, should, against their serious intentions, be otherwise perverted, they may countenance opinions which (as I have said before, and could wish over and over again to press) they may in vain attempt to control. In their theory, these doctrines admit no limit, no qualification whatsoever. No man can say how far he will go, who joins with those who are avowedly going to the utmost extremities. What security is there for stopping short at all in these wild conceits? Why, neither more nor less than this—that the moral sentiments of some few amongst them do put some check on their savage theories. But let us take care. The moral sentiments, so nearly connected with early prejudice as to be almost one and the same thing, will assuredly not live long under a discipline, which has for its basis the destruction of all prejudices, and the making the mind proof against all dread of consequences flowing from the pretended truths that are taught by their philosophy.

In this school the moral sentiments must grow weaker and weaker every day. The more cautious of these teachers, in laying down their maxims, draw as much of the conclusion as suits, not with their premises, but with their policy. They trust the rest to the sagacity of their pupils. Others, and these are the most vaunted for their spirit, not only lay down the same premises, but boldly draw the conclusions to the destruction of our whole constitution in church and state. But are these conclusions truly drawn? Yes, most certainly. Their principles are wild and wicked. But let justice be done even to phrensy and villainy. These teachers are perfectly systematic. No man who assumes their grounds can tolerate the British constitution in church or state. These teachers profess to scorn all mediocrity; to engage for perfection; to proceed by the simplest and shortest course. They build their politics, not on convenience but on truth; and they profess to conduct men to certain happiness by the assertion of their undoubted rights. With them there is no compromise. All other governments are usurpations, which justify and even demand resistance.

Their principles always go to the extreme. They who go with the principles of the ancient Whigs, which are those contained in Mr. Burke's book, never can go too far. They may indeed stop short of some hazardous and ambiguous excellence, which they will be taught to postpone to any reasonable degree of good they may actually possess. The opinions maintained in that book never can lead to an extreme, because their foundation is laid in an opposition to extremes. The foundation of government is there laid, not in imaginary rights of men (which at best is a confusion of judicial with civil principles), but in political convenience, and in human nature; either as that nature is universal, or as it is modified by local habits and social aptitudes. The foundation of government (those who have read that book will recollect), is laid in a provision for our wants, and in a conformity to our duties; it is to purvey for the one; it is to enforce the other. These doctrines do of themselves gravitate to a middle point, or to some point near a middle. They suppose indeed a certain portion of liberty to be essential to all good government; but they infer that this liberty is to be blended into the government; to harmonize with its forms and its rules; and to be made subordinate to its end. Those who are not with that book are with its opposite. For there is no medium besides the medium itself. That medium is not such, because it is found there; but it is found there, because it is conformable to truth and nature. In this we do not follow the author; but we and the author travel together upon the same safe and middle path.

The theory contained in his book is not to furnish principles for making a new constitution, but for illustrating the principles of a constitution already made. It is a theory drawn from the *fact* of our government. They who oppose it are bound to shew, that his theory militates with that fact. Otherwise, their quarrel is not with his book, but with the constitution of their country. The whole scheme of our mixed constitution is to prevent any one of its principles from being carried as far, as taken by itself, and theoretically, it would go. Allow that to be the true policy of the British system, then most of the faults with which that system stands charged will appear to be, not imperfections into which it has inadvertently fallen, but excellencies which it has studiously sought. To avoid the perfections of extreme, all its several parts are so constituted, as not alone to answer their own several ends, but also each to limit and control the others: insomuch, that take which of the principles you please—you will find its operation checked and stopped at a certain point. The whole movement stands still rather than that any part should proceed beyond its boundary. From thence it results, that in the British constitution, there is a perpetual treaty and compromise going on, sometimes openly, sometimes with less observation. To him who contemplates the British constitution, as to him who contemplates the subordinate material world, it will always be a matter of his most curious investigation, to discover the secret of this mutual limitation.

> ——— *Finita* potestas denique *cuique*
> Quanam sit ratione, atque alte terminus haerens?[50]

They who have acted, as in France they have done, upon a scheme wholly different, and who aim at the abstract and unlimited perfection of power in the popular part, can be of no service to us in any of our political arrangements. They who in their headlong career have overpassed the goal, can furnish no example to those who aim to go no further. The temerity of such speculators is no more an example than the timidity of others. The one sort scorns the right; the other fears it; both miss it. But those who by violence go beyond the barrier, are without question the most mischievous; because to go beyond it they overturn and destroy it. To say they have spirit, is to say nothing in their praise. The untempered spirit of madness, blindness, immorality, and impiety, deserves no commendation. He that sets his house on fire because his fingers are frostbitten, can never be a fit instructor in the method of providing our habitations with a cheerful and salu-

---

[50] ["How the powers and ultimate limits of each thing have been established." Lucretius, *De Rerum Natura* 1.76–77. Burke customarily uses question marks after indirect questions, contrary to modern practice.]

tary warmth. We want no foreign examples to rekindle in us the flame of liberty. The example of our own ancestors is abundantly sufficient to maintain the spirit of freedom in its full vigour, and to qualify it in all its exertions. The example of a wise, moral, well-natured, and well-tempered spirit of freedom, is that alone which can be useful to us, or in the least degree reputable or safe. Our fabric is so constituted; one part of it bears so much on the other, the parts are so made for one another, and for nothing else, that to introduce any foreign matter into it, is to destroy it.

What has been said of the Roman empire, is at least as true of the British constitution—"*Octingentorum annorum fortuna, disciplinaque, compages haec coaluit; quae convelli sine convellentium exitio non potest.*"[51] This British constitution has not been struck out at an heat by a set of presumptuous men, like the assembly of pettifoggers run mad in Paris.

> 'Tis not the hasty product of a day,
> But the well-ripen'd fruit of wise delay.[52]

It is the result of the thoughts of many minds, in many ages. It is no simple, no superficial thing, nor to be estimated by superficial understandings. An ignorant man, who is not fool enough to meddle with his clock, is however sufficiently confident to think he can safely take to pieces, and put together at his pleasure, a moral machine of another guise, importance and complexity, composed of far other wheels, and springs, and balances, and counteracting and co-operating powers. Men little think how immorally they act in rashly meddling with what they do not understand. Their delusive good intention is no sort of excuse for their presumption. They who truly mean well must be fearful of acting ill. The British constitution may have its advantages pointed out to wise and reflecting minds; but it is of too high an order of excellence to

---

[51] ["This mighty structure has come together thanks to eight hundred years of good fortune and discipline, which cannot be uprooted without destroying the uprooters." Tacitus, *Histories* 4.74 (altered)]

[52] [John Dryden, *Astraea Redux*, ll. 169–170]

be adapted to those which are common. It takes in too many views, it makes too many combinations, to be so much as comprehended by shallow and superficial understandings. Profound thinkers will know it in its reason and spirit. The less enquiring will recognize it in their feelings and their experience. They will thank God they have a standard, which, in the most essential point of this great concern, will put them on a par with the most wise and knowing.

If we do not take to our aid the foregone studies of men reputed intelligent and learned, we shall be always beginners. But men must learn somewhere; and the new teachers mean no more than what they effect, as far as they succeed, that is, to deprive men of the benefit of the collected wisdom of mankind, and to make them blind disciples of their own particular presumption. Talk to these deluded creatures (all the disciples and most of the masters) who are taught to think themselves so newly fitted up and furnished, and you will find nothing in their houses but the refuse of *Knaves Acre*; nothing but the rotten stuff, worn out in the service of delusion and sedition in all ages, and which being newly furbished up, patched, and varnished, serves well enough for those who being unacquainted with the conflict which has always been maintained between the sense and the nonsense of mankind, know nothing of the former existence and the antient refutation of the same follies. It is near two thousand years since it has been observed, that these devices of ambition, avarice, and turbulence, were antiquated. They are, indeed, the most antient of all common places; common places, sometimes of good and necessary causes; more frequently of the worst, but which decide upon neither. *Eadem semper causa, libido et avaritia, et mutandarum rerum amor. Ceterum libertas et speciosa nomina pretexuntur; nec quisquam alienum servitium, et dominationem sibi concupivit, ut non eadem ista vocabula usurparet.*[53]

---

[53] ["The reason is always the same: lust and avarice, and a desire to change their circumstances. Still, liberty and specious words provide the pretext; and yet no one ever lusted after slavery for others and dominion for himself without using the very same cant." Tacitus, *Histories* 4.73]

An Appeal from the New to the Old Whigs

Rational and experienced men, tolerably well know, and have always known, how to distinguish between true and false liberty; and between the genuine adherence and the false pretence to what is true. But none, except those who are profoundly studied, can comprehend the elaborate contrivance of a fabric fitted to unite private and public liberty with public force, with order, with peace, with justice, and, above all, with the institutions formed for bestowing permanence and stability through ages, upon this invaluable whole.

Place, for instance, before your eyes, such a man as Montesquieu. Think of a genius not born in every country, or every time; a man gifted by nature with a penetrating aquiline eye; with a judgment prepared with the most extensive erudition; with an herculean robustness of mind, and nerves not to be broken with labour; a man who could spend twenty years in one pursuit. Think of a man, like the universal patriarch in Milton[54] (who had drawn up before him in his prophetic vision the whole series of the generations which were to issue from his loins) a man capable of placing in review, after having brought together, from the east, the west, the north, and the south, from the coarseness of the rudest barbarism to the most refined and subtle civilization, all the schemes of government which had ever prevailed amongst mankind, weighing, measuring, collating, and comparing them all, joining fact with theory, and calling into council, upon all this infinite assemblage of things, all the speculations which have fatigued the understandings of profound reasoners in all times! Let us then consider, that all these were but so many preparatory steps to qualify a man, and such a man, tinctured with no national prejudice, with no domestic affection, to admire, and to hold out to the admiration of mankind the constitution of England! And shall we Englishmen revoke to such a suit? Shall we, when so much more than he has produced, remains still to be understood and admired, instead of keeping ourselves in the schools of real science,

---

[54] [Adam in *Paradise Lost* 11:423ff. Montesquieu discusses the English Constitution in *The Spirit of Laws* 11.6.]

choose for our teachers men incapable of being taught, whose only claim to know is, that they have never doubted; from whom we can learn nothing but their own indocility; who would teach us to scorn what in the silence of our hearts we ought to adore?

Different from them are all the great critics. They have taught us one essential rule. I think the excellent and philosophic artist, a true judge, as well as a perfect follower of nature, Sir Joshua Reynolds has somewhere applied it, or something like it, in his own profession. It is this, That if ever we should find ourselves disposed not to admire those writers or artists, Livy and Virgil for instance, Raphael or Michael Angelo, whom all the learned had admired, not to follow our own fancies, but to study them until we know how and what we ought to admire; and if we cannot arrive at this combination of admiration with knowledge, rather to believe that we are dull, than that the rest of the world has been imposed on. It is as good a rule, at least, with regard to this admired constitution. We ought to understand it according to our measure; and to venerate where we are not able presently to comprehend.

Such admirers were our fathers to whom we owe this splendid inheritance. Let us improve it with zeal, but with fear. Let us follow our ancestors, men not without a rational, though without an exclusive confidence in themselves; who, by respecting the reason of others, who, by looking backward as well as forward, by the modesty as well as by the energy of their minds, went on, insensibly drawing this constitution nearer and nearer to its perfection by never departing from its fundamental principles, nor introducing any amendment which had not a subsisting root in the laws, constitution, and usages of the kingdom. Let those who have the trust of political or of natural authority ever keep watch against the desperate enterprizes of innovation: Let even their benevolence be fortified and armed. They have before their eyes the example of a monarch, insulted, degraded, confined, deposed; his family dispersed, scattered, imprisoned; his wife insulted to his face like the vilest of the sex, by the vilest of all populace; himself three times dragged by these wretches in an infamous triumph; his children torn from him, in violation of the first right of nature, and given into the tuition of the most desperate and impious of the leaders of desperate and impious clubs; his revenues dilapidated and plundered; his magistrates murdered; his clergy proscribed, persecuted, famished; his nobility degraded in their rank, undone in their fortunes, fugitives in their persons; his armies corrupted and ruined; his whole people impoverished, disunited, dissolved; whilst through the bars of his prison, and amidst the bayonets of his keepers, he hears the tumult of two conflicting factions, equally wicked and abandoned, who agree in principles, in dispositions, and in objects, but who tear each other to pieces about the most effectual means of obtaining their common end; the one contending to preserve for a while his name and his person, the more easily to destroy the royal authority—the other clamouring to cut off the name, the person, and the monarchy together, by one sacrilegious execution. All this accumulation of calamity, the greatest that ever fell upon one man, has fallen upon his head, because he had left his virtues unguarded by caution; because he was not taught that where power is concerned, he who will confer benefits must take security against ingratitude.

I have stated the calamities which have fallen upon a great prince and nation, because they were not alarmed at the approach of danger, and because, what commonly happens to men surprised, they lost all resource when they were caught in it. When I speak of danger, I certainly mean to address myself to those who consider the prevalence of the new Whig doctrines as an evil.

The Whigs of this day have before them, in this Appeal, their constitutional ancestors: They have the doctors of the modern school. They will choose for themselves. The author of the Reflections has chosen for himself. If a new order is coming on, and all the political opinions must pass away as dreams, which our ancestors have worshipped as revelations,

I say for him, that he would rather be the last (as certainly he is the least) of that race of men, than the first and greatest of those who have coined to themselves Whig principles from a French die, unknown to the impress of our fathers in the constitution.

FINIS

5

THOUGHTS ON FRENCH AFFAIRS

December 1791

*A*fter the breach with Fox and the leadership of the Whig party
in May 1791, Burke's independence gave him more freedom to influence opinion, as he saw fit, among Tory ministers and disenchanted
Whigs. Between 1791 and 1793 he wrote three works—Thoughts on
French Affairs, Heads for Consideration on the Present State of
Affairs *(1792), and* Remarks on the Policy of the Allies *(1793)—*
*"with one single principle to guide me," he said in 1794, "namely that
the extinction of Jacobinism in France was the sole worthy object of
Arms and politicks of this time" (Corr. Copeland 7:517–518).*

*Since the work is a private communication intended for the small
audience of Whig and Tory leaders he still hoped to sway, Burke's
style here is quite different from that of the other works in this volume:
There are no classical allusions, far fewer appeals to the terrible sublimity of the Revolution, and no sustained portraits of historical personages such as one finds in each of the longer works. Still, Burke
makes some of his most insightful comments on the psychology of those
who make their living by talking about ideas—the "knowledge class"
or "new class."*

*Burke's hopes for an international coalition of the monarchies
against France had been forwarded by the Declaration of Pillnitz,
signed in August 1791 by Frederick William II (1744–1797, ruled
1786–1797) of Prussia, and Marie Antoinette's brother, Leopold II
(1747–1792, ruled 1790–1792) of Austria. These two German powers
had long been competitors in the areas of modern Belgium (the Austri-*

an Netherlands, which Burke sometimes calls the Belgic provinces) and the Netherlands (which Burke sometimes calls Holland): The Austrian Netherlands had returned to the emperor's control under Leopold's predecessor and brother, Joseph II (1741–1790, ruled 1765–1790), while to the north, Holland's Stadtholder, William V, Prince of Orange, had married Frederick William's sister. To further complicate matters, Prussia and Russia found it difficult to cooperate on French affairs when their real desire was to carve up Poland between them. The German heads of state declared at Pillnitz that "they regard the present position of [Louis XVI] as a matter of common concern to all the sovereigns of Europe." They made any military intervention contingent on the cooperation of the other European sovereigns. Under the circumstances, however, Britain was very unlikely to participate. The opening paragraphs of Thoughts allude to a letter from the French Foreign Minister, Armand-Marc, Comte de Montmorin de Saint-Hérem, telling French ambassadors to inform Europe's heads of state of Louis XVI's acceptance of the French constitution. The letter was dated April 1791, just two months before the King disavowed his compliance with the Revolution and attempted to flee the country.

Thoughts on French Affairs consists primarily of a survey of revolutionary sentiment in the various European countries, arguing that the absence of a credible, counter-revolutionary movement in France would force Britain and the other European monarchies to eliminate Jacobinism militarily.

Thoughts on French Affairs

December 1791

In all our transactions with France, and at all periods, we have treated with that State on the footing of a Monarchy. Monarchy was considered in all the external relations of that kingdom with every Power in Europe as it's legal and constitutional Government, and that in which alone it's federal capacity was vested.

It is not yet a year since Monsieur de Montmorin, formally, and with as little respect as can be imagined, to the King, and to all crowned heads, announced a total revolution in that country. He has informed the British Ministry that it's frame of Government is wholly altered; that he is one of the Ministers of the new system; and in effect, that the King is no longer his master (nor does he even call him such) but the *"first of the Ministers"* in the new system.

Montmorin's Letter.

The second notification was that of the King's acceptance of the new Constitution; accompanied with fanfaronades in the modern style of the French bureaus, things which have much more the air and character of the saucy declamations of their clubs, than the tone of regular office.

Acceptance of the Constitution ratified.

It has not been very usual to notify to foreign Courts, any thing concerning the internal arrangements of any State. In the present case, the circumstance of these two notifications, with the observations with which they are attended, does not

[205]

leave it in the choice of the Sovereigns of Christendom to appear ignorant either of this French Revolution, or (what is more important) of it's principles.

We know that very soon after this Manifesto of Monsieur de Montmorin, the King of France, in whose name it was made, found himself obliged to fly, with his whole family; leaving behind him a Declaration, in which he disavows and annuls that Constitution, as having been the effect of force on his person and usurpation on his authority. It is equally notorious that this unfortunate Prince was, with many circumstances of insult and outrage, brought back prisoner, by a deputation of the pretended National Assembly, and afterwards suspended by their authority, from his Government. Under equally notorious constraint, and under menaces of total deposition, he has been compelled to accept what they call a Constitution, and to agree to whatever else the usurped power which holds him in confinement, thinks proper to impose.

His next brother, who had fled with him, and his third brother, who had fled before him,[1] all the Princes of his blood, who remained faithful to him, and the flower of his Magistracy, his Clergy, and his Nobility, continue in foreign countries, protesting against all acts done by him in his present situation, on the grounds upon which he had himself protested against them at the time of his flight; with this addition, that they deny his very competence (as on good grounds they may), to abrogate the Royalty, or the ancient constitutional Orders of the Kingdom. In this protest they are joined by three hundred of the late Assembly itself, and in effect, by a great part of the French Nation. The new Government (so far as the people dare to disclose their sentiments) is disdained, I am persuaded, by the greater number; who as M. de la Fayette complains, and as the truth is, have declined to take any

---

[1] [The oldest brother of the king, later Louis XVIII, also fled Paris on June 20, 1791, but was not captured. His youngest brother, later Charles X, had already emigrated.]

share in the new elections to the National Assembly, either as candidates or electors.

In this state of things (that is in the case of a *divided* kingdom) by the law of nations,[2] Great Britain, like every other Power, is free to take any part she pleases. She may decline, with more or less formality, according to her discretion, to acknowledge this new system; or she may recognize it as a Government *de facto,* setting aside all discussion of it's original legality, and considering the ancient Monarchy as at an end. The law of nations leaves our Court open to it's choice. We have no direction but what is found in the well-understood policy of the King and kingdom.

This Declaration of a *new species* of Government, on new principles (such it professes itself to be) is a real crisis in the politicks of Europe. The conduct which prudence ought to dictate to Great-Britain, will not depend (as hitherto our connexion or quarrel with other States has for some time depended) upon merely *external* relations; but, in a great measure also upon the system which we may think it right to adopt for the internal government of our own country.

If it be our policy to assimilate our Government to that of France, we ought to prepare for this change, by encouraging the schemes of authority established there. We ought to wink at the captivity and deposition of a Prince, with whom, if not in close alliance, we were in friendship. We ought to fall in with the ideas of Mons. Montmorin's circular Manifesto; and to do business of course with the functionaries who act under the new power, by which that King to whom his Majesty's Minister has been sent to reside, has been deposed and imprisoned. On that idea we ought also to with-hold all sorts of direct or indirect countenance from those who are treating in Germany for the re-establishment of the French Monarchy

---

[2] See Vattel, b. ii. c. 4. sect. 56. and b. iii. c 18. sect. 296. [Burke owned a copy of *Droit des Gens* (1758) by Emmerich von Vattel (1714–1767). He prepared and edited a series of "extracts" from Vattel, as an appendix to his *Remarks on the Policy of the Allies* (written in the autumn of 1793), particularly to justify English intervention in France.]

and the ancient Orders of that State. This conduct is suitable to this policy.

The question is, whether this policy be suitable to the interests of the Crown and subjects of Great Britain. Let us therefore a little consider the true nature and probable effects of the Revolution which, in such a very unusual manner, has been twice diplomatically announced to his Majesty.

Difference between this Revolution and others.

There have been many internal revolutions in the Government of countries, both as to persons and forms, in which the neighbouring States have had little or no concern. Whatever the Government might be with respect to those persons and those forms, the stationary interests of the nation concerned, have most commonly influenced the new Governments in the same manner in which they influenced the old; and the Revolution, turning on matter of local grievance or of local accommodation, did not extend beyond it's territory.

Nature of the French Revolution.

The present Revolution in France seems to me to be quite of another character and description; and to bear little resemblance or analogy to any of those which have been brought about in Europe, upon principles merely political. *It is a Revolution of doctrine and theoretick dogma.* It has a much greater resemblance to those changes which have been made upon religious grounds, in which a spirit of proselytism makes an essential part.

The last Revolution of doctrine and theory which has happened in Europe, is the Reformation. It is not for my purpose to take any notice here of the merits of that Revolution, but to state one only of it's effects.

It's effects.

That effect was *to introduce other interests into all countries, than those which arose from their locality and natural circumstances.* The principle of the Reformation was such, as by it's essence, could not be local or confined to the country in which it had it's origin. For instance, the doctrine of "Justification by Faith or by Works," which was the original basis of the Reformation, could not have one of it's alternatives true as to Germany, and false as to every other country. Neither are questions of theoretick truth and falsehood governed by circumstances any more than by places. On that occasion, therefore, the spirit of proselytism expanded itself with great elasticity upon all sides; and great divisions were every where the result.

These divisions however, in appearance merely dogmatick, soon became mixed with the political; and their effects were rendered much more intense from this combination. Europe was for a long time divided into two great factions, under the name of Catholick and Protestant, which not only often alienated State from State, but also divided almost every State within itself. The warm parties in each State were more affectionately attached to those of their own doctrinal interest in some other country than to their fellow citizens, or to their natural Government, when they or either of them happened to be of a different persuasion. These factions, wherever they prevailed, if they did not absolutely destroy, at least weakened and distracted the locality of patriotism. The publick affections came to have other motives and other ties.

It would be to repeat the history of the two last centuries to exemplify the effects of this Revolution.

Although the principles to which it gave rise, did not operate with a perfect regularity and constancy, they never wholly ceased to operate. Few wars were made, and few treaties were entered into in which they did not come in for some part. They gave a colour, a character, and direction to all the politicks of Europe.

These principles of internal, as well as external division and coalition, are but just now extinguished. But they who will examine into the true character and genius of some late events, must be satisfied that other sources of faction, combining parties among the inhabitants of different countries into one connexion, are opened, and that from these sources are likely to arise effects full as important as those which had formerly arisen from the jarring interests of the religious sects. The intention of the several actors in the change in France, is not a matter of doubt. It is very openly professed.

In the modern world, before this time, there has been no instance of this spirit of general political faction, separated

New system of Politicks.

from religion, pervading several countries, and forming a principle of union between the partizans in each. But the thing is not less in human nature. The antient world has furnished a strong and striking instance of such a ground for faction, full as powerful and full as mischievous as our spirit of religious system had ever been, exciting in all the States of Greece (European and Asiatick) the most violent animosities, and the most cruel and bloody persecutions and proscriptions. These ancient factions in each commonwealth of Greece, connected themselves with those of the same description in some other States; and secret cabals and publick alliances were carried on and made, not upon a conformity of general political interests, but for the support and aggrandizement of the two leading States which headed the Aristocratick and Democratick Factions. For, as in later times, the King of Spain was at the head of a Catholick, and the King of Sweden of a Protestant interest, France (though Catholick, acting subordinately to the latter), in the like manner the Lacedemonians were every where at the head of the Aristocratick interests, and the Athenians of the Democratick. The two leading Powers kept alive a constant cabal and conspiracy in every State, and the political dogmas concerning the constitution of a Republick, were the great instruments by which these leading States chose to aggrandize themselves. Their choice was not unwise; because the interest in opinions (merely as opinions, and without any experimental reference to their effects) when once they take strong hold of the mind, become the most operative of all interests and indeed very often supercede every other.

I might further exemplify the possibility of a political sentiment running through various states and combining factions in them, from the history of the middle ages in the Guelfs and Ghibellines. These were political factions originally in favour of the Emperor and the Pope, with no mixture of religious dogmas; or if any thing religiously doctrinal they had in them originally, it very soon disappeared; as their first political objects disappeared also, though the spirit remained. They became no more than names to distinguish factions; but they were not the less powerful in their operation, when they had no direct point of doctrine, either religious or civil, to assert. For a long time, however, those factions gave no small degree of influence to the foreign Chiefs in every commonwealth in which they existed. I do not mean to pursue further the track of these parties. I allude to this part of history only, as it furnishes an instance of that species of faction which broke the locality of publick affections, and united descriptions of citizens more with strangers than with their countrymen of different opinions.

The political dogma, which upon the new French system, is to unite the factions of different nations, is this, "That the majority told, by the head, of the taxable people in every country, is the perpetual, natural, unceasing, indefeasible sovereign; that this majority is perfectly master of the form, as well as the administration of the state, and that the magistrates, under whatever names they are called, are only functionaries to obey the orders (general as laws or particular as decrees), which that majority may make; that this is the only natural government; that all others are tyranny and usurpation." French fundamental principle.

In order to reduce this dogma into practice, the Republicans in France, and their associates in other countries, make it always their business, and often their publick profession, to destroy all traces of antient establishments, and to form a new commonwealth in each country, upon the basis of the French *Rights of Men*. On the principle of these rights, they mean to institute in every country, and as it were, the germe of the whole, parochial governments, for the purpose of what they call equal representation. From them is to grow, by some media, a general council and representative of all the parochial governments. In that representative is to be vested the whole national power; totally abolishing hereditary name and office, levelling all conditions of men (except where money *must* make a difference), breaking all connexion between territory and dignity, and abolishing every species of nobility, gentry, Practical project.

and church establishments; all their priests, and all their magistrates being only creatures of election, and pensioners at will.

Knowing how opposite a permanent landed interest is to that scheme, they have resolved, and it is the great drift of all their regulations, to reduce that description of men to a mere peasantry, for the sustenance of the towns, and to place the true effective government in cities, among the tradesmen, bankers, and voluntary clubs of bold, presuming young persons; advocates, attornies, notaries, managers of newspapers, and those cabals of literary men, called academies. Their Republick is to have a first functionary (as they call him), under the name of King, or not, as they think fit. This officer, when such an officer is permitted, is however, neither in fact nor name, to be considered as sovereign, nor the people as his subjects. The very use of these appellations is offensive to their ears.

Partizans of the French system.

This system, as it has first been realized, dogmatically as well as practically, in France, makes France the natural head of all factions formed on a similar principle, wherever they may prevail, as much as Athens was the head and settled ally of all democratick factions, wherever they existed. The other system has no head.

This system has very many partizans in every country in Europe, but particularly in England, where they are already formed into a body, comprehending most of the dissenters of the three leading denominations; to these are readily aggregated all who are dissenters in character, temper, and disposition, though not belonging to any of their congregations—that is, all the restless people who resemble them, of all ranks and all parties—Whigs, and even Tories—the whole race of half-bred speculators; all the Atheists, Deists, and Socinians; all those who hate the Clergy, and envy the Nobility, a good many among the monied people; the East Indians almost to a man, who cannot bear to find that their present importance does not bear a proportion to their wealth. These latter have united themselves into one great, and in my opinion, formi-

Thoughts on French Affairs

dable Club,[3] which, though now quiet, may be brought into action with considerable unanimity and force.

Formerly few, except the ambitious great, or the desperate and indigent, were to be feared as instruments in revolutions. What has happened in France teaches us, with many other things, that there are more causes than have commonly been taken into our consideration, by which Government may be subverted. The monied men, merchants, principal tradesmen, and men of letters (hitherto generally thought the peaceable and even timid part of society) are the chief actors in the French Revolution. But the fact is, that as money increases and circulates, and as the circulation of news, in politicks and letters, becomes more and more diffused, the persons who diffuse this money, and this intelligence, become more and more important. This was not long undiscovered. Views of *ambition* were in France, for the first time, presented to these classes of men. Objects in the State, in the Army, in the system of civil offices of every kind. Their eyes were dazzled with this new prospect. They were, as it were, electrified and made to lose the natural spirit of their situation. A bribe, great without example in the history of the world, was held out to them—the whole government of a very large kingdom.

There are several who are persuaded that the same thing cannot happen in England, because here (they say), the occupations of merchants, tradesmen, and manufacturers, are not held as degrading situations. I once thought that the low estimation in which commerce was held in France, might be reckoned among the causes of the late revolution; and I am still of opinion, that the exclusive spirit of the French nobility, did irritate the wealthy of other classes. But I found long since, that persons in trade and business were by no means despised in France in the manner I had been taught to believe. As to men of letters, they were so far from being de-

Grounds of security supposed for England.

---

[3] Originally called the Bengal Club, but since opened to persons from the other Presidencies, for the purpose of consolidating the whole Indian interest.

spised or neglected, that there was no country perhaps in the universe, in which they were so highly esteemed, courted, caressed, and even feared; tradesmen naturally were not so much sought in society (as not furnishing so largely to the fund of conversation as they do to the revenues of the state) but the latter description got forward every day. M. Bailly, who made himself the popular Mayor on the rebellion of the Bastile, and is a principal actor in the revolt, before the change possessed a pension or office under the Crown, of six hundred pound English, a year, for that country, no contemptible provision: And this he obtained solely as a man of letters, and on no other title. As to the monied men—whilst the Monarchy continued, there is no doubt, that merely as such, they did not enjoy the *privileges* of nobility, but nobility was of so easy an acquisition, that it was the fault or neglect of all of that description, who did not obtain it's privileges, for their lives at least, in virtue of office. It attached under the royal government to an innumerable multitude of places, real and nominal, that were vendible; and such nobility were as capable of every thing as their degree of influence or interest could make them, that is, as nobility of no considerable rank or consequence. M. Necker, so far from being a French gentleman, was not so much as a Frenchman born, and yet we all know the rank in which he stood on the day of the meeting of the States.

As to the mere matter of estimation of the mercantile or any other class, this is regulated by opinion and prejudice. In England a security against the envy of men in these classes, is not so very complete as we may imagine. We must not impose upon ourselves. What institutions and manners together had done in France, manners alone do here. It is the natural operation of things where there exists a Crown, a Court, splendid Orders of Knighthood, and an Hereditary Nobility; where there exists a fixed, permanent, landed Gentry, continued in greatness and opulence by the law of primogeniture, and by a protection given to family settlements; where there exists a standing Army and Navy; where there exists a Church Estab-

Literary interest.

Monied interest.

Mercantile interest.

Thoughts on French Affairs

lishment, which bestows on learning and parts an interest combined with that of Religion and the State; in a country where such things exist, wealth, new in it's acquisition, and precarious in it's duration, can never rank first, or even near the first; though wealth has it's natural weight, further, than as it is balanced and even preponderated amongst us as amongst other nations, by artificial institutions and opinions growing out of them. At no period in the history of England have so few Peers been taken out of trade or from families newly created by commerce. In no period has so small a number of noble families entered into the counting-house. I can call to mind but one in all England, and his is of near fifty years standing. Be that as it may, it appears plain to me from my best observation, that envy and ambition may by art, management and disposition, be as much excited amongst these descriptions of men in England, as in any other country; and that they are just as capable of acting a part in any great change.

What direction the French spirit of proselytism is likely to take, and in what order it is likely to prevail in the several parts of Europe, it is not easy to determine. The seeds are sown almost every where, chiefly by newspaper circulations, infinitely more efficacious and extensive than ever they were. And they are a more important instrument than generally is imagined. They are a part of the reading of all, they are the whole of the reading of the far greater number. There are thirty of them in Paris alone. The language diffuses them more widely than the English, though the English too are much read. The writers of these papers indeed, for the greater part, are either unknown or in contempt, but they are like a battery in which the stroke of any one ball produces no great effect, but the amount of continual repetition is decisive. Let us only suffer any person to tell us his story, morning and evening, but for one twelvemonth, and he will become our master.

Progress of the French Spirit. It's course.

All those countries in which several States are comprehended under some general geographical description, and loosely united by some federal constitution; countries of which the members are small, and greatly diversified in their forms of government, and in the titles by which they are held—these countries, as it might be well expected, are the principal objects of their hopes and machinations. Of these, the chief are Germany and Switzerland: after them, Italy has it's place as in circumstances somewhat similar.

Germany.

As to Germany (in which from their relation to the Emperor, I comprehend the Belgick provinces) it appears to me to be from several circumstances, internal and external, in a very critical situation, and the laws and liberties of the Empire are by no means secure from the contagion of the French doctrines and the effect of French intrigues; or from the use which two of the greater German powers may make of a general derangement, to the general detriment. I do not say that the French do not mean to bestow on these Germany States, liberties and laws too, after their mode; but those are not what have hitherto been understood as the laws and liberties of the Empire. These exist and have always existed under the principles of feodal tenure and succession, under Imperial constitutions, grants and concessions of Sovereigns, family compacts and publick treaties, made under the sanction, and some of them guaranteed by the Sovereign Powers of other nations, and particularly the old Government of France, the author and natural support of the treaty of Westphalia.

In short, the Germanick body is a vast mass of heterogeneous States, held together by that heterogeneous body of old principles which formed the publick law positive and doctrinal. The modern laws and liberties which the new power in France proposes to introduce into Germany, and to support with all it's force, of intrigue and of arms, is of a very different nature, utterly irreconcileable with the first, and indeed fundamentally the reverse of it: I mean the *Rights and Liberties of the Man,* the *Droit de l'Homme.* That this doctrine has made an amazing progress in Germany, there cannot be a shadow of doubt. They are infected by it along the whole course of the Rhine, the Maese, the Moselle, and in the greater part of

THOUGHTS ON FRENCH AFFAIRS

Suabia and Franconia. It is particularly prevalent amongst all the lower people, churchmen and laity, in the dominions of the Ecclesiastical Electors. It is not easy to find or to conceive Governments more mild and indulgent than these Church Sovereignties; but good government is as nothing when the Rights of Man take possession of the mind. Indeed the loose rein held over the people in these provinces, must be considered as one cause of the facility with which they lend themselves to any schemes of innovation, by inducing them to think lightly of their governments, and to judge of grievances not by feeling, but by imagination. *Ecclesiastical State.*

It is in these Electorates that the first impressions of France are likely to be made, and if they succeed, it is over with the Germanick body as it stands at present. A great revolution is preparing in Germany; and a revolution, in my opinion, likely to be more decisive upon the general fate of nations than that of France itself; other than as in France is to be found the first source of all the principles which are in any way likely to distinguish the troubles and convulsions of our age. If Europe does not conceive the independence, and the equilibrium of the Empire to be in the very essence of the system of balanced power in Europe, and if the scheme of publick law, or mass of laws upon which that independence and equilibrium are founded, be of no leading consequence as they are preserved or destroyed, all the politicks of Europe for more than two Centuries have been miserably erroneous. *Balance of Germany.*

If the two great leading Powers of Germany do not regard this danger (as apparently they do not) in the light in which it presents itself so naturally, it is because they are powers too great to have a social interest. That sort of interest belongs only to those, whose state of weakness or mediocrity is such, as to give them greater cause of apprehension from what may destroy them, than of hope from any thing by which they may be aggrandized. *Prussia and Emperor.*

As long as those two Princes are at variance, so long the liberties of Germany are safe. But if ever they should so far understand one another as to be persuaded that they have a more direct and more certainly defined interest in a proportioned mutual aggrandizement than in a reciprocal reduction, that is, if they come to think that they are more likely to be enriched by a division of spoil, than to be rendered secure by keeping to the old policy of preventing others from being spoiled by either of them, from that moment the liberties of Germany are no more.

That a junction of two in such a scheme is neither impossible nor improbable, is evident from the partition of Poland in 1773, which was effected by such a junction as made the interposition of other nations to prevent it, not easy. Their circumstances at that time hindered any other three States, or indeed any two, from taking measures in common to prevent it, though France was at that time an existing power, and had not yet learned to act upon a system of politicks of her own invention. The geographical position of Poland was a great obstacle to any movements of France in opposition to this, at that time unparalleled league. To my certain knowledge, if Great Britain had at that time been willing to concur in preventing the execution of a project so dangerous in the example, even exhausted as France then was by the preceding war, and under a lazy and unenterprizing Prince, she would have at every risque taken an active part in this business. But a languor with regard to so remote an interest, and the principles and passions which were then strongly at work at home, were the causes why Great Britain would not give France any encouragement in such an enterprize. At that time, however, and with regard to that object, in my opinion, Great Britain and France had a common interest.

But the position of Germany is not like that of Poland, with regard to France, either for good or for evil. If a conjunction between Prussia and the Emperor should be formed for the purpose of secularising and rendering hereditary the Ecclesiastical Electorates and the Bishoprick of Munster, for settling two of them on the children of the Emperor, and uniting Cologne and Munster to the dominions of the King of Prussia on the Rhine, or if any other project of mutual aggrandize-

Possible project of the Emperor and K. of Prussia.

ment should be in prospect, and that to facilitate such a scheme, the modern French should be permitted and encouraged to shake the internal and external security of these Ecclesiastical Electorates, Great Britain is so situated that she could not with any effect set herself in opposition to such a design. Her principal arm, her marine, could here be of no sort of use.

France, the author of the treaty of Westphalia, is the natural guardian of the independence and balance of Germany. Great Britain (to say nothing of the King's concern as one of that august body) has a serious interest in preserving it; but, except through the power of France, *acting upon the common old principles of State policy,* in the case we have supposed, she has no sort of means of supporting that interest. It is always the interest of Great Britain that the power of France should be kept within the bounds of moderation. It is not her interest that that power should be wholly annihilated in the system of Europe. Though at one time through France the independence of Europe was endangered, it is and ever was through her alone that the common liberty of Germany can be secured against the single or the combined ambition of any other power. In truth, within this century the aggrandizement of other Sovereign Houses has been such that there has been a great change in the whole state of Europe, and other nations as well as France may become objects of jealousy and apprehension.

In this state of things, a new principle of alliances and wars is opened. The treaty of Westphalia is, with France, an antiquated fable. The rights and liberties she was bound to maintain are now a system of wrong and tyranny which she is bound to destroy. Her good and ill dispositions are shewn by the same means. *To communicate peaceably* the rights of men is the true mode of her shewing her *friendship*; to force Sovereigns to *submit* to those rights is her mode of *hostility*. So that either as friend or foe her whole scheme has been and is, to throw the Empire into confusion: and those Statesmen, who follow the old routine of politicks, may see in this general confusion, and in the danger of the *lesser* Princes, an occasion

To be resisted only by France.

New principles of alliance.

as protectors or enemies, of connecting their territories to one or the other of the *two great* German Powers. They do not take into consideration that the means which they encourage, as leading to the event they desire, will with certainty not only ravage and destroy the Empire, but if they should for a moment seem to aggrandize the two great houses, will also establish principles, and confirm tempers amongst the people, which will preclude the two Sovereigns from the possibility of holding what they acquire, or even the dominions which they have inherited. It is on the side of the Ecclesiastical Electorates that the dykes, raised to support the German liberty, first will give way.

The French have begun their general operations by seizing upon those territories of the Pope, the situation of which was the most inviting to the enterprize. Their method of doing it was by exciting sedition and spreading massacre and desolation thro' these unfortunate places, and then under an idea of kindness and protection, bringing forward an antiquated title of the Crown of France and annexing Avignon and the two cities of the Comtat with their territory to the French Republick. They have made an attempt on Geneva, in which they very narrowly failed of success. It is known that they hold out from time to time the idea of uniting all the other provinces of which Gaul was antiently composed, including Savoy on the other side, and on this side bounding themselves by the Rhine.

Geneva.

Savoy.

As to Switzerland, it is a country whose long union rather than it's possible division, is the matter of wonder. Here I know they entertain very sanguine hopes. The aggregation to France of the Democratick Swiss Republicks appears to them to be a work half done by their very form; and it might seem to them rather an encrease of importance to these little Commonwealths, than a derogation from their independency, or a change in the manner of their Government. Upon any quarrel amongst the Cantons nothing is more likely than such an event. As to the Aristocratick Republicks, the general clamour and hatred which the French excite against the very name (and

Switzerland.

THOUGHTS ON FRENCH AFFAIRS

with more facility and success than against Monarchs), and the utter impossibility of their Government making any sort of resistance against an insurrection, where they have no troops, and the people are all armed and trained, render their hopes in that quarter, far indeed from unfounded. It is certain that the Republick of Berne thinks itself obliged to a vigilance next to hostile, and to imprison or expel all the French whom they find in their territories. But indeed those Aristocracies which comprehend whatever is considerable, wealthy, and valuable in Switzerland, do now so wholly depend upon opinion, and the humour of their multitude, that the lightest puff of wind is sufficient to blow them down. If France, under it's antient regimen, and upon the antient principles of policy, was the support of the Germanick Constitution, it was much more so of that of Switzerland, which almost from the very origin of that confederacy rested upon the closeness of it's connexion with France, on which the Swiss Cantons wholly reposed themselves for the preservation of the parts of their body in their respective rights and permanent forms, as well as for the maintenance of all in their general independency. *Old French maxims the security of its independence.*

Switzerland and Germany are the first objects of the new French politicians. When I contemplate what they have done at home, which is in effect little less than an amazing conquest wrought by a change of opinion, in a great part (to be sure far from altogether) very sudden, I cannot help letting my thoughts run along with their designs, and without attending to geographical order, to consider the other States of Europe so far as they may be any way affected by this astonishing Revolution. If early steps are not taken in some way or other to prevent the spreading of this influence, I scarcely think any of them perfectly secure.

Italy is divided, as Germany and Switzerland are, into many smaller States, and with some considerable diversity as to forms of Government; but as these divisions and varieties in Italy are not so considerable, so neither do I think the danger altogether so imminent there as in Germany and Switzerland. Savoy I know that the French consider as in a very hope- *Italy.*

Lombardy.

ful way, and I believe not at all without reason. They view it as an old member of the Kingdom of France which may be easily re-united in the manner, and on the principles of the re-union of Avignon. This country communicates with Piedmont; and as the King of Sardinia's dominions were long the key of Italy, and as such long regarded by France, whilst France acted on her old maxims, and with views on Italy; so in this new French empire of sedition, if once she gets that key into her hands, she can easily lay open the barrier which hinders the entrance of her present politicks into that inviting region. Milan, I am sure, nourishes great disquiets—and if Milan should stir, no part of Lombardy is secure to the present possessors—whether the Venetian or the Austrian. Genoa is closely connected with France.

Bourbon
Princes in
Italy.

The first Prince of the House of Bourbon has been obliged to give himself up entirely to the new system, and to pretend even to propagate it with all zeal; at least that Club of intriguers who assemble at the Feuillans,[4] and whose cabinet meets at Madame Stahl's, and makes and directs all the Ministers, is the real Executive Government of France. The Emperor is perfectly in concert, and they will not long suffer any Prince of the House of Bourbon, to keep by force the French emissaries out of their dominions; nor whilst France has a commerce with them, especially thro' Marseilles (the hottest focus of sedition in France), will it be long possible to prevent the intercourse or the effects.

Naples has an old inveterate disposition to Republicanism, and (however for some time past quiet) is as liable to explosion as it's own Vesuvius. Sicily I think has these dispositions in full as strong a degree. In neither of these countries

[4] [The "first Prince" of the Bourbons is the King, Louis XVI. The Club of the Feuillants was formed in July 1791 by Jacobins who refused to sign a petition demanding the deposition of the King after his attempted flight. Madame "Stahl" is the writer Anne-Louise-Germaine Necker, Baronne de Staël-Holstein (1766-1817), daughter of Jacques Necker. Her salon attracted the moderate constitutionalists. She fled Paris in 1792, on the eve of the September massacres.]

exists any thing which very well deserves the name of Government or exact police.

In the Estates of the Church, notwithstanding their strictness in banishing the French out of that country, there are not wanting the seeds of a revolution. The spirit of Nepotism prevails there nearly as strong as ever. Every Pope of course is to give origin or restoration to a great family, by the means of large donations. The foreign revenues have long been gradually on the decline, and seem now in a manner dried up. To supply this defect the resource of vexatious and impolitick jobbing at home, if any thing, is rather encreased than lessened. Various, well intended but ill understood practices, some of them existing, in their spirit at least, from the time of the old Roman empire, still prevail; and that Government is as blindly attached to old abusive customs, as others are wildly disposed to all sorts of innovations and experiments. These abuses were less felt whilst the Pontificate drew riches from abroad, which in some measure counterbalanced the evils of their remiss and jobbish Government at home. But now it can subsist only on the resources of domestick management; and abuses in that management of course will be more intimately and more severely felt.

In the midst of the apparently torpid languor of the Ecclesiastical State, those who have had opportunity of a near observation, have seen a little rippling in that smooth water, which indicates something alive under it. There is in the Ecclesiastical State, a personage who seems capable of acting (but with more force and steadiness) the part of the Tribune Rienzi.[5] The people once inflamed will not be destitute of a leader. They have such an one already in the Cardinal or Archbishop *Buon Campagna*. He is, of all men, if I am not ill informed, the most turbulent, seditious, intriguing, bold, and

Ecclesiastical state.

[5] [Cola di Rienzi (1313–1354) took the title of tribune after displacing the nobles and seizing power in Rome in 1347. He proposed a new Roman empire in which sovereignty would come from the will of the people, but ended up fleeing the city at the end of the year. Burke compares him to Cardinal Ignazio Boncompagni (1743–1790) of Bologna. Burke seems not to have known that the Cardinal was dead.]

desperate. He is not at all made for a Roman of the present day. I think he lately held the first office of their State, that of Great Chamberlain, which is equivalent to High Treasurer. At present he is out of employment, and in disgrace. If he should be elected Pope, or even come to have any weight with a new Pope, he will infallibly conjure up a democratick spirit in that country. He may indeed be able to effect it without these advantages. The next interregnum will probably shew more of him. There may be others of the same character, who have not come to my knowledge. This much is certain, that the Roman people, if once the blind reverence they bear to the sanctity of the Pope, which is their only bridle, should relax, are naturally turbulent, ferocious, and headlong, whilst the police is defective, and the Government feeble and resourceless beyond all imagination.

Spain.

As to Spain, it is a nerveless country. It does not possess the use, it only suffers the abuse of a nobility. For some time, and even before the settlement of the Bourbon Dynasty, that body has been systematically lowered, and rendered incapable by exclusion, and for incapacity excluded from affairs. In this circle the body is in a manner annihilated—and so little means have they of any weighty exertion either to controul or to support the crown, that if they at all interfere, it is only by abetting desperate and mobbish insurrections like that at Madrid which drove Squillace from his place. Florida Blanca is a creature of office, and has little connexion, and no sympathy with that body.

As to the Clergy, they are the only thing in Spain that looks like an independent order, and they are kept in some respect by the Inquisition, the sole but unhappy resource of publick tranquillity and order now remaining in Spain. As in Venice, it is become mostly an engine of State, which indeed to a degree it has always been in Spain. It wars no longer with Jews and Hereticks: It has no such war to carry on. It's great object is to keep atheistick and republican doctrines from making their way in that kingdom. No French book upon any subject can enter there which does not contain such matter. In Spain, the clergy are of moment from their influence, but at the same time with the envy and jealousy that attend great riches and power. Though the Crown has by management with the Pope got a very great share of the ecclesiastical revenues into it's own hands, much still remains to them. There will always be about that Court those who look out to a farther division of the Church property as a resource, and to be obtained by shorter methods than those of negotiations with the Clergy and their Chief. But at present I think it likely that they will stop, lest the business should be taken out of their hands; and lest that body in which remains the only life that exists in Spain, and is not a fever, may with their property lose all the influence necessary to preserve the Monarchy, or being poor and desperate, may employ whatever influence remains to them as active agents in it's destruction.

The Castilians have still remaining a good deal of their old character, their *Gravidad, Lealdad,* and *il Timor de Dios*;[6] but that character neither is, or ever was exactly true, except of the Castilians only. The several kingdoms which compose Spain, have perhaps some features which run through the whole; but they are in many particulars as different as nations who go by different names; the Catalans, for instance, and the Arragonians too, in a good measure have the spirit of the Miquelets, and much more of republicanism than of an attachment to royalty. They are more in the way of trade and intercourse with France; and upon the least internal movement, will disclose and probably let loose a spirit that may throw the whole Spanish Monarchy into convulsions.

Castile different from Catalonia & Arragon.

It is a melancholy reflection that the spirit of melioration which has been going on in that part of Europe, more or less during this century, and the various schemes very lately on foot for further advancement are all put a stop to at once. Reformation certainly is nearly connected with innovation— and where that latter comes in for too large a share, those who

[6] [Gravity, Loyalty, and the Fear of God.]

THOUGHTS ON FRENCH AFFAIRS

undertake to improve their country may risque their own safety. In times where the correction, which includes the confession of an abuse, is turned to criminate the authority which has long suffered it, rather than to honour those who would amend it (which is the spirit of this malignant French distemper) every step out of the common course becomes critical, and renders it a task full of peril for Princes of moderate talents to engage in great undertakings. At present the only safety of Spain is the old national hatred to the French. How far that can be depended upon, if any great ferments should be excited, it is impossible to say.

As to Portugal, she is out of the high road of these politicks—I shall, therefore, not divert my thoughts that way; but return again to the North of Europe, which at present seems the part most interested, and there it appears to me that the French speculation on the northern countries, may be valued in the following, or some such manner.

Denmark.

Sweden.

Denmark and Norway do not appear to furnish any of the materials of a democratick revolution, or the dispositions to it. Denmark can only be *consequentially* affected by any thing done in France; but of Sweden I think quite otherwise. The present power in Sweden is too new a system, and too green and too sore from it's late Revolution, to be considered as perfectly assured. The King by his astonishing activity, his boldness, his decision, his ready versatility, and by rouzing and employing the old military spirit of Sweden, keeps up the top with continual agitation and lashing. The moment it ceases to spin, the Royalty is a dead bit of box. Whenever Sweden is quiet externally for some time, there is great danger that all the republican elements she contains will be animated by the new French spirit, and of this I believe the King is very sensible.

Russia.

The Russian Government is of all others the most liable to be subverted by military seditions, by Court conspiracies, and sometimes by headlong rebellions of the people, such as the turbinating movement of Pugatchef.[7] It is not quite so proba-

[7] [The Pugachev Rebellion (1773–1775) was a large peasant uprising.]

ble that in any of these changes the spirit of system may mingle in the manner it has done in France. The Muscovites are no great speculators—But I should not much rely on their uninquisitive disposition, if any of their ordinary motives to sedition should arise. The little catechism of the Rights of Men is soon learned; and the inferences are in the passions.

Poland, from one cause or another, is always unquiet. **Poland.** The new Constitution only serves to supply that restless people with new means, at least new modes, of cherishing their turbulent disposition. The bottom of the character is the same. It is a great question, whether the joining that Crown with the Electorate of Saxony, will contribute most to **Saxony.** strengthen the Royal authority of Poland, or to shake the Ducal in Saxony. The Elector is a Catholick;[8] the people of Saxony are, six sevenths at the very least, Protestants. He *must* continue a Catholick according to the Polish law, if he accepts that Crown. The pride of the Saxons, formerly flattered by having a Crown in the House of their Prince, though an honour which cost them dear; the German probity, fidelity and loyalty; the weight of the Constitution of the Empire under the Treaty of Westphalia; the good temper and good nature of the Princes of the House of Saxony; had formerly removed from the people all apprehension with regard to their religion, and kept them perfectly quiet, obedient, and even affectionate. The seven years war made some change in the minds of the Saxons. They did not, I believe, regret the loss of what might be considered almost as the succession to the Crown of Poland, the possession of which, by annexing them to a foreign interest, had often obliged them to act an arduous part, towards the support of which that foreign interest afforded no proportionable strength. In this very delicate situation of their political interests, the speculations of the French and German *Oeconomists,* and the cabals, and the secret, as well as public doctrines of the *Illuminatenordens* and *Free Masons,* have made a considerable progress in that country; and a

---

[8] [Frederick Augustus III (1750–1827). His grandfather and great-grandfather, also electors of Saxony, had been elected Kings of Poland.]

turbulent spirit under colour of religion, but in reality arising from the French Rights of Man, has already shewn itself, and is ready on every occasion to blaze out.

The present Elector is a Prince of a safe and quiet temper, of great prudence, and goodness. He knows that in the actual state of things, not the power and respect belonging to Sovereigns, but their very existence depends on a reasonable frugality. It is very certain that not one Sovereign in Europe can either promise for the continuance of his authority in a state of indigence and insolvency, or dares to venture on a new imposition to relieve himself. Without abandoning wholly the ancient magnificence of his Court, the Elector has conducted his affairs with infinitely more oeconomy than any of his predecessors, so as to restore his finances beyond what was thought possible from the state in which the seven years war had left Saxony. Saxony during the whole of that dreadful period having been in the hands of an exasperated enemy, rigorous by resentment, by nature and by necessity, was obliged to bear in a manner the whole burthen of the war; in the intervals when their allies prevailed, the inhabitants of that country were not better treated.

The moderation and prudence of the present Elector, in my opinion, rather perhaps respites the troubles than secures the peace of the Electorate. The offer of the succession to the Crown of Poland is truly critical, whether he accepts, or whether he declines it. If the States will consent to his acceptance, it will add to the difficulties, already great, of his situation between the King of Prussia and the Emperor. But these thoughts lead me too far, when I mean to speak only of the interior condition of these Princes. It has always however some necessary connexion with their foreign politicks.

Holland.

With regard to Holland and the ruling party there, I do not think it at all tainted, or likely to be so except by fear; or that it is likely to be misled unless indirectly and circuitously. But the predominant party in Holland is not Holland. The suppressed faction, though suppressed, exists. Under the ashes, the embers of the late commotion are still warm. This

THOUGHTS ON FRENCH AFFAIRS

Anti-Orange party has from the day of it's origin been French, though alienated in some degree for some time, through the pride and folly of Louis the Fourteenth. It will ever hanker after a French connexion; and now that the internal Government in France has been assimilated in so considerable a degree to that which the immoderate Republicans began so very lately to introduce into Holland, their connexion, as still more natural, will be more desired. I do not well understand the present exterior politicks of the Stadtholder, nor the Treaty into which the newspapers say he has entered for the States with the Emperor. But the Emperor's own politicks with regard to the Netherlands seem to me to be exactly calculated to answer the purpose of the French Revolutionists. He endeavours to crush the Aristocratick party—and to nourish one in avowed connexion with the most furious Democratists in France.

These Provinces in which the French game is so well played, they consider as part of the Old French Empire: certainly they were amongst the oldest parts of it. These they think very well situated, as their party is well-disposed to a re-union. As to the greater nations, they do not aim at making a direct conquest of them, but by disturbing them through a propagation of their principles, they hope to weaken, as they will weaken them, and to keep them in perpetual alarm and agitation, and thus render all their efforts against them utterly impracticable, whilst they extend the dominion of their sovereign anarchy on all sides.

As to England, there may be some apprehension from *England.* vicinity, from constant communication, and from the very name of Liberty, which, as it ought to be very dear to us, in it's worst abuses carries something seductive. It is the abuse of the first and best of the objects which we cherish. I know that many who sufficiently dislike the system of France, have yet no apprehensions of it's prevalence here. I say nothing to the ground of this security in the attachment of the people to their Constitution, and their satisfaction in the discreet portion of liberty which it measures out to them. Upon this I have said all I have to say, in the Appeal I have published. That security is something, and not inconsiderable. But if a storm arises I should not much rely upon it.

There are other views of things which may be used to give us a perfect (though in my opinion a delusive) assurance of our own security. The first of these is from the weakness and ricketty nature of the new system in the place of it's first formation. It is thought that the monster of a Commonwealth cannot possibly live—that at any rate the ill contrivance of their fabrick will make it fall in pieces of itself—that the Assembly must be bankrupt, and that this bankruptcy will totally destroy that system, from the contagion of which apprehensions are entertained.

For my part I have long thought that one great cause of the stability of this wretched scheme of things in France was an opinion that it could not stand; and, therefore, that all external measures to destroy it were wholly useless.

As to the bankruptcy, that event has happened long ago, as much as it is ever likely to happen. So soon as a nation compels a creditor to take paper currency in discharge of his debt, there is a bankruptcy. The compulsory paper has in some degree answered; not because there was a surplus from Church lands, but because faith has not been kept with the Clergy. As to the holders of the old funds, to them the payments will be dilatory, but they will be made, and whatever may be the discount on paper, whilst paper is taken, paper will be issued.

As to the rest, they have shot out three branches of revenue to supply all those which they have destroyed, that is, *the Universal Register of all Transactions,* the heavy and universal *Stamp Duty,* and the new *Territorial Impost,* levied chiefly on the reduced estates of the gentlemen. These branches of the revenue, especially as they take assignats in payment, answer their purpose in a considerable degree, and keep up the credit of their paper; for as they receive it in their treasury, it is in reality funded upon all their taxes and future resources of all kinds, as well as upon the church estates. As this paper is

Thoughts on French Affairs

become in a manner the only visible maintenance of the whole people, the dread of a bankruptcy is more apparently connected with the delay of a counter-revolution, than with the duration of this Republick; because the interest of the new Republick manifestly leans upon it; and in my opinion, the counter-revolution cannot exist along with it. The above three projects ruined some Ministers under the old Government, merely for having conceived them. They are the salvation of the present Rulers.

As the Assembly has laid a most unsparing and cruel hand on all men who have lived by the bounty, the justice, or the abuses of the old Government, they have lessened many expences. The royal establishment, though excessively and ridiculously great for *their* scheme of things, is reduced at least one half; the estates of the King's Brothers, which under the ancient Government had been in truth royal revenues, go to the general stock of the confiscation; and as to the crown lands, though under the Monarchy they never yielded two hundred and fifty thousand a year, by many they are thought at least worth three times as much.

As to the ecclesiastical charge, whether as a compensation for losses, or a provision for religion, of which they made at first a great parade, and entered into a solemn engagement in favour of it, it was estimated at a much larger sum than they could expect from the church property, moveable or immoveable: they are completely bankrupt as to that article. It is just what they wish; and it is not productive of any serious inconvenience. The non-payment produces discontent and occasional sedition; but is only by fits and spasms, and amongst the country people who are of no consequence. These seditions furnish new pretexts for non-payment to the church establishment, and help the Assembly wholly to get rid of the Clergy, and indeed of any form of religion, which is not only their real, but avowed object.

They are embarrassed indeed in the highest degree, but not wholly resourceless. They are without the species of money. Circulation of money is a great convenience, but a substi-

Want of Money how supplied.

tute for it may be found. Whilst the great objects of production and consumption, corn, cattle, wine, and the like, exist in a country, the means of giving them circulation with more or less convenience, cannot be *wholly* wanting. The great confiscation of the church and of the crown lands, and of the appenages of the princes, for the purchase of all which their paper is always received at par, gives means of continually destroying and continually creating, and this perpetual destruction and renovation feeds the speculative market, and prevents, and will prevent, till that fund of confiscation begins to fail, a *total* depreciation.

But all consideration of public credit in France is of little avail at present. The action indeed of the monied interest was of absolute necessity at the beginning of this Revolution; but the French Republicks can stand without any assistance from that description of men, which, as things are now circumstanced, rather stands in need of assistance itself from the power which alone substantially exists in France; I mean the several districts and municipal republicks, and the several clubs which direct all their affairs and appoint their magistrates. This is the power now paramount to every thing, even to the Assembly itself called National, and that to which tribunals, priesthood, laws, finances, and both descriptions of military power, are wholly subservient, so far as the military power of either description yields obedience to any name of authority.

Monied Interest not necessary to them.

The world of contingency and political combination is much larger than we are apt to imagine. We never can say what may, or may not happen, without a view to all the actual circumstances. Experience upon other data than those, is of all things the most delusive. Prudence in new cases can do nothing on grounds of retrospect. A constant vigilance and attention to the train of things as they successively emerge, and to act on what they direct, are the only sure courses. The physician that let blood, and by blood-letting cured one kind of plague, in the next added to it's ravages. That power goes with property is not universally true, and the idea that the operation of it is certain and invariable, may mislead us very fatally.

Whoever will take an accurate view of the state of those Republicks, and of the composition of the present Assembly deputed by them (in which Assembly there are not quite fifty persons possessed of an income amounting to 100l. sterling yearly) must discern clearly, *that the political and civil power of France is wholly separated from it's property of every description*; and of course that neither the landed nor the monied interest possesses the smallest weight or consideration in the direction of any publick concern. The whole kingdom is directed by the *refuse of it's chicane,* with the aid of the bustling, presumptuous young clerks of counting-houses and shops, and some inter-mixture of young gentlemen of the same character in the several towns. The rich peasants are bribed with church lands; and the poorer of that description are, and can be, counted for nothing. They may rise in ferocious, ill-directed tumults—but they can only disgrace themselves and signalize the triumph of their adversaries.

Power separated from Property.

The *truly* active citizens, that is, the above descriptions, are all concerned in intrigue respecting the various objects in their local or their general government. The rota which the French have established for their National Assembly, holds out the highest objects of ambition to such vast multitudes as, in an unexampled measure, to widen the bottom of a new species of interest merely political, and wholly unconnected with birth or property. This scheme of a rota, though it enfee-bles the state, considered as one solid body, and indeed whol-ly disables it from acting as such, gives a great, an equal, and a diffusive strength to the democratick scheme. Seven hun-dred and fifty people, every two years raised to the supreme power, has already produced at least fifteen hundred bold, acting politicians; a great number for even so great a country as France. These men never will quietly settle in ordinary occupations, nor submit to any scheme which must reduce them to an entirely private condition, or to the exercise of a steady, peaceful, but obscure and unimportant industry.

Effect of the Rota.

Whilst they sit in the Assembly they are denied offices of trust and profit—but their short duration makes this no restraint—during their probation and apprenticeship they are all salaried with an income to the greatest part of them immense; and after they have passed the novitiate, those who take any sort of lead are placed in very lucrative offices, according to their influence and credit, or appoint those who divide their profits with them.

This supply of recruits to the corps of the highest civil ambition, goes on with a regular progression. In very few years it must amount to many thousands. These, however, will be as nothing in comparison to the multitude of municipal officers, and officers of district and department, of all sorts, who have tasted of power and profit, and who hunger for the periodical return of the meal. To these needy agitators, the glory of the state, the general wealth and prosperity of the nation, and the rise or fall of publick credit, are as dreams; nor have arguments deduced from these topicks any sort of weight with them. The indifference with which the Assembly regards the state of their Colonies, the only valuable part of the French commerce, is a full proof how little they are likely to be affected by any thing but the selfish game of their own ambition, now universally diffused.

It is true, amidst all these turbulent means of security to their system, very great discontents every where prevail. But they only produce misery to those who nurse them at home, or exile, beggary, and in the end, confiscation, to those who are so impatient as to remove from them. Each Municipal Republick has a Committee, or something in the nature of a *Committee of Research.* In these petty Republicks the tyranny is so near it's object, that it becomes instantly acquainted with every act of every man. It stifles conspiracy in it's very first movements. Their power is absolute and uncontroulable. No stand can be made against it. These Republicks are besides so disconnected, that very little intelligence of what happens in them is to be obtained, beyond their own bounds, except by the means of their clubs, who keep up a constant correspon-

Impractica-
bility of Re-
sistance.

dence, and who give what colour they please to such facts as they choose to communicate out of the track of their correspondence. They all have some sort of communication, just as much or as little as they please, with the center. By this confinement of all communication to the ruling faction, any combination grounded on the abuses and discontents in one, scarcely can reach the other. There is not one man, in any one place, to head them. The old Government had so much abstracted the Nobility from the cultivation of provincial interest, that no man in France exists, whose power, credit or consequence extends to two districts, or who is capable of uniting them in any design, even if any man could assemble ten men together, without being sure of a speedy lodging in a prison. One must not judge of the state of France by what has been observed elsewhere. It does not in the least resemble any other country. Analogical reasoning from history or from recent experience in other places is wholly delusive.

In my opinion there never was seen so strong a government internally as that of the French Municipalities. If ever any rebellion can arise against the present system, it must begin, where the Revolution which gave birth to it did, at the Capital. Paris is the only place in which there is the least freedom of intercourse. But even there, so many servants as any man has, so many spies, and irreconcileable domestick enemies.

But that place being the chief seat of the power and intelligence of the ruling faction, and the place of occasional resort for their fiercest spirits, even there a revolution is not likely to have any thing to feed it. The leaders of the aristocratick party have been drawn out of the kingdom by order of the Princes, on the hopes held out by the Emperor and the King of Prussia at Pilnitz;[9] and as to the democratick factions in Paris, amongst them there are no leaders possessed of an

Gentlemen are Fugitives.

[9] [On August 27, 1791, two months after the attempted flight and recapture of Louis XVI, the Emperor Leopold II and King Frederick William II issued the Declaration of Pillnitz. Leopold, like his predecessor, Joseph II, was brother to Marie Antoinette.]

influence for any other purpose but that of maintaining the present state of things. The moment they are seen to warp, they are reduced to nothing. They have no attached army— no party that is at all personal.

It is not to be imagined because a political system is, under certain aspects, very unwise in it's contrivance, and very mischievous in it's effects, that it therefore can have no long duration. It's very defects may tend to it's stability, because they are agreeable to it's nature. The very faults in the constitution of Poland made it last; the *veto* which destroyed all it's energy preserved it's life. What can be conceived so monstrous as the Republick of Algiers? and that no less strange Republick of the Mammalukes in Egypt? They are of the worst form imaginable, and exercised in the worst manner, yet they have existed as a nuisance on the earth for several hundred years.

From all these considerations, and many more, that croud

Conclusions.
upon me, three conclusions have long since arisen in my mind—

First, that no counter-revolution is to be expected in France from internal causes solely.

Secondly, that the longer the present system exists, the greater will be it's strength; the greater it's power to destroy discontents at home, and to resist all foreign attempts in favour of these discontents.

Thirdly, that as long as it exists in France, it will be the interest of the managers there, and it is in the very essence of their plan, to disturb and distract all other governments, and their endless succession of restless politicians will continually stimulate them to new attempts.

Proceedings
of Princes;
Defensive
Plans.
Princes are generally sensible that this is their common cause; and two of them have made a publick declaration of their opinion to this effect. Against this common danger, some of them, such as the King of Spain, the King of Sardinia, and the Republick of Berne, are very diligent in using defensive measures.

If they were to guard against an invasion from France, the merits of this plan of a merely defensive resistance might be supported by plausible topicks; but as the attack does not operate against these countries externally, but by an internal corruption (a sort of dry rot); they who pursue this merely defensive plan, against a danger which the plan itself supposes to be serious, cannot possibly escape it. For it is in the nature of all defensive measures to be sharp and vigorous under the impressions of the first alarm, and to relax by degrees; until at length the danger, by not operating instantly, comes to appear as a false alarm; so much so that the next menacing appearance will look less formidable, and will be less provided against. But to those who are on the offensive it is not necessary to be always alert. Possibly it is more their interest not to be so. For their unforeseen attacks contribute to their success.

In the mean time a system of French conspiracy is gaining ground in every country. This system happening to be founded on principles the most delusive indeed, but the most flattering to the natural propensities of the unthinking multitude, and to the speculations of all those who think, without thinking very profoundly, must daily extend it's influence. A predominant inclination towards it appears in all those who have no religion, when otherwise their disposition leads them to be advocates even for despotism. Hence Hume, though I cannot say that he does not throw out some expressions of disapprobation on the proceedings of the levellers in the reign of Richard the Second, yet affirms that the doctrines of *John Ball* were "conformable to the ideas of primitive equality, *which are engraven in the hearts of all men.*"

Boldness formerly was not the character of Atheists as such. They were even of a character nearly the reverse; they were formerly like the old Epicureans, rather an unenterprizing race. But of late they are grown active, designing, turbulent and seditious. They are sworn enemies to Kings, Nobility and Priesthood. We have seen all the Academicians at Paris, with Condorcet, the friend and correspondent of Priestley, at their head, the most furious of the extravagant Republicans.

> The French Party how composed.

THOUGHTS ON FRENCH AFFAIRS

Condorcet.

The late Assembly, after the last captivity of the King, had actually chosen this Condorcet by a majority on the ballot, for Preceptor to the Dauphin, who was to be taken out of the hands and direction of his parents, and to be delivered over to this fanatick Atheist, and furious democratick Republican. His untractability to these leaders, and his figure in the Club of Jacobins, which at that time they wished to bring under, alone prevented that part of the arrangement, and others in the same style, from being carried into execution. Whilst he was candidate for this office, he produced his title to it by promulgating the following ideas of the title of his royal pupil to the crown. In a paper written by him, and published with his name, against the re-establishment, even of the appearance of monarchy under any qualifications, He says,

Doctrine of the French.

Jusqu'à ce moment ils [l'Assemblée Nationale] n'ont rien préjugé encore. En se reservant de nommer un Gouverneur au Dauphin, ils n'ont pas prononcé *que cet enfant dût regner*; mais seulement quil *étoit possible* que la Constitution l'y destinât; ils ont voulu que l'éducation, effaçant tout ce que *les prestiges du Trône* ont pu lui inspirer de préjugés sur les droits prétendus de sa naissance, qu'elle lui fit connoître de bonne heure, et *l'Egalité naturelle des Hommes, et la Souveraineté du peuple*; qu'elle lui apprit à ne pas oublier que c'est *du peuple* qu'il tiendra le tître de Roi, et que *le peuple n'a pas même le droit de renoncer à celui de l'en depouiller*.

Ils ont voulu que cette éducation le rendit également digne, par ses lumières, et ses vertus, de recevoir *avec resignation*, le fardeau dangereux d'une couronne, ou de la *déposer avec joie* entre les mains de ces frères, qu'il sentit que le devoir, et la gloire du Roi d'un peuple libre, est de hâter le moment de n'être plus qu'un citoyen ordinaire.

Ils ont voulu que *l'inutilité d'un Roi*, la nécessité de chercher les moyens de remplacer *un pouvoir fondé sur les illusions*, fut une des premières vérités offertes à sa raison; *l'obligation d'y concourir lui même un des premières devoirs de sa morale; et le desir, de n'être plus affranchi du joug de la loi, par une injurieuse inviolabilité, le premier sentiment de son coeur*. Ils n'ignorent pas que dans ce moment il s'agit bien moins de former un Roi que de lui apprendre à *savoir, à vouloir ne plus l'être*.[10]

[10] Until now, they (the National Assembly) have prejudged nothing. Reserving to themselves a right to appoint a Preceptor to the Dauphin, they

THOUGHTS ON FRENCH AFFAIRS

Such are the sentiments of the man who has occasionally filled the chair of the National Assembly, who is their perpetual secretary, their only standing officer, and the most important by far. He leads them to peace or war. He is the great theme of the Republican faction in England. These ideas of M. Condorcet, are the principles of those to whom Kings are to entrust their successors, and the interests of their succession. This man would be ready to plunge the poignard in the heart of his pupil, or to whet the axe for his neck. Of all men, the most dangerous is a warm, hot-headed, zealous Atheist. This sort of man aims at dominion, and his means are, the words he always has in his mouth, "L'égalité naturelle des Hommes, et la Souveraineté du Peuple."

All former attempts grounded on these Rights of Men, had proved unfortunate. The success of this last makes a mighty difference in the effect of the doctrine. Here is a principle of a nature, to the multitude, the most seductive, always existing before their eyes, *as a thing feasible in practice*. After so many failures, such an enterprize previous to the French experiment, carried ruin to the contrivers, on the face of it; and if any enthusiast was so wild as to wish to engage in a scheme of that nature, it was not easy for him to find followers: Now

did not declare that *this child was* to reign; but only that *possibly* the Constitution *might* destine him to it: they willed that while education should efface from his mind all the prejudices arising from *the delusions of the throne* respecting his pretended birth-right, it should also teach him not to forget, that it is *from the people* he is to receive the title of King, and that *the people do not even possess the right of giving up their power to take it from him.*

They willed that this education should render him worthy by his knowledge, and by his virtues, both to receive *with submission* the dangerous burden of a crown, and *to resign* it *with pleasure* into the hands of his brethren; that he should be conscious that the hastening of that moment when he is to be only a common citizen, constitutes the duty and the glory of a King of a free people.

They willed that the *uselessness of a King*, the necessity of seeking means to establish something in lieu of *a power founded on illusions*, should be one of the first truths offered to his reason; *the obligation of conforming himself to this, the first of his moral duties; and the desire of no longer being freed from the yoke of the law, by an injurious inviolability, the first and chief sentiment of his heart.* They are not ignorant that in the present moment the object is less to form a King than to teach him *that he should know how to wish no longer to be such.*

there is a party almost in all countries, ready made, animated with success, with a sure Ally in the very center of Europe. There is no cabal so obscure in any place, that they do not protect, cherish, foster, and endeavour to raise it into importance at home and abroad. From the lowest, this intrigue will creep up to the highest. Ambition, as well as enthusiasm, may find it's account in the party and in the principle.

Character of Ministers.

The Ministers of other Kings, like those of the King of France (not one of whom was perfectly free from this guilt, and some of whom were very deep in it) may themselves be the persons to foment such a disposition and such a faction. Hertzberg, the King of Prussia's late Minister, is so much of what is called a philosopher, that he was of a faction with that sort of politicians in every thing, and in every place. Even when he defends himself from the imputation of giving extravagantly into these principles, he still considers the revolution of France as a great publick good, by giving credit to their fraudulent declaration of their universal benevolence, and love of peace. Nor are his Prussian Majesty's present ministers at all disinclined to the same system. Their ostentatious preamble to certain late edicts, demonstrates (if their actions had not been sufficiently explanatory of their cast of mind) that they are deeply infected with the same distemper of dangerous, because plausible, though trivial, and shallow speculation.

Ministers turning their backs on the reputation which properly belongs to them, aspire at the glory of being speculative writers. The duties of these two situations are, in general, directly opposite to each other. Speculators ought to be neutral. A Minister cannot be so. He is to support the interest of the publick as connected with that of his master. He is his master's trustee, advocate, attorney, and steward—and he is not to indulge in any speculation which contradicts that character or even detracts from its efficacy. Necker had an extreme thirst for this sort of glory; so had others; and this pursuit of a misplaced and misunderstood reputation, was one of the causes of the ruin of these ministers, and of their

THOUGHTS ON FRENCH AFFAIRS

unhappy master. The Prussian ministers in foreign courts, have (at least not long since) talked the most democratick language with regard to France, and in the most unmanaged terms.

The whole corps diplomatique, with very few exceptions, leans that way. What cause produces in them a turn of mind, which at first one would think unnatural to their situation, it is not impossible to explain. The discussion would however be somewhat long and somewhat invidious. The fact itself is indisputable, however they may disguise it to their several courts. This disposition is gone to so very great a length in that corps, in itself so important, and so important as *furnishing* the intelligence which sways all cabinets, that if Princes and States do not very speedily attend with a vigorous controul to that source of direction and information, very serious evils are likely to befal them.

Corps diplomatique.

But indeed Kings are to guard against the same sort of dispositions in themselves. They are very easily alienated from all the higher orders of their subjects, whether civil or military, laick or ecclesiastical. It is with persons of condition that Sovereigns chiefly come into contact. It is from them that they generally experience opposition to their will. It is with *their* pride and impracticability, that Princes are most hurt; it is with *their* servility and baseness, that they are most commonly disgusted; it is from their humours and cabals, that they find their affairs most frequently troubled and distracted. But of the common people in pure monarchical governments, Kings know little or nothing; and therefore being unacquainted with their faults (which are as many as those of the great, and much more decisive in their effects when accompanied with power) Kings generally regard them with tenderness and favour, and turn their eyes towards that description of their subjects, particularly when hurt by opposition from the higher orders. It was thus that the King of France (a perpetual example to all sovereigns) was ruined. I have it from very sure information (and it was indeed obvious enough from the measures which were taken previous to the assem-

Sovereigns—their dispositions.

bly of the States and afterwards) that the King's counsellors had filled him with a strong dislike to his nobility, his clergy, and the corps of his magistracy. They represented to him, that he had tried them all severally, in several ways, and found them all untractable. That he had twice called an Assembly (the Notables) composed of the first men of the clergy, the nobility, and the magistrates; that he had himself named every one member in those assemblies, and that though so picked out, he had not, in this their collective state, found them more disposed to a compliance with his will than they had been separately. That there remained for him, with the least prospect of advantage to his authority in the States General, which were to be composed of the same sorts of men, but not chosen by him, only the *Tiers Etat*. In this alone he could repose any hope of extricating himself from his difficulties, and of settling him in a clear and permanent authority. They represented (these are the words of one of my informants) "That the Royal Authority compressed with the weight of these aristocratick bodies, full of ambition, and of faction, when once unloaded, would rise of itself, and occupy it's natural place without disturbance or controul": That the common people would protect, cherish, and support, instead of crushing it. "The people," (it was said) "could entertain no objects of ambition"; they were out of the road of intrigue and cabal; and could possibly have no other view than the support of the mild and parental authority by which they were invested, for the first time collectively with real importance in the State, and protected in their peaceable and useful employments.

King of
France.

This unfortunate King (not without a large share of blame to himself) was deluded to his ruin by a desire to humble and reduce his Nobility, Clergy, and his corporate Magistracy; not that I suppose he meant wholly to eradicate these bodies, in the manner since effected by the Democratick power: I rather believe that even Necker's designs did not go to that extent. With his own hand, however, Louis the XVIth pulled down the pillars which upheld his throne; and this he did, because he could not bear the inconveniences which are attached to every thing human; because he found himself cooped up, and in durance by those limits which nature prescribes to desire and imagination; and was taught to consider as low and degrading, that mutual dependance which Providence has ordained that all men should have on one another. He is not at this minute perhaps cured of the dread of the power and credit like to be acquired by those who would save and rescue him. He leaves those who suffer in his cause to their fate; and hopes by various mean delusive intrigues in which I am afraid he is encouraged from abroad, to regain, among Traitors and Regicides, the power he has joined to take from his own family, whom he quietly sees proscribed before his eyes, and called to answer to the lowest of his rebels, as the vilest of all criminals.

It is to be hoped that the Emperor may be taught better things by this fatal example. But it is sure that he has advisers who endeavour to fill him with the ideas which have brought his brother-in-law to his present situation. Joseph the Second was far gone in this philosophy, and some, if not most who serve the Emperor, would kindly initiate him into all the mysteries of this free-masonry. They would persuade him to look on the National Assembly not with the hatred of an enemy, but the jealousy of a rival. They would make him desirous of doing, in his own dominions, by a Royal despotism, what has been done in France by a Democratick. Rather than abandon such enterprises, they would persuade him to a strange alliance between those extremes. Their grand object being now, as in his brother's time, at any rate to destroy the higher orders, they think he cannot compass this end, as certainly he cannot, without elevating the lower. By depressing the one and by raising the other, they hope in the first place to encrease his treasures and his army; and with these common instruments of Royal Power they flatter him that the Democracy which they help, in his name, to create, will give him but little trouble. In defiance of the freshest experience, which might shew him that old impossibilities are become modern

Emperor.

probabilities, and that the extent to which evil principles may go, when left to their own operation, is beyond the power of calculation, they will endeavour to persuade him that such a Democracy is a thing which cannot subsist by itself; that in whosever hands the military command is placed, he must be in the necessary course of affairs, sooner or later the master; and that being the master of various unconnected countries, he may keep them all in order by employing a military force, which to each of them is foreign. This maxim too, however formerly plausible, will not now hold water. This scheme is full of intricacy, and may cause him every where to lose the hearts of his people. These Counsellors forget that a corrupted army was the very cause of the ruin of his brother-in-law; and that he is himself far from secure from a similar corruption.

Brabant.

Instead of reconciling himself heartily and *bona fide* according to the most obvious rules of policy to the States of Brabant *as they are constituted,* and who in the *present state of things* stand on the same foundation with the Monarchy itself, and who might have been gained with the greatest facility, they have advised him to the most unkingly proceeding which, either in a good or in a bad light, has ever been attempted.[11] Under a pretext taken from the spirit of the lowest chicane, they have counselled him wholly to break the publick faith, to annul the amnesty, as well as the other conditions through which he obtained an entrance into the Provinces of the Netherlands, under the guarantee of Great Britain and Prussia. He is made to declare his adherence to the indemnity in a criminal sense, but he is to keep alive in his own name, and to encourage in others a *civil* process in the nature of an action of damages for what has been suffered during the troubles. Whilst he keeps up this hopeful law-suit in view of the damages he may recover against individuals, he loses the hearts of a whole people, and the vast subsidies which his ancestors had been used to receive from them.

[11] [In November 1789, Joseph II abolished the constitution of Brabant.]

Thoughts on French Affairs

This design once admitted, unriddles the mystery of the whole conduct of the Emperor's Ministers with regard to France. As soon as they saw the life of the King and Queen of France no longer as they thought in danger, they entirely changed their plan with regard to the French nation. I believe that the chiefs of the Revolution (those who led the Constituting Assembly) have contrived as far as they can do it, to give the Emperor satisfaction on this head. He keeps a continual tone and posture of menace to secure this his only point. But it must be observed, that he all along grounds his departure from the engagement at Pilnitz to the Princes, on the will and actions of *the King* and the majority of the people, without any regard to the natural and constitutional orders of the State, or to the opinions of the whole House of Bourbon. Though it is manifestly under the constraint of imprisonment and the fear of death, that this unhappy man has been guilty of all those humilities which have astonished mankind, the advisers of the Emperor will consider nothing but the *physical* person of Louis, which, even in his present degraded and infamous state, they regard as of sufficient authority to give a compleat sanction to the persecution and utter ruin of all his family, and of every person who has shewn any degree of attachment or fidelity to him, or to his cause; as well as competent to destroy the whole antient constitution and frame of the French monarchy.

The present policy therefore of the Austrian politicians, is to recover despotism through democracy; or at least, at any expence, every where to ruin the description of men who are every where the objects of their settled and systematick aversion, but more especially in the Netherlands. Compare this with the Emperor's refusing at first all intercourse with the present powers in France, with his endeavouring to excite all Europe against them, and then his not only withdrawing all assistance and all countenance from the fugitives who had been drawn by his declarations from their houses, situations, and military commissions, many even from the means of

Emperor's conduct with regard to France.

THOUGHTS ON FRENCH AFFAIRS

their very existence, but treating them with every species of insult and outrage.

Combining this unexampled conduct in the Emperor's advisers, with the timidity (operating as perfidy) of the King of France, a fatal example is held out to all subjects, tending to shew what little support, or even countenance they are to expect from those for whom their principle of fidelity may induce them to risque life and fortune. The Emperor's advisers would not for the world rescind one of the acts of this or of the late French Assembly; nor do they wish any thing better at present for their master's brother of France, than that he should really be, as he is nominally, at the head of the system of persecution of religion and good order, and of all descriptions of dignity, natural and instituted; they only wish all this done with a little more respect to the King's person, and with more appearance of consideration for his new subordinate office; in hopes that yielding himself for the present, to the persons who have effected these changes, he may be able to game for the rest hereafter. On no other principles than these, can the conduct of the Court of Vienna be accounted for. The subordinate Court of Brussels talks the language of a club of Feuillans and Jacobins.

In this state of general rottenness among subjects, and of delusion and false politicks in Princes, comes a new experiment. The King of France is in the hands of the Chiefs of the Regicide Faction, the Barnaves, Lameths, Fayettes, Perigords, Duports, Robespierre's, Camus's, &c. &c. &c. They who had imprisoned, suspended, and conditionally deposed him, are his confidential counsellors. The next desperate of the desperate rebels, call themselves the *Moderate* Party. They are the Chiefs of the first Assembly, who are confederated to support their power during their suspension from the present, and to govern the existent body with as sovereign a sway as they had done the last. They have, for the greater part, succeeded; and they have many advantages towards procuring their success in future. Just before the close of their regular power, they bestowed some appearance of prerogatives

Moderate party.

THOUGHTS ON FRENCH AFFAIRS

on the King, which in their first plans they had refused to him; particularly the mischievous, and in his situation, dreadful prerogative of a *Veto*. This prerogative (which they hold as their bit in the mouth of the National Assembly for the time being) without the direct assistance of their Club, it was impossible for the King to shew even the desire of exerting with the smallest effect, or even with safety to his person. However, by playing through this *Veto*, the Assembly against the King, and the King against the Assembly, they have made themselves masters of both. In this situation, having destroyed the old Government by their sedition, they would preserve as much of order as is necessary for the support of their own usurpation.

It is believed that this, by far the worst party of the miscreants of France, has received direct encouragement from the counsellors who betray the Emperor. Thus strengthened by the possession of the captive King (now captive in his mind as well as in body) and by a good hope of the Emperor, they intend to send their Ministers to every Court in Europe; having sent before them such a denunciation of terror and superiority to every nation without exception, as has no example in the diplomatick world. Hitherto the Ministers to foreign Courts had been of the appointment of the Sovereign of France *previous to the Revolution*; and either from inclination, duty or decorum, most of them were contented with a merely passive obedience to the new power. At present the King being entirely in the hands of his jailors, and his mind broken to his situation, can send none but the enthusiasts of the system—men framed by the secret Committee of the Feuillans, who meet in the house of Madame de Stahl, Mr. Necker's daughter. Such is every man whom they have talked of sending hither. These Ministers will be so many spies and incendiaries; so many active emissaries of Democracy. Their houses will become places of rendezvous here, as every where else, and centers of cabal for whatever is mischievous and malignant in this country, particularly among those of rank and fashion. As the Minister of the National Assembly will be ad-

French Ambassador.

THOUGHTS ON FRENCH AFFAIRS

mitted at this Court, at least with his usual rank, and as enter-
tainments will be naturally given and received by the King's
own Ministers, any attempt to discountenance the resort of
other people to that Minister would be ineffectual, and indeed absurd, and full of contradiction. The women who come
with these Ambassadors will assist in fomenting factions
amongst ours, which cannot fail of extending the evil. Some
of them I hear are already arrived. There is no doubt they will
do as much mischief as they can.

Connexion
of Clubs.

    Whilst the publick Ministers are received under the gener-
al law of the communication between nations, the correspondences between the factious clubs in France and ours, will be,
as they now are, kept up: but this pretended embassy will be a
closer, more steady and more effectual link between the partizans of the new system on both sides of the water. I do not
mean that these Anglo Gallick clubs in London, Manchester,
&c. are not dangerous in a high degree. The appointment of
festive anniversaries has ever in the sense of mankind been
held the best method of keeping alive the spirit of any institution. We have one settled in London; and at the last of them,
that of the 14th of July, the strong discountenance of Government, the unfavourable time of the year, and the then uncertainty of the disposition of foreign Powers, did not hinder the
meeting of at least nine hundred people, with good coats on
their backs, who could afford to pay half a guinea a head to
shew their zeal for the new principles. They were with great
difficulty, and all possible address, hindered from inviting the
French Ambassador. His real indisposition, besides the fear of
offending any party, sent him out of town. But when our
Court shall have recognized a Government in France, founded on the principles announced in Montmorin's Letter, how
can the French Ambassador be frowned upon for an attend-
ance on those meetings wherein the establishment of the Government he represents is celebrated? An event happened a
few days ago, which in many particulars was very ridiculous;
yet even from the ridicule and absurdity of the proceedings, it
marks the more strongly the spirit of the French Assembly. I

mean the reception they have given to the Frith-Street Alliance.[12] This, though the delirium of a low, drunken alehouse-club, they have publicly announced as a formal alliance with the people of England, as such ordered it to be presented to their King, and to be published in every province in France. This leads more directly and with much greater force than any proceeding with a regular and rational appearance, to two very material considerations. First, it shews that they are of opinion that the current opinions of the English have the greatest influence on the minds of the people in France, and indeed of all the people in Europe, since they catch with such astonishing eagerness at every the most trifling shew of such opinions in their favour. Next, and what appears to me to be full as important, it shews that they are willing publickly to countenance and even to adopt every factious conspiracy that can be formed in this nation, however low and base in itself, in order to excite in the most miserable wretches here, an idea of their own sovereign importance, and to encourage them to look up to France, whenever they may be matured into something of more force, for assistance in the subversion of their domestick Government. This address of the alehouse-club was actually proposed and accepted by the Assembly as an *alliance*. The procedure was in my opinion a high misdemeanor in those who acted thus in England, if they were not so very low and so very base, that no acts of theirs can be called high, even as a description of criminality; and the Assembly in accepting, proclaiming and publishing this forged alliance, has been guilty of a plain aggression, which would justify our Court in demanding a direct disavowal, if our policy should not lead us to wink at it.

Whilst I look over this paper to have it copied, I see a Manifesto of the Assembly, as a preliminary to a declaration

[12] [The "Frith Street Alliance" or "Club of Constitutional Whigs" had written, on October 15, 1791, to the National Assembly, who mistook them for the Whig Club. *The Times* reported that it was made up of "fifteen or sixteen journeymen Barbers, Bakers, and Carpenters." See *Corr.* Copeland 6:465n4.]

of war against the German Princes on the Rhine. This Manifesto contains the whole substance of the French politicks with regard to foreign States. They have ordered it to be circulated amongst the people in every country of Europe— even previously to it's acceptance by the King and his new Privy Council, the club of the Feuillans. Therefore, as a summary of their policy avowed by themselves, let us consider some of the circumstances attending that piece, as well as the spirit and temper of the piece itself.

It was preceded by a speech from Brissot, full of unexampled insolence towards all the Sovereign States of Germany, if not of Europe. The Assembly, to express their satisfaction in the sentiments which it contained, ordered it to be printed. This Brissot had been in the lowest and basest employ under the deposed Monarchy; a sort of thieftaker, or spy of police, in which character he acted after the manner of persons in that description. He had been employed by his master, the Lieutenant de Police, for a considerable time in London, in the same or some such honourable occupation. The Revolution which has brought forward all merit of that kind, raised him, with others of a similar class and disposition, to fame and eminence. On the Revolution he became a publisher of an infamous newspaper, which he still continues. He is charged, and I believe justly, as the first mover of the troubles in Hispaniola. There is no wickedness, if I am rightly informed, in which he is not versed, and of which he is not perfectly capable. His quality of news-writer, now an employment of the first dignity in France, and his practices and principles, procured his election into the Assembly, where he is one of the leading members. Mr. Condorcet produced on the same day a draft of a Declaration to the King, which the Assembly published before it was presented.

Condorcet (though no Marquis, as he styled himself before the Revolution) is a man of another sort of birth, fashion, and occupation from Brissot; but in every principle, and in every disposition to the lowest as well as the highest and most determined villainies, fully his equal. He seconds Bris-

Declaration against the Emperor.

THOUGHTS ON FRENCH AFFAIRS

sot in the Assembly, and is at once his coadjutor and his rival in a newspaper, which in his own name and as successor to Mr. Garat, a Member also of the Assembly, he has just set up in that Empire of Gazettes. Condorcet was chosen to draw the first Declaration presented by the Assembly to the King, as a threat to the Elector of Treves, and the other Princes on the Rhine. In that piece, in which both Feuillans and Jacobins concurred, they declared publickly, and most proudly and insolently, the principle on which they mean to proceed in their future disputes with any of the Sovereigns of Europe, for they say, "That it is not with fire and sword they mean to attack their territories, but by what will be *more dreadful* to them, the introduction of liberty." I have not the paper by me to give the exact words—but I believe they are nearly as I state them. *Dreadful* indeed will be their hostility, if they should be able to carry it on according to the example of *their* modes of introducing liberty. They have shewn a perfect model of their whole design, very complete, though in little. This gang of murderers and savages have wholly laid waste and utterly ruined the beautiful and happy country of the Comtat Venaissin and the city of Avignon. This cruel and treacherous outrage the Sovereigns of Europe, in my opinion, with a great mistake of their honour and interest, have permitted even without a remonstrance to be carried to the desired point, on the principles on which they are now themselves threatened in their own States; and this, because, according to the poor and narrow spirit now in fashion, their brother Sovereign, whose subjects have been thus traiterously and inhumanly treated in violation of the law of nature and of nations, has a name somewhat different from theirs, and instead of being styled King or Duke, or Landgrave, is usually called Pope.

The Electors of Treves and Mentz were frightened with the menace of a similar mode of war. The Assembly, however, not thinking that the Electors of Treves and Mentz had done enough under their first terror, have again brought forward Condorcet, preceded by Brissot, as I have

State of the Empire.

just stated. The Declaration which they have ordered now to be circulated in all countries, is in substance the same as the first, but still more insolent, because more full of detail. There they have the impudence to state that they aim at no conquest; insinuating that all the old lawful Powers of the World had each made a constant open profession of a design of subduing his neighbours. They add, that if they are provoked, their war will be directed only against those who assume to be *Masters*. But to the *People* they will bring peace, law, liberty, &c. &c. There is not the least hint that they consider those whom they call persons *"assuming to be Masters,"* to be the lawful Government of their country, or persons to be treated with the least management or respect. They regard them as usurpers and enslavers of the people. If I do not mistake they are described by the name of tyrants in Condorcet's first draft. I am sure they are so in Brissot's speech, ordered by the Assembly to be printed at the same time and for the same purposes. The whole is in the same strain, full of false philosophy and false rhetorick, both however calculated to captivate and influence the vulgar mind, and to excite sedition in the countries in which it is ordered to be circulated. Indeed it is such, that if any of the lawful acknowledged Sovereigns of Europe had publickly ordered such a manifesto to be circulated in the dominions of another, the Ambassador of that power would instantly be ordered to quit every Court without an audience.

Effect of Fear on the Sovereign Powers.

The powers of Europe have a pretext for concealing their fears, by saying that this language is not used by the King; though they well know that there is in effect no such person, that the Assembly is in reality, and by that King is acknowledged to be *the Master,* that what he does is but matter of formality, and that he can neither cause nor hinder, accelerate or retard any measure whatsoever, nor add to or soften the manifesto which the Assembly has directed to be published, with the declared purpose of exciting mutiny and rebellion in the several countries governed by these powers. By the generality also of the menaces contained in this paper (though infinitely aggravating the outrage) they hope to re-move from each power separately the idea of a distinct af-front. The persons first pointed at by the menace are certain-ly the Princes of Germany, who harbour the persecuted house of Bourbon and the Nobility of France; the declara-tion, however, is general, and goes to every state with which they may have a cause of quarrel. But the terror of France has fallen upon all nations. A few months since all Sovereigns seemed disposed to unite against her, at present they all seem to combine in her favour. At no period has the power of France ever appeared with so formidable an aspect. In partic-ular the liberties of the Empire can have nothing more than an existence the most tottering and precarious, whilst France exists with a great power of fomenting rebellion, and the greatest in the weakest; but with neither power nor disposi-tion to support the smaller states in their independence against the attempts of the more powerful.

I wind up all in a full conviction within my own breast, and the substance of which I must repeat over and over again, that the state of France is the first consideration in the politicks of Europe, and of each state, externally as well as internally con-sidered.

Most of the topicks I have used are drawn from fear and apprehension. Topicks derived from fear or addressed to it, are, I well know, of doubtful appearance. To be sure, hope is in general the incitement to action. Alarm some men— you do not drive them to provide for their security; you put them to a stand; you induce them not to take measures to prevent the approach of danger, but to remove so unpleas-ant an idea from their minds; you persuade them to remain as they are, from a new fear that their activity may bring on the apprehended mischief before it's time. I confess freely that this evil sometimes happens from an overdone precau-tion; but it is when the measures are rash, ill chosen, or ill combined, and the effects rather of blind terror than of enlightened foresight. But the few to whom I wish to submit my thoughts, are of a character which will enable them to see danger without astonishment, and to provide against it without perplexity.

To what lengths this method of circulating mutinous manifestos, and of keeping emissaries of sedition in every Court under the name of Ambassadors, to propagate the same principles and to follow the practices, will go, and how soon they will operate, it is hard to say—but go on it will—more or less rapidly, according to events, and to the humour of the time. The Princes menaced with the revolt of their subjects, at the same time that they have obsequiously obeyed the sovereign mandate of the new Roman Senate, have received with distinction, in a publick character, Ambassadors from those who in the same act had circulated the manifesto of sedition in their dominions. This was the only thing wanting to the degradation and disgrace of the Germanick Body.

The Ambassadors from the Rights of Man, and their admission into the diplomatick system, I hold to be a new aera in this business. It will be the most important step yet taken to affect the existence of Sovereigns, and the higher classes of life—I do not mean to exclude it's effects upon all classes—but the first blow is aimed at the more prominent parts in the ancient order of things.

What is to be done?

It would be presumption in me to do more than to make a case. Many things occur. But as they, like all political measures, depend on dispositions, tempers, means, and external circumstances, for all their effect, not being well assured of these, I do not know how to let loose any speculations of mine on the subject. The evil is stated in my opinion as it exists. The remedy must be where power, wisdom and information, I hope are more united with good intentions than they can be with me. I have done with this subject, I believe for ever. It has given me many anxious moments for the two last years. If a great change is to be made in human affairs, the minds of men will be fitted to it; the general opinions and feelings will draw that way. Every fear, every hope, will forward it; and

THOUGHTS ON FRENCH AFFAIRS

then they who persist in opposing this mighty current in human affairs, will appear rather to resist the decrees of Providence itself, than the mere designs of men. They will not be resolute and firm, but perverse and obstinate.

6

LETTER TO WILLIAM ELLIOT

May 1795

*A*s the revolutionary decade wore on, Burke grew increasingly
despondent over the aptitude of the British revolutionaries for forming clubs, societies, and informal ideological alliances, while his political allies either languished or lashed out in shortsighted reaction.
Burke had hoped his son Richard would become a leader, especially
among younger men, to oppose radicals like Joseph Priestley, Thomas
Paine, and their followers in the Revolution Society. Richard's death
in August 1794, however, forced Burke to turn to others, including
William Elliot.

Burke's hopes were being dashed on the international as well as
on the domestic front. The German powers and Russia had never been
able to overcome their mutual suspicion or their desire for Polish land.
By late 1794 the First Coalition had broken up when Prussia sued for
peace with France. The resulting Treaty of Basle (April 5, 1795), to
which this letter refers, effectively annulled the Declaration of
Pillnitz, which had united the Austrian Emperor and Prussian King
since August 1791.

The immediate motive for Burke's letter was a speech on May 8,
1795, by the Duke of Norfolk, designated in the text below by "His
Grace" and by asterisks. The speech had condemned the **Reflections**
for "inculcating principles and broaching doctrines, not only subversive of the constitutional rights of Englishmen, but diametrically contradictory to the whig principles which he in common with his party,
professed."

The Letter *laments the willingness of the European monarchies to abandon their principles in the face of revolutionary propaganda. It describes the fundamental importance of a proper education, of the security of property, and of religion to a free people. Finally, it calls for a new leader possessed of civic courage and piety toward ancient practices, symbolized by Judas Maccabeus.*

LETTER TO WILLIAM ELLIOT

Beaconsfield, May 26, 1795

M Y DEAR SIR,

I have been told of the voluntary, which, for the entertainment of the House of Lords, has been lately played by His
Grace the **** of *******, a great deal at my expence, and a
little at his own. I confess I should have liked the composition
rather better, if it had been quite new. But every man has his
taste, and His Grace is an admirer of antient musick.

There may be sometimes too much even of a good thing.
A toast is good, and a bumper is not bad: but the best toasts
may be so often repeated as to disgust the palate, and cease-
less rounds of bumpers may nauseate and overload the stomach. The ears of the most steady-voting politicians may at last
be stunned with three times three. I am sure I have been very
grateful for the flattering remembrance made of me in the
toasts of the Revolution Society, and of other clubs formed on
the same laudable plan. After giving the brimming honours
to Citizen Thomas Paine, and to Citizen Dr. Priestley, the
gentlemen of these clubs seldom failed to bring me forth in
my turn, and to drink, "Mr. Burke, and thanks to him for the
discussion he has provoked."

I found myself elevated with this honour; for even by the
collision of resistance, to be the means of striking out sparkles
of truth, if not merit, is at least felicity.

LETTER TO WILLIAM ELLIOT

Here I might have rested. But when I found that the great advocate, Mr. Erskine,[1] condescended to resort to these bumper toasts, as the pure and exuberant fountains of politicks and of rhetorick (as I hear he did, in three or four speeches made in defence of certain worthy citizens), I was rather let down a little. Though still somewhat proud of myself, I was not quite so proud of my voucher. Though he is no idolater of fame, in some way or other, Mr. Erskine will always do himself honour. Methinks, however, in following the precedents of these toasts, he seemed to do more credit to his diligence, as a special pleader, than to his invention as an orator. To those who did not know the abundance of his resources, both of genius and erudition, there was something in it that indicated the want of a good assortment, with regard to richness and variety, in the magazine of topicks and commonplaces, which I suppose he keeps by him, in imitation of Cicero and other renowned declaimers of antiquity.

Mr. Erskine supplied something, I allow, from the stores of his imagination, in metamorphosing the jovial toasts of clubs, into solemn special arguments at the bar. So far the thing shewed talent: however I must still prefer the bar of the tavern to the other bar. The toasts at the first hand were better than the arguments at the second. Even when the toasts began to grow old as sarcasms, they were washed down with still older pricked election port; then the acid of the wine made some amends for the want of any thing piquant in the wit. But when His Grace gave them a second transformation, and brought out the vapid stuff, which had wearied the clubs and disgusted the courts; the drug made up of the bottoms of rejected bottles, all smelling so woefully of the cork and of the cask, and of every thing except the honest old lamp, and when that sad draught had been farther infected with the gaol pollution of the Old Bailey, and was dashed and brewed,

---

[1] [Thomas Erskine, first Baron Erskine (1750–1823), was a Whig member of Parliament and an early admirer of the French Revolution. In the autumn of 1794, at the Old Bailey, he successfully defended the radicals Thomas Hardy, John Horne Tooke, and John Thelwall against criminal charges.]

Letter to William Elliot

and ineffectually stummed again into a senatorial exordium in the House of Lords, I found all the high flavour and mantling of my honours, tasteless, flat, and stale. Unluckily, the new tax on wine is felt even in the greatest fortunes, and His Grace submits to take up with the heel-taps of Mr. Erskine.

I have had the ill or good fortune to provoke two great men of this age to the publication of their opinions; I mean, Citizen Thomas Paine, and His Grace the **** of *******. I am not so great a leveller as to put these two great men on a par, either in the state, or the republick of letters: but, "the field of glory is a field for all."² It is a large one indeed, and we all may run, God knows where, in chace of glory, over the boundless expanse of that wild heath, whose horizon always flies before us. I assure His Grace (if he will yet give me leave to call him so) whatever may be said on the authority of the clubs, or of the bar, that Citizen Paine (who, they will have it, hunts with me in couples, and who only moves as I drag him along), has a sufficient activity in his own native benevolence to dispose and enable him to take the lead for himself. He is ready to blaspheme his God, to insult his king, and to libel the constitution of his country, without any provocation from me, or any encouragement from His Grace. I assure him, that I shall not be guilty of the injustice of charging Mr. Paine's next work against religion and human society, upon His Grace's excellent speech in the House of Lords. I farther assure this noble Duke, that I neither encouraged nor provoked that worthy citizen to seek for plenty, liberty, safety, justice or lenity, in the famine, in the prisons, in the decrees of convention, in the revolutionary tribunal, and in the guillotine of Paris, rather than quietly to take up with what he could find in the glutted markets, the unbarricadoed streets, the drowsy Old Bailey judges, or, at worst, the airy, wholesome pillory of Old England. The choice of country was his own taste. The writings were the effects of his own zeal. In spite of his friend Dr. Priestley, he was a free agent. I admit, indeed, that my

² [Alexander Pope, *The Dunciad* (1743) 2:32.]

praises of the British government loaded with all its encumbrances; clogged with its peers and its beef; its parsons and its pudding; its Commons and its beer; and its dull slavish liberty of going about just as one pleases, had something to provoke a Jockey of Norfolk,[3] who was inspired with the resolute ambition of becoming a citizen of France, to do something which might render him worthy of naturalization in that grand asylum of persecuted merit: something which should intitle him to a place in the senate of the adoptive country of all the gallant, generous and humane. This, I say, was possible. But the truth is (with great deference to His Grace I say it) Citizen Paine acted without any provocation at all; he acted solely from the native impulses of his own excellent heart.

His Grace, like an able orator, as he is, begins with giving me a great deal of praise for talents which I do not possess. He does this to intitle himself, on the credit of this gratuitous kindness, to exaggerate my abuse of the parts which his bounty, and not that of nature has bestowed upon me. In this, too, he has condescended to copy Mr. Erskine. These priests (I hope they will excuse me: I mean priests of the Rights of Man) begin by crowning me with their flowers and their fillets, and bedewing me with their odours, as a preface to their knocking me on the head with their consecrated axes. I have injured, say they, the Constitution; and I have abandoned the whig party and the whig principles that I professed. I do not mean, my dear sir, to defend myself against His Grace. I have not much interest in what the world shall think or say of me; as little has the world an interest in what I shall think or say of any one in it; and I wish that His Grace had suffered an unhappy man to enjoy, in his retreat, the melancholy privileges of obscurity and sorrow. At any rate, I have spoken, and I have written on the subject. If I have written or spoken so poorly as to be quite forgot, a fresh apology will not make a more lasting impression. "I must let the tree lie as it falls." Perhaps I must take some shame to myself. I confess that I

[3] Mr. Paine is a Norfolk man, from Thetford.

LETTER TO WILLIAM ELLIOT

have acted on my own principles of government, and not on those of His Grace, which are, I dare say, profound and wise; but which I do not pretend to understand. As to the party to which he alludes, and which has long taken its leave of me, I believe the principles of the book which he condemns, are very conformable to the opinions of many of the most considerable and most grave in that description of politicians. A few indeed, who, I admit, are equally respectable in all points, differ from me, and talk His Grace's language. I am too feeble to contend with them. They have the field to themselves. There are others very young and very ingenious persons, who form, probably, the largest part of what His Grace, I believe, is pleased to consider as that party. Some of them were not born into the world, and all of them were children, when I entered into that connexion. I give due credit to the censorial brow, to the broad phylacteries, and to the imposing gravity of those magisterial rabbins and doctors in the cabala of political science. I admit that "wisdom is as the grey hair to man, and that learning is like honourable old age."[4] But, at a time when liberty is a good deal talked of, perhaps I might be excused, if I caught something of the general indocility. It might not be surprising, if I lengthened my chain a link or two, and in an age of relaxed discipline, gave a trifling indulgence to my own notions. If that could be allowed, perhaps I might sometimes (by accident, and without an unpardonable crime) trust as much to my own very careful and very laborious, though, perhaps, somewhat purblind disquisitions, as to their soaring, intuitive, eagle-eyed authority; but the modern liberty is a precious thing. It must not be profaned by too vulgar an use. It belongs only to the chosen few, who are born to the hereditary representation of the whole democracy, and who leave nothing at all, no, not the offal, to us poor outcasts of the plebeian race.

Amongst those gentlemen who came to authority, as soon, or sooner than they came of age, I do not mean to

4 [Cf. Ecclesiasticus. 6:18.]

include His Grace. With all those native titles to empire over our minds which distinguish the others, he has a large share of experience. He certainly ought to understand the British Constitution better than I do. He has studied it in the fundamental part. For one election I have seen, he has been concerned in twenty.[5] Nobody is less of a visionary theorist; nobody has drawn his speculations more from practice. No Peer has condescended to superintend with more vigilance the declining franchises of the poor Commons. "With thrice great Hermes he has out-watched the bear."[6] Often have his candles been burned to the snuff, and glimmered and stunk in the sockets, whilst he grew pale at his constitutional studies; long sleepless nights has he wasted; long, laborious, shiftless journies has he made, and great sums has he expended, in order to secure the purity, the independence, and the sobriety of elections, and to give a check, if possible, to the ruinous charges that go nearly to the destruction of the right of election itself.

Amidst these his labours, his Grace will be pleased to forgive me, if my zeal, less enlightened to be sure than his by midnight lamps and studies, has presumed to talk too favourably of this Constitution, and even to say something sounding like approbation of that body which has the honour to reckon his Grace at the head of it. Those who dislike this partiality, or, if his Grace pleases, this flattery of mine, have a comfort at hand. I may be refuted and brought to shame by the most convincing of all refutations, a practical refutation. Every individual Peer for himself may shew that I was ridiculously wrong; the whole body of those noble persons may refute me for the whole corps. If they please, they are more powerful advocates against themselves, than a thousand scribblers like me can be in their favour. If I were even possessed of those powers which his Grace, in order to heighten my offence, is

[5] [Burke's remark refers to the nobility's increasingly unpopular practice (of which Burke himself had benefited) of bestowing the parliamentary seats in pocket boroughs upon their party associates.]

[6] [See Milton, "Il Penseroso," ll. 87–88.]

LETTER TO WILLIAM ELLIOT

pleased to attribute to me, there would be little difference. The eloquence of Mr. Erskine might save Mr. ***** from the gallows, but no eloquence could save Mr. Jackson from the effects of his own potion.[7]

In that unfortunate book of mine, which is put in the *index expurgatorius* of the modern whigs, I might have spoken too favourably not only of those who wear coronets, but of those who wear crowns. Kings however have not only long arms, but strong ones too. A great Northern Potentate for instance, is able in one moment, and with one bold stroke of his diplomatick pen, to efface all the volumes which I could write in a century, or which the most laborious publicists of Germany ever carried to the fair of Leipsick, as an apology for monarchs and monarchy. Whilst I, or any other poor puny private sophist, was defending the declaration of Pilnitz, his Majesty might refute me by the treaty of Bâsle. Such a monarch may destroy one republick because it had a king at its head, and he may balance this extraordinary act by founding another republick that has cut off the head of its king. I defended that great Potentate for associating in a grand alliance for the preservation of the old governments of Europe; but he puts me to silence by delivering up all those governments (his own virtually included) to the new system of France. If he is accused before the Parisian tribunal (constituted for the trial of kings) for having polluted the soil of liberty by the tracks of his disciplined slaves, he clears himself by surrendering the finest parts of Germany (with a handsome cut of his own territories) to the offended majesty of the regicides of France. Can I resist this? Am I responsible for it, if with a torch in his hand, and a rope about his neck, he makes *amende honorable* to the *Sans-Culotterie* of the republick one and indivisible? In that humiliating attitude, in spite of my protests, he may supplicate pardon for his menacing proclamations;

[7] [The Rev. William Jackson, a French agent who had communicated with leading Irish radicals, was brought to trial for treason in 1795 but committed suicide before his sentence could be passed. See *Corr.* Copeland 8:41. In the next paragraph, Burke's "unfortunate book" is the *Reflections*.]

and as an expiation to those whom he failed to terrify with his threats, he may abandon those whom he had seduced by his promises. He may sacrifice the Royalists of France whom he had called to his standard, as a salutary example to those who shall adhere to their native Sovereign, or shall confide in any other who undertakes the cause of oppressed kings and of loyal subjects.

How can I help it, if this high-minded Prince will subscribe to the invectives which the regicides have made against all kings, and particularly against himself? How can I help it, if this Royal propagandist will preach the doctrine of the rights of men? Is it my fault, if his professors of literature read lectures on that code in all his academies, and if all the pensioned managers of the news-papers in his dominions diffuse it throughout Europe in an hundred journals? Can it be attributed to me, if he will initiate all his grenadiers, and all his hussars in these high mysteries? Am I responsible, if he will make *le Droit de l'Homme,* or *la Souveraineté du Peuple* the favourite parole of his military orders? Now that his troops are to act with the brave legions of freedom, no doubt he will fit them for their fraternity. He will teach the Prussians to think, to feel and to act like them, and to emulate the glories of the *Regiment de l'Echaffaut.* He will employ the illustrious Citizen Santerre, the general of his new allies, to instruct the dull Germans how they shall conduct themselves toward persons who, like Louis the XVIth (whose cause and person, he once took into his protection), shall dare without the sanction of the people, or with it, to consider themselves as hereditary kings. Can I arrest this great Potentate in his career of glory? Am I blameable in recommending virtue and religion as the true foundation of all monarchies, because the Protector of the three religions of the Westphalian arrangement, to ingratiate himself with the Republic of Philosophy, shall abolish all the three? It is not in my power to prevent the grand Patron of the reformed church, if he chuses it, from annulling the Calvinistick Sabbath, and establishing the Decadi of Atheism in all his states.[8] He may even renounce and abjure his favourite mysticism in the temple of reason. In these things, at least, he is truly despotick. He has now shaken hands with every thing which at first had inspired him with horrour. It would be curious indeed to see (what I shall not however travel so far to see), the ingenious devices, and the elegant transparencies which on the restoration of peace and the commencement of Prussian liberty are to decorate Potzdam and Charlottenburg *festigiante*. What shades of his armed ancestors of the House of Brandenburgh will the Committee of *Illuminés* raise up in the opera-house of Berlin, to dance a grand ballet in the rejoicings for this auspicious event? Is it a Grand Master of the Teutonick Order, or is it the great Elector? Is it the first King of Prussia or the last? or is the whole long line (long, I mean *a parte antè*) to appear like Banquo's royal procession in the tragedy of Macbeth?

How can I prevent all these arts of Royal policy and all these displays of Royal magnificence? How can I prevent the Successor of Frederick the Great from aspiring to a new, and in this age unexampled kind of glory? Is it in my power to say, that he shall not make his confessions in the style of St. Austin[9] or of Rousseau? That he shall not assume the character of the penitent and flagellant, and grafting monkery on philosophy, strip himself of his regal purple, clothe his gigantick limbs in the sackcloth and the *hair-shirt*, and exercise on his broad shoulders the disciplinary scourge of the holy order of the *Sans-Culottes*? It is not in me to hinder Kings from making new orders of religious and martial knighthood. I am not Hercules enough to uphold those orbs which the Atlasses of the world are so desirous of shifting from their weary shoulders. What can be done against the magnanimous resolution of the great to accomplish the degradation and the ruin of their own character and situation?

---

[8] [Earlier in 1795, the newly founded Batavian Republic revoked the 1618 Synod of Dort, which had established the Reformed faith in the Netherlands.]

[9] [St. Augustine.]

LETTER TO WILLIAM ELLIOT

What I say of the German Princes, that I say of all the other dignities and all the other institutions of the Holy Roman Empire. If they have a mind to destroy themselves, they may put their advocates to silence and their advisers to shame. I have often praised the Aulick Council.[10] It is very true I did so. I thought it a tribunal, as well formed as human wisdom could form a tribunal, for coercing the great, the rich and the powerful; for obliging them to submit their necks to the imperial laws, and to those of nature and of nations; a tribunal well conceived for extirpating peculation, corruption and oppression, from all the parts of that vast heterogeneous mass called the Germanic Body. I should not be inclined to retract these praises upon any of the ordinary lapses into which human infirmity will fall; they might still stand, though some of their *conclusums* should taste of the prejudices of country or of faction, whether political or religious. Some degree, even of corruption, should not make me think them guilty of suicide; but if we could suppose, that the Aulick Council not regarding duty, or even common decorum, listening neither to the secret admonitions of conscience, nor to the publick voice of fame, some of the members basely abandoning their post, and others continuing in it, only the more infamously to betray it, should give a judgment so shameless and so prostitute, of such monstrous and even portentous corruption, that no example in the history of human depravity, or even in the fictions of poëtick imagination, could possibly match it; if it should be a judgment which with cold unfeeling cruelty, after long deliberations should condemn millions of innocent people to extortion, to rapine and to blood, and should devote some of the finest countries upon earth to ravage and desolation—does any one think that any servile apologies of mine, or any strutting and bullying insolence of their own, can save them from the ruin that must fall on all institutions of dignity or of authority that are perverted from their purport to the oppression of human nature in

[10] [One of the two supreme courts of the Holy Roman Empire, dissolved in 1806.]

others, and to its disgrace in themselves. As the wisdom of men makes such institutions, the folly of men destroys them. Whatever we may pretend, there is always more in the soundness of the materials, than in the fashion of the work. The order of a good building is something. But if it be wholly declined from its perpendicular; if the cement is loose and incoherent; if the stones are scaling with every change of the weather, and the whole toppling on our heads, what matter is it whether we are crushed by a Corinthian or a Dorick ruin? The fine form of a vessel is a matter of use and of delight. It is pleasant to see her decorated with cost and art. But what signifies even the mathematical truth of her form? What signify all the art and cost with which she can be carved, and painted, and gilded, and covered with decorations from stem to stern; what signify all her rigging and sails, her flags, her pendants and her streamers? what signify even her cannon, her stores and her provisions, if all her planks and timbers be unsound and rotten?

> *Quamvis Pontica pinus*
> *Silvae filia nobilis*
> *Jactes & genus & nomen inutile.*[11]

I have been stimulated, I know not how, to give you this trouble by what very few, except myself, would think worth any trouble at all. In a speech in the House of Lords, I have been attacked for the defence of a scheme of government, in which that body inheres, and in which alone it can exist. Peers of Great Britain may become as penitent as the Sovereign of Prussia. They may repent of what they have done in assertion of the honour of their King, and in favour of their own safety. But never the gloom that lowers over the fortune of the cause, nor any thing which the great may do towards hastening their own fall, can make me repent of what I have done by pen or

[11] ["Although you are built of the pine of Pontus, child of noble forests, you boast of a worthless pedigree and name." Horace, *Odes* 1.14:11–13]

voice (the only arms I possess) in favour of the order of things into which I was born, and in which I fondly hoped to die.

In the long series of ages which have furnished the matter of history, never was so beautiful and so august a spectacle presented to the moral eye, as Europe afforded the day before the revolution in France. I knew indeed that this prosperity contained in itself the seeds of its own danger. In one part of the society it caused laxity and debility. In the other it produced bold spirits and dark designs. A false philosophy passed from academies into courts, and the great themselves were infected with the theories which conducted to their ruin. Knowledge which in the two last centuries either did not exist at all, or existed solidly on right principles and in chosen hands, was now diffused, weakened and perverted. General wealth loosened morals, relaxed vigilance, and increased presumption. Men of talent began to compare, in the partition of the common stock of public prosperity, the proportions of the dividends, with the merits of the claimants. As usual, they found their portion not equal to their estimate (or perhaps to the public estimate) of their own worth. When it was once discovered by the revolution in France that a struggle between establishment and rapacity could be maintained, though but for one year, and in one place, I was sure that a practicable breach was made in the whole order of things and in every country. Religion, that held the materials of the fabrick together, was first systematically loosened. All other opinions, under the name of prejudices, must fall along with it; and Property, left undefended by principles, became a repository of spoils to tempt cupidity, and not a magazine to furnish arms for defence. I knew, that attacked on all sides by the infernal energies of talents set in action by vice and disorder, authority could not stand upon authority alone. It wanted some other support than the poise of its own gravity. Situations formerly supported persons. It now became necessary that personal qualities should support situations. Formerly, where authority was found, wisdom and virtue were presumed. But now the veil was torn, and to keep off sacrilegious intrusion, it was necessary that in the sanctuary of government something should be disclosed not only venerable, but dreadful. Government was at once to shew itself full of virtue and full of force. It was to invite partizans by making it appear to the world that a generous cause was to be asserted; one fit for a generous people to engage in. From passive submission was it to expect resolute defence? No! It must have warm advocates and passionate defenders, which an heavy, discontented acquiescence never could produce. What a base and foolish thing is it for any consolidated body of authority to say, or to act as if it said, "I will put my trust not in my own virtue, but in your patience; I will indulge in effeminacy, in indolence, in corruption; I will give way to all my perverse and vitious humours, because you cannot punish me without the hazard of ruining yourselves?"

I wished to warn the people against the greatest of all evils: a blind and furious spirit of innovation, under the name of reform. I was indeed well aware that power rarely reforms itself. So it is undoubtedly when all is quiet about it. But I was in hopes that provident fear might prevent fruitless penitence. I trusted that danger might produce at least circumspection; I flattered myself in a moment like this that nothing would be added to make authority top-heavy; that the very moment of an earth-quake would not be the time chosen for adding a story to our houses. I hoped to see the surest of all reforms, perhaps the only sure reform, the ceasing to do ill. In the mean time I wished to the people, the wisdom of knowing how to tolerate a condition which none of their efforts can render much more than tolerable. It was a condition, however, in which every thing was to be found that could enable them to live to nature, and if so they pleased, to live to virtue and to honour.

I do not repent that I thought better of those to whom I wished well, than they will suffer me long to think that they deserved. Far from repenting, I would to God, that new faculties had been called up in me, in favour not of this or that man, or this or that system, but of the general vital principle that whilst it was in its vigour produced the state of things transmitted to us from our fathers; but which, through the joint operation of the abuses of authority and liberty, may perish in our hands. I am not of opinion that the race of men, and the commonwealths they create, like the bodies of individuals, grow effete and languid and bloodless, and ossify by the necessities of their own conformation, and the fatal operation of longevity and time. These analogies between bodies natural and politick, though they may some times illustrate arguments, furnish no argument of themselves. They are but too often used under the colour of a specious philosophy, to find apologies for the despair of laziness and pusillanimity, and to excuse the want of all manly efforts, when the exigencies of our country call for them the more loudly.

How often has public calamity been arrested on the very brink of ruin by the seasonable energy of a single man? Have we no such man amongst us? I am as sure as I am of my being, that one vigorous mind without office, without situation, without public functions of any kind (at a time when the want of such a thing is felt, as I am sure it is) I say, one such man, confiding in the aid of God, and full of just reliance in his own fortitude, vigour, enterprize and perseverance, would first draw to him some few like himself, and then that multitudes, hardly thought to be in existence, would appear and troop about him.

If I saw this auspicious beginning, baffled and frustrated as I am, yet on the very verge of a timely grave, abandoned abroad and desolate at home, stripped of my boast, my hope, my consolation, my helper, my counsellor and my guide[12] (you know in part what I have lost, and would to God I could clear myself of all neglect and fault in that loss), yet thus, even thus, I would rake up the fire under all the ashes that oppress it. I am no longer patient of the public eye; nor am I of force to win my way and to justle and elbow in a crowd. But even in solitude, something may be done for society. The meditations

[12] [A reference to the death of his son, Richard, in August 1794. Burke refers to his son again in the final paragraph of this work.]

of the closet have infected senates with a subtle frenzy, and inflamed armies with the brands of the furies. The cure might come from the same source with the distemper. I would add my part to those who would animate the people (whose hearts are yet right) to new exertions in the old cause.

Novelty is not the only source of zeal. Why should not a Maccabeus and his brethren arise to assert the honour of the ancient law, and to defend the temple of their forefathers, with as ardent a spirit, as can inspire any innovator to destroy the monuments of the piety and the glory of antient ages? It is not a hazarded assertion, it is a great truth, that when once things are gone out of their ordinary course, it is by acts out of the ordinary course they can alone be re-established. Republican spirit can only be combated by a spirit of the same nature: of the same nature, but informed with another principle and pointing to another end. I would persuade a resistance both to the corruption and to the reformation that prevails. It will not be the weaker, but much the stronger, for combating both together. A victory over real corruptions would enable us to baffle the spurious and pretended reformations. I would not wish to excite, or even to tolerate, that kind of evil spirit which evokes the powers of hell to rectify the disorders of the earth. No! I would add my voice with better, and I trust, more potent charms, to draw down justice and wisdom and fortitude from heaven, for the correction of human vice, and the recalling of human errour from the devious ways into which it has been betrayed. I would wish to call the impulses of individuals at once to the aid and to the controul of authority. By this which I call the true republican spirit, paradoxical as it may appear, monarchies alone can be rescued from the imbecillity of courts and the madness of the crowd. This republican spirit would not suffer men in high place to bring ruin on their country and on themselves. It would reform, not by destroying, but by saving, the great, the rich and the powerful. Such a republican spirit, we perhaps fondly conceive to have animated the distinguished heroes and patriots of old, who knew no mode of policy but religion and virtue. These, they would have paramount to all constitutions; they would not suffer Monarchs or Senates or popular Assemblies, under pretences of dignity or authority, or freedom, to shake off those moral riders which reason has appointed to govern every sort of rude power. These, in appearance loading them by their weight, do by that pressure augment their essential force. The momentum is encreased by the extraneous weight. It is true in moral, as it is in mechanical science. It is true, not only in the draught, but in the race. These riders of the great, in effect, hold the reins which guide them in their course, and wear the spur that stimulates them to the goals of honour and of safety. The great must submit to the dominion of prudence and of virtue; or none will long submit to the dominion of the great.

"Dîs te minorem quod geris imperas."[13]

This is the feudal tenure which they cannot alter.

Indeed, my dear Sir, things are in a bad state. I do not deny a good share of diligence, a very great share of ability, and much publick virtue to those who direct our affairs. But they are encumbered, not aided, by their very instruments, and by all the apparatus of the state. I think that our Ministry (though there are things against them, which neither you nor I can dissemble, and which grieve to the heart) is by far the most honest and by far the wisest system of administration in Europe. Their fall would be no trivial calamity.

Not meaning to depreciate the Minority in Parliament, whose talents are also great, and to whom I do not deny virtues, their system seems to me to be fundamentally wrong. But whether wrong or right, they have not enough of coherence among themselves, nor of estimation with the publick, nor of numbers. They cannot make up an administration. Nothing is more visible. Many other things are against them,

[13] ["Inasmuch as you submit yourself to the gods, you rule." Horace, *Odes* 3.6:5]

which I do not charge as faults, but reckon among national misfortunes. Extraordinary things must be done, or one of the parties cannot stand as a Ministry, nor the other even as an Opposition. They cannot change their situations, nor can any useful coalition be made between them. I do not see the mode of it, nor the way to it. This aspect of things I do not contemplate with pleasure.

I well know that every thing of the daring kind which I speak of, is critical—But the times are critical. New things in a new world! I see no hopes in the common tracks. If men are not to be found who can be got to feel within them some impulse

> "—— *quod nequeo monstrare, & sentio tantum,*"[14]

and which makes them impatient of the present; if none can be got to feel that private persons may sometimes assume that sort of magistracy which does not depend on the nomination of Kings, or the election of the people, but has an inherent and self-existent power which both would recognize; I see nothing in the world to hope.

If I saw such a group beginning to cluster, such as they are, they should have (all that I can give) my prayers and my advice. People talk of war, or cry for peace—have they to the bottom considered the questions either of war, or peace, upon the scale of the existing world? No. I fear they have not.

Why should not you, yourself, be one of those to enter your name in such a list as I speak of. You are young; you have great talents, you have a clear head, you have a natural, fluent and unforced elocution; your ideas are just, your sentiments benevolent, open and enlarged—but this is too big for your modesty. Oh! this modesty in time and place is a charming virtue, and the grace of all other virtues. But it is sometimes the worst enemy they have. Let him, whose print I gave you

[14] ["I cannot point to such a man, but I feel sure he is out there." Juvenal, *Satires* 7:56]

the other day, be engraved in your memory! Had it pleased Providence to have spared him for the trying situations that seem to be coming on, notwithstanding that he was sometimes a little dispirited by the disposition which we thought shewn to depress him and set him aside; yet he was always buoyed up again; and on one or two occasions, he discovered what might be expected from the vigour and elevation of his mind, from his unconquerable fortitude, and from the extent of his resources for every purpose of speculation and of action. Remember him, my friend, who in the highest degree honoured and respected you, and remember that great parts are a great trust. Remember too that mistaken or misapplied virtues, if they are not as pernicious as vice, frustrate at least their own natural tendencies, and disappoint the purposes of the great giver.

Adieu. My dreams are finished.

7

A LETTER TO A NOBLE LORD

February 1796

When Burke retired from Parliament in June 1794, his finances were, as always, in a perilous state. Members of Parliament were not paid for their service. A member could hope to earn money for his labors only if, while his party was in power, he was chosen for a government post. The Rockingham Whigs had been in power only twice during Burke's thirty-year career—for brief periods in 1765 and 1782. Generous to a fault and surrounded with impecunious friends and relatives, Burke faced the prospect in 1794 of selling his beloved home in Beaconsfield. In late August, however, his fears were allayed by Pitt's decision to grant Burke £1,200 per year from the civil list, the statutory maximum. Political opposition to this act of generosity was so great, however, that Pitt chose not to apply to Parliament for a further grant on Burke's behalf, deciding, in the summer of 1795, in favor of two annuities available directly from the crown, bringing Burke's annual pension up to £3,700.

In November 1795, Burke's pension was attacked in the House of Lords by James Maitland, 8th Earl of Lauderdale, and Francis Russell, 5th Duke of Bedford. Like the Duc d'Orléans in France—now styling himself Philippe-Egalité—these men were attracted by the image of themselves as radicals. Lauderdale had even met Brissot during a political pilgrimage to France. "Never was a man so unfortunate in picking either a cause or an opponent as Bedford," writes W. Jackson Bate. "For his attack provoked Burke's magnificent reply, A Letter to a Noble Lord, surely the most splendid valedictory that *any statesman ever wrote." The "noble lord" to whom the letter is addressed is Burke's friend and patron, the 4th Earl Fitzwilliam, nephew to Lord Rockingham.*

A Letter to a Noble Lord has three sections. First, Burke is compelled to defend his consistency in accepting a pension from the crown in light of his "Speech on Economical Reform" (1780), which had argued that the crown was wasting enormous amounts of public money by bestowing pensions and sinecures that were neither merited in themselves nor subject to parliamentary oversight. Next, Burke discusses the Bedford family, comparing its questionable history to his own rise and his family's tragic loss in the untimely death of his son. Finally, Burke invokes the spirit of Bedford's uncle, Augustus Keppel, who was appointed First Lord of the Admiralty by Rockingham, and imagines how he would have viewed the French Revolution. The work contains some of Burke's most eloquent prose, particularly in his description of the British constitution.

A Letter to a Noble Lord

1796

Mᴀ LORD,

I could hardly flatter myself with the hope, that so very early in the season I should have to acknowledge obligations to the Duke of Bedford and to the Earl of Lauderdale. These noble persons have lost no time in conferring upon me, that sort of honour, which it is alone within their competence, and which it is certainly most congenial to their nature and their manners to bestow.

To be ill spoken of, in whatever language they speak, by the zealots of the new sect in philosophy and politicks, of which these noble persons think so charitably, and of which others think so justly, to me, is no matter of uneasiness or surprise. To have incurred the displeasure of the Duke of Orleans or the Duke of Bedford, to fall under the censure of Citizen Brissot or of his friend the Earl of Lauderdale, I ought to consider as proofs, not the least satisfactory, that I have produced some part of the effect I proposed by my endeavours. I have laboured hard to earn, what the noble Lords are generous enough to pay. Personal offence I have given them none. The part they take against me is from zeal to the cause. It is well! It is perfectly well! I have to do homage to their justice. I have to thank the Bedfords and the Lauderdales for having so faithfully and so fully acquitted towards me whatever arrear of debt was left undischarged by the Priestleys and the Paines.

Some, perhaps, may think them executors in their own wrong: I at least have nothing to complain of. They have gone beyond the demands of justice. They have been (a little perhaps beyond their intention) favourable to me. They have been the means of bringing out, by their invectives, the handsome things which Lord Grenville has had the goodness and condescension to say in my behalf. Retired as I am from the world, and from all it's affairs and all it's pleasures, I confess it does kindle, in my nearly extinguished feelings, a very vivid satisfaction to be so attacked and so commended. It is soothing to my wounded mind, to be commended by an able, vigorous, and well informed statesman, and at the very moment when he stands forth with a manliness and resolution, worthy of himself and of his cause, for the preservation of the person and government of our Sovereign, and therein for the security of the laws, the liberties, the morals, and the lives of his people. To be in any fair way connected with such things, is indeed a distinction. No philosophy can make me above it: no melancholy can depress me so low, as to make me wholly insensible to such an honour.

Why will they not let me remain in obscurity and inaction? Are they apprehensive, that if an atom of me remains, the sect has something to fear? Must I be annihilated, lest, like old *John Zisca's*,[1] my skin might be made into a drum, to animate Europe to eternal battle, against a tyranny that threatens to overwhelm all Europe, and all the human race?

My Lord, it is a subject of awful meditation. Before this of France, the annals of all time have not furnished an instance of a *compleat* revolution. That revolution seems to have extended even to the constitution of the mind of man. It has this of wonderful in it, that it resembles what Lord Verulam[2]

[1] [John Zisca (*c.* 1360–1424) was a Bohemian nobleman and military leader of the Hussites. He is said to have ordered his skin to be made into a drumhead after his death.]

[2] [Francis Bacon (1561–1626).]

says of the operations of nature: It was perfect, not only in all its elements and principles, but in all it's members and it's organs from the very beginning. The moral scheme of France furnishes the only pattern ever known, which they who admire will *instantly* resemble. It is indeed an inexhaustible repertory of one kind of examples. In my wretched condition, though hardly to be classed with the living, I am not safe from them. They have tygers to fall upon animated strength. They have hyenas to prey upon carcasses. The national menagerie is collected by the first physiologists of the time; and it is defective in no description of savage nature. They pursue, even such as me, into the obscurest retreats, and haul them before their revolutionary tribunals. Neither sex, nor age—nor the sanctuary of the tomb is sacred to them. They have so determined a hatred to all privileged orders, that they deny even to the departed, the sad immunities of the grave. They are not wholly without an object. Their turpitude purveys to their malice; and they unplumb the dead for bullets to assassinate the living. If all revolutionists were not proof against all caution, I should recommend it to their consideration, that no persons were ever known in history, either sacred or profane, to vex the sepulchre, and by their sorceries, to call up the prophetic dead, with any other event, than the prediction of their own disastrous fate, "Leave, oh leave me to repose!"[3]

In one thing I can excuse the Duke of Bedford for his attack upon me and my mortuary pension. He cannot readily comprehend the transaction he condemns. What I have obtained was the fruit of no bargain; the production of no intrigue; the result of no compromise; the effect of no solicitation. The first suggestion of it never came from me, mediately or immediately, to his Majesty or any of his Ministers. It was long known that the instant my engagements would permit it, and before the heaviest of all calamities had for ever con-

[3] [Paraphrased from Thomas Gray, "The Descent of Odin," l.50.]

demned me to obscurity and sorrow, I had resolved on a total retreat.[4] I had executed that design. I was entirely out of the way of serving or of hurting any statesman, or any party, when the Ministers so generously and so nobly carried into effect the spontaneous bounty of the Crown. Both descriptions have acted as became them. When I could no longer serve them, the Ministers have considered my situation. When I could no longer hurt them, the revolutionists have trampled on my infirmity. My gratitude, I trust, is equal to the manner in which the benefit was conferred. It came to me indeed, at a time of life, and in a state of mind and body, in which no circumstance of fortune could afford me any real pleasure. But this was no fault in the Royal Donor, or in his Ministers, who were pleased, in acknowledging the merits of an invalid servant of the publick, to assuage the sorrows of a desolate old man.

It would ill become me to boast of any thing. It would as ill become me, thus called upon, to depreciate the value of a long life, spent with unexampled toil in the service of my country. Since the total body of my services, on account of the industry which was shewn in them, and the fairness of my intentions, have obtained the acceptance of my Sovereign, it would be absurd in me to range myself on the side of the Duke of Bedford and the Corresponding Society, or, as far as in me lies, to permit a dispute on the rate at which the authority appointed by *our* Constitution to estimate such things, has been pleased to set them.

Loose libels ought to be passed by in silence and contempt. By me they have been so always. I knew that as long as I remained in publick, I should live down the calumnies of malice, and the judgments of ignorance. If I happened to be now and then in the wrong, as who is not, like all other men, I must bear the consequence of my faults and my mistakes. The

[4] [The engagements to which Burke refers are the proceedings in the impeachment trial of Warren Hastings, which had engaged him until June 1794. The "heaviest of all calamities" of which Burke speaks is the sudden death of his son Richard on August 2 of that year.]

A LETTER TO A NOBLE LORD

libels of the present day, are just of the same stuff as the libels of the past. But they derive an importance from the rank of the persons they come from, and the gravity of the place where they were uttered. In some way or other I ought to take some notice of them. To assert myself thus traduced is not vanity or arrogance. It is a demand of justice; it is a demonstration of gratitude. If I am unworthy, the Ministers are worse than prodigal. On that hypothesis, I perfectly agree with the Duke of Bedford.

For whatever I have been (I am now no more) I put myself on my country. I ought to be allowed a reasonable freedom, because I stand upon my deliverance; and no culprit ought to plead in irons. Even in the utmost latitude of defensive liberty, I wish to preserve all possible decorum. Whatever it may be in the eyes of these noble persons themselves, to me, their situation calls for the most profound respect. If I should happen to trespass a little, which I trust I shall not, let it always be supposed, that a confusion of characters may produce mistakes; that in the masquerades of the grand carnival of our age, whimsical adventures happen; odd things are said and pass off. If I should fail a single point in the high respect I owe to those illustrious persons, I cannot be supposed to mean the Duke of Bedford and the Earl of Lauderdale of the House of Peers, but the Duke of Bedford and the Earl of Lauderdale of Palace Yard—the Dukes and Earls of Brentford.5 There they are on the pavement; there they seem to come nearer to my humble level; and, virtually at least, to have waved their high privilege.

Making this protestation, I refuse all revolutionary tribunals, where men have been put to death for no other reason, than that they had obtained favours from the Crown. I claim, not the letter, but the spirit of the old English law, that is, to be tried by my peers. I decline his Grace's jurisdiction as a judge. I challenge the Duke of Bedford as a juror to pass upon the value of my services. Whatever his natural parts may be, I

5 [The kings of Brentford are two characters in Buckingham's *The Rehearsal* (1672), appropriately absurd, Frenchified, and alike.]

cannot recognize in his few and idle years, the competence to judge of my long and laborious life. If I can help it, he shall not be on the inquest of my *quantum meruit*.[6] Poor rich man! He can hardly know any thing of publick industry in it's exertions, or can estimate it's compensations when it's work is done. I have no doubt of his Grace's readiness in all the calculations of vulgar arithmetick; but I shrewdly suspect, that he is very little studied in the theory of moral proportions; and has never learned the Rule of Three in the arithmetick of policy and state.

His Grace thinks I have obtained too much. I answer, that my exertions, whatever they have been, were such as no hopes of pecuniary reward could possibly excite; and no pecuniary compensation can possibly reward them. Between money and services of this kind (I said it long since,[7] when I was not myself concerned), there is no common measurer. Money is made for the comfort and convenience of animal life. It cannot be a reward for what, mere animal life must indeed sustain, but never can inspire. With submission to his Grace, I have not had more than sufficient. As to any noble use, I trust I know how to employ, as well as he, a much greater fortune than he possesses. In a more confined application, I certainly stand in need of every kind of relief and easement much more than he does. When I say I have not received more than I deserve, is this the language I hold to Majesty? No! Far, very far, from it! Before that presence, I claim no merit at all. Every thing towards me is favour, and bounty. One style to a gracious benefactor; another to a proud and insulting foe.

His Grace is pleased to aggravate my guilt, by charging my acceptance of his Majesty's grant as a departure from my ideas, and the spirit of my conduct with regard to oeconomy. If it be, my ideas of oeconomy were false and ill founded. But they are the Duke of Bedford's ideas of oeconomy I have

---

[6] ["As much as he deserves." A legal term used to describe the extent of one's liability.]

[7] Speech on Oeconomical Reform, 1780.

contradicted, and not my own. If he means to allude to certain bills brought in by me on a message from the throne in 1782, I tell him, that there is nothing in my conduct that can contradict either the letter or the spirit of those acts. Does he mean the pay-office act? I take it for granted he does not. The act to which he alludes is, I suppose, the establishment act. I greatly doubt whether his Grace has ever read the one or the other. The first of these systems cost me, with every assistance which my then situation gave me, pains incredible. I found an opinion common through all the offices, and general in the publick at large, that it would prove impossible to reform and methodize the office of Paymaster General. I undertook it, however; and I succeeded in my undertaking. Whether the military service, or whether the general oeconomy of our finances have profited by that act, I leave to those who are acquainted with the army, and with the treasury, to judge.

An opinion full as general prevailed also at the same time, that nothing could be done for the regulation of the civil-list establishment. The very attempt to introduce method into it, and any limitations to it's services, was held absurd. I had not seen the man, who so much as suggested one oeconomical principle, or an oeconomical expedient, upon that subject. Nothing but coarse amputation, or coarser taxation, were then talked of, both of them without design, combination, or the least shadow of principle. Blind and headlong zeal, or factious fury, were the whole contribution brought by the most noisy on that occasion, towards the satisfaction of the publick, or the relief of the Crown.

Let me tell my youthful Censor, that the necessities of that time required something very different from what others then suggested, or what his Grace now conceives. Let me inform him, that it was one of the most critical periods in our annals.

Astronomers have supposed, that if a certain comet, whose path intersected the ecliptick, had met the earth in some (I forget what) sign, it would have whirled us along with it, in it's excentrick course, into God knows what regions of heat and cold. Had the portentous comet of the rights of man (which "from it's horrid hair shakes pestilence, and war," and "with fear of change perplexes Monarchs"),[8] had that comet crossed upon us in that internal state of England, nothing human could have prevented our being irresistibly hurried, out of the highway of heaven, into all the vices, crimes, horrours and miseries of the French revolution.

Happily, France was not then jacobinized. Her hostility was at a good distance. We had a limb cut off; but we preserved the body: We lost our Colonies; but we kept our Constitution. There was, indeed, much intestine heat, there was a dreadful fermentation. Wild and savage insurrection quitted the woods, and prowled about our streets in the name of reform. Such was the distemper of the publick mind, that there was no madman, in his maddest ideas, and maddest projects, who might not count upon numbers to support his principles and execute his designs.

Many of the changes, by a great misnomer called parliamentary reforms, went, not in the intention of all the professors and supporters of them, undoubtedly, but went in their certain, and, in my opinion, not very remote effect, home to the utter destruction of the Constitution of this kingdom. Had they taken place, not France, but England, would have had the honour of leading up the death-dance of Democratick Revolution. Other projects, exactly coincident in time with those, struck at the very existence of the kingdom under any constitution. There are who remember the blind fury of some, and the lamentable helplessness of others; here, a torpid confusion, from a panic fear of the danger; there, the same inaction from a stupid insensibility to it; here, well-wishers to the mischief; there, indifferent lookers-on. At the same time, a sort of National Convention, dubious in its nature, and perilous in its example, nosed Parliament in the very seat of its authority; sat with a sort of superintendance over it; and little less than dictated to it, not only laws, but the very form

[8] [*Paradise Lost* 2:710-11, 1:598-99.]

and essence of Legislature itself. In Ireland things ran in a still more eccentrick course. Government was unnerved, confounded, and in a manner suspended. It's equipoise was totally gone. I do not mean to speak disrespectfully of Lord North. He was a man of admirable parts; of general knowledge; of a versatile understanding fitted for every sort of business; of infinite wit and pleasantry; of a delightful temper; and with a mind most perfectly disinterested. But it would be only to degrade myself by a weak adulation, and not to honour the memory of a great man, to deny that he wanted something of the vigilance, and spirit of command, that the time required. Indeed, a darkness, next to the fog of this awful day, loured over the whole region. For a little time the helm appeared abandoned—

Ipse diem noctemque negat discernere coelo
Nec meminisse viae mediâ Palinurus in undâ.[9]

At that time I was connected with men of high place in the community. They loved Liberty as much as the Duke of Bedford can do; and they understood it at least as well. Perhaps their politicks, as usual, took a tincture from their character, and they cultivated what they loved. The Liberty they pursued was a Liberty inseparable from order, from virtue, from morals, and from religion, and was neither hypocritically nor fanatically followed. They did not wish, that Liberty, in itself one of the first of blessings, should in it's perversion become the greatest curse which could fall upon mankind. To preserve the Constitution entire, and practically equal to all the great ends of it's formation, not in one single part, but in all it's parts, was to them the first object. Popularity and power they regarded alike. These were with them only different means of obtaining that object; and had no preference over each other in their minds, but as one or the other might afford a surer or a less certain prospect of arriving at that end. It

[9] ["Even Palinurus said he could neither distinguish night from day in the heavens, nor remember a course in mid-ocean." Vergil, *Aeneid* 3:201-02]

---

is some consolation to me, in the chearless gloom which darkens the evening of my life, that with them I commenced my political career, and never for a moment, in reality, nor in appearance, for any length of time, was separated from their good wishes and good opinion.

By what accident it matters not, nor upon what desert, but just then, and in the midst of that hunt of obloquy, which ever has pursued me with a full cry through life, I had obtained a very considerable degree of publick confidence. I know well enough how equivocal a test this kind of popular opinion forms of the merit that obtained it. I am no stranger to the insecurity of it's tenure. I do not boast of it. It is mentioned, to shew, not how highly I prize the thing, but my right to value the use I made of it. I endeavoured to turn that short-lived advantage to myself into a permanent benefit to my Country. Far am I from detracting from the merit of some Gentlemen, out of office or in it, on that occasion. No! It is not my way to refuse a full and heaped measure of justice to the aids that I receive. I have, through life, been willing to give every thing to others; and to reserve nothing for myself, but the inward conscience, that I had omitted no pains to discover, to animate, to discipline, to direct the abilities of the Country for it's service, and to place them in the best light to improve their age, or to adorn it. This conscience I have. I have never suppressed any man; never checked him for a moment in his course, by any jealousy, or by any policy. I was always ready, to the height of my means (and they were always infinitely below my desires) to forward those abilities which overpowered my own. He is an ill-furnished undertaker, who has no machinery but his own hands to work with. Poor in my own faculties, I ever thought myself rich in theirs. In that period of difficulty and danger, more especially, I consulted, and sincerely co-operated with men of all parties, who seemed disposed to the same ends, or to any main part of them. Nothing, to prevent disorder, was omitted: when it appeared, nothing to subdue it, was left uncounselled, nor unexecuted, as far as I could prevail. At the time I speak of, and having a momentary lead, so aided and so encouraged, and as a feeble instrument in a mighty hand—I do not say, I saved my Country; I am sure I did my Country important service. There were few, indeed, that did not at that time acknowledge it, and that time was thirteen years ago. It was but one voice, that no man in the kingdom better deserved an honourable provision should be made for him.

So much for my general conduct through the whole of the portentous crisis from 1780 to 1782, and the general sense then entertained of that conduct by my country. But my character, as a reformer, in the particular instances which the Duke of Bedford refers to, is so connected in principle with my opinions on the hideous changes, which have since barbarized France, and spreading thence, threaten the political and moral order of the whole world, that it seems to demand something of a more detailed discussion.

My oeconomical reforms were not, as his Grace may think, the suppression of a paltry pension or employment, more or less. Oeconomy in my plans was, as it ought to be, secondary, subordinate, instrumental. I acted on state principles. I found a great distemper in the commonwealth; and, according to the nature of evil and of the object, I treated it. The malady was deep; it was complicated, in the causes and in the symptoms. Throughout it was full of contra-indicants. On one hand Government, daily growing more invidious for an apparent increase of the means of strength, was every day growing more contemptible by real weakness. Nor was this dissolution confined to Government commonly so called. It extended to Parliament; which was losing not a little in it's dignity and estimation, by an opinion of it's not acting on worthy motives. On the other hand, the desires of the People (partly natural and partly infused into them by art), appeared in so wild and inconsiderate a manner, with regard to the oeconomical object (for I set aside for a moment the dreadful tampering with the body of the Constitution itself) that if their petitions had literally been complied with, the State would have been convulsed; and a gate would have been opened, through which all property might be sacked and ravaged. Nothing could have saved the Publick from the mischiefs of the false reform but it's absurdity; which would soon have brought itself, and with it all real reform, into discredit. This would have left a rankling wound in the hearts of the people who would know they had failed in the accomplishment of their wishes, but who, like the rest of mankind in all ages, would impute the blame to any thing rather than to their own proceedings. But there were then persons in the world, who nourished complaint; and would have been thoroughly disappointed if the people were ever satisfied. I was not of that humour. I wished that they *should* be satisfied. It was my aim to give to the People the substance of what I knew they desired, and what I thought was right whether they desired it or not, before it had been modified for them into senseless petitions. I knew that there is a manifest marked distinction, which ill men, with ill designs, or weak men incapable of any design, will constantly be confounding, that is, a marked distinction between Change and Reformation. The former alters the substance of the objects themselves; and gets rid of all their essential good, as well as of all the accidental evil annexed to them. Change is novelty; and whether it is to operate any one of the effects of reformation at all, or whether it may not contradict the very principle upon which reformation is desired, cannot be certainly known beforehand. Reform is, not a change in the substance, or in the primary modification of the object, but a direct application of a remedy to the grievance complained of. So far as that is removed, all is sure. It stops there; and if it fails, the substance which underwent the operation, at the very worst, is but where it was.

All this, in effect, I think, but am not sure, I have said elsewhere. It cannot at this time be too often repeated; line upon line; precept upon precept; until it comes into the currency of a proverb, *To innovate is not to reform*. The French revolutionists complained of every thing; they refused to reform any thing; and they left nothing, no, nothing at all *un-*

changed. The consequences are *before* us, not in remote history; not in future prognostication: they are about us; they are upon us. They shake the publick security; they menace private enjoyment. They dwarf the growth of the young; they break the quiet of the old. If we travel, they stop our way. They infest us in town; they pursue us to the country. Our business is interrupted; our repose is troubled; our pleasures are saddened; our very studies are poisoned and perverted, and knowledge is rendered worse than ignorance, by the enormous evils of this dreadful innovation. The revolution harpies of France, sprung from night and hell, or from that chaotick anarchy, which generates equivocally "all monstrous, all prodigious things,"[10] cuckoo-like, adulterously lay their eggs, and brood over, and hatch them in the nest of every neighbouring State. These obscene harpies, who deck themselves, in I know not what divine attributes, but who in reality are foul and ravenous birds of prey (both mothers and daughters) flutter over our heads, and souse down upon our tables, and leave nothing unrent, unrifled, unravaged, or unpolluted with the slime of their filthy offal.[11]

---

[10] [*Paradise Lost* 2:625.]

[11] Tristius haud illis monstrum, nec saevior ulla.
  Pestis, & ira Deûm Stygiis sese extulit undis.
  Virginei volucrum vultus; faedissima ventris
  Proluvies; uncaeque manus; & pallida semper
  Ora fame—

Here the Poet breaks the line, because he (and that He is Virgil) had not verse or language to describe that monster even as he had conceived her. Had he lived to our time, he would have been more overpowered with the reality than he was with the imagination. Virgil only knew the horror of the times before him. Had he lived to see the Revolutionists and Constitutionalists of France, he would have had more horrid and disgusting features of his harpies to describe, and more frequent failures in the attempt to describe them.

  ["Monsters more fierce offended Heav'n ne'er sent
  From hell's abyss, for human punishment:
  With virgin faces, but with wombs obscene,
  Foul paunches, and with ordure still unclean;
  With claws for hands, and looks for ever lean."

  Aeneid 3:214–18, trans. Dryden]

If his Grace can contemplate the result of this compleat innovation, or, as some friends of his will call it, *reform*, in the whole body of it's solidity and compound mass, at which, as Hamlet says, the face of Heaven glows with horrour and indignation, and which, in truth, makes every reflecting mind, and every feeling heart, perfectly thought-sick, without a thorough abhorrence of every thing they say, and every thing they do, I am amazed at the morbid strength, or the natural infirmity of his mind.

It was then not my love, but my hatred to innovation, that produced my Plan of Reform. Without troubling myself with the exactness of the logical diagram, I considered them as things substantially opposite. It was to prevent that evil, that I proposed the measures, which his Grace is pleased, and I am not sorry he is pleased, to recall to my collection. I had (what I hope that Noble Duke will remember in all his operations) a State to preserve, as well as a State to reform. I had a People to gratify, but not to inflame, or to mislead. I do not claim half the credit for what I did, as for what I prevented from being done. In that situation of the publick mind, I did not undertake, as was then proposed, to new model the House of Commons or the House of Lords; or to change the authority under which any officer of the Crown acted, who was suffered at all to exist. Crown, Lords, Commons, judicial system, system of administration, existed as they had existed before; and in the mode and manner in which they had always existed. My measures were, what I then truly stated them to the House to be, in their intent, healing and mediatorial. A complaint was made of too much influence in the House of Commons; I reduced it in both Houses; and I gave my reasons article by article for every reduction, and shewed why I thought it safe for the service of the State. I heaved the lead every inch of way I made. A disposition to expence was complained of; to that I opposed, not mere retrenchment, but a system of oeconomy, which would make a random expence without plan or foresight, in future not easily practicable. I proceeded upon principles of research to put me in posses-

---

A LETTER TO A NOBLE LORD

sion of my matter; on principles of method to regulate it; and on principles in the human mind and in civil affairs to secure and perpetuate the operation. I conceived nothing arbitrarily; nor proposed any thing to be done by the will and pleasure of others, or my own; but by reason, and by reason only. I have ever abhorred, since the first dawn of my understanding to this it's obscure twilight, all the operations of opinion, fancy, inclination, and will, in the affairs of Government, where only a sovereign reason, paramount to all forms of legislation and administration, should dictate. Government is made for the very purpose of opposing that reason to will and to caprice, in the reformers or in the reformed, in the governors or in the governed, in Kings, in Senates, or in People.

On a careful review, therefore, and analysis of all the component parts of the Civil List, and on weighing them each against other, in order to make, as much as possible, all of them a subject of estimate (the foundation and cornerstone of all regular provident oeconomy) it appeared to me evident, that this was impracticable, whilst that part, called the Pension List, was totally discretionary in it's amount. For this reason, and for this only, I proposed to reduce it, both in it's gross quantity, and in it's larger individual proportions, to a certainty: lest, if it were left without a *general* limit, it might eat up the Civil List service; if suffered to be granted in portions too great for the fund, it might defeat it's own end; and by unlimited allowances to some, it might disable the Crown in means of providing for others. The Pension List was to be kept as a sacred fund; but it could not be kept as a constant open fund, sufficient for growing demands, if some demands could wholly devour it. The tenour of the Act will shew that it regarded the Civil List *only*, the reduction of which to some sort of estimate was my great object.

No other of the Crown funds did I meddle with, because they had not the same relations. This of the four and a half per cents[12] does his Grace imagine had escaped me, or had

---

[12] [The annuity fund from which the bulk of Burke's pension was drawn.]

A LETTER TO A NOBLE LORD

escaped all the men of business, who acted with me in those regulations? I knew that such a fund existed, and that pensions had been always granted on it, before his Grace was born. This fund was full in my eye. It was full in the eyes of those who worked with me. It was left on principle. On principle I did what was then done; and on principle what was left undone was omitted. I did not dare to rob the nation of all funds to reward merit. If I pressed this point too close, I acted contrary to the avowed principles on which I went. Gentlemen are very fond of quoting me; but if any one thinks it is worth his while to know the rules that guided me in my plan of reform, he will read my printed speech on that subject; at least what is contained from page 230 to page 241 in the second Volume of the collection which a friend has given himself the trouble to make of my publications. Be this as it may, these two Bills (though atchieved with the greatest labour, and management of every sort, both within and without the House) were only a part, and but a small part, of a very large system, comprehending all the objects I stated in opening my proposition, and indeed many more, which I just hinted at in my Speech to the Electors of Bristol, when I was put out of that representation. All these, in some state or other of forwardness, I have long had by me.

But do I justify his Majesty's grace on these grounds? I think them the least of my services! The time gave them an occasional value: What I have done in the way of political oeconomy was far from confined to this body of measures. I did not come into Parliament to con my lesson. I had earned my pension before I set my foot in St. Stephen's Chapel.[13] I was prepared and disciplined to this political warfare. The first session I sat in Parliament, I found it necessary to analyze the whole commercial, financial, constitutional and foreign interests of Great Britain and it's Empire. A great deal was then done; and more, far more would have been done, if more had been permitted by events. Then in the vigour of my

[13] [Where the House of Commons met, until it was burnt in 1834.]

manhood, my constitution sunk under my labour. Had I then died (and I seemed to myself very near death), I had then earned for those who belonged to me, more than the Duke of Bedford's ideas of service are of power to estimate. But in truth, these services I am called to account for, are not those on which I value myself the most. If I were to call for a reward (which I have never done) it should be for those in which for fourteen years, without intermission, I shewed the most industry, and had the least success; I mean in the affairs of India. They are those on which I value myself the most; most for the importance; most for the labour; most for the judgment; most for constancy and perseverance in the pursuit. Others may value them most for the *intention*. In that, surely, they are not mistaken.

Does his Grace think, that they who advised the Crown to make my retreat easy, considered me only as an oeconomist? That, well understood, however, is a good deal. If I had not deemed it of some value, I should not have made political oeconomy an object of my humble studies, from my very early youth to near the end of my service in parliament, even before (at least to any knowledge of mine), it had employed the thoughts of speculative men in other parts of Europe. At that time, it was still in it's infancy in England, where, in the last century, it had it's origin. Great and learned men thought my studies were not wholly thrown away, and deigned to communicate with me now and then on some particulars of their immortal works. Something of these studies may appear incidentally in some of the earliest things I published. The House has been witness to their effect, and has profited of them more or less, for above eight and twenty years.

To their estimate I leave the matter. I was not, like his Grace of Bedford, swaddled, and rocked, and dandled into a Legislator; *"Nitor in adversum"*[14] is the motto for a man like me. I possessed not one of the qualities, nor cultivated one of the arts, that recommend men to the favour and protection of

[14] ["I strive against adversity." Ovid, *Metamorphoses* 2:72]

the great. I was not made for a minion or a tool. As little did I follow the trade of winning the hearts, by imposing on the understandings, of the people. At every step of my progress in life (for in every step was I traversed and opposed), and at every turnpike I met, I was obliged to shew my passport, and again and again to prove my sole title to the honour of being useful to my Country, by a proof that I was not wholly unacquainted with it's laws, and the whole system of it's interests both abroad and at home. Otherwise no rank, no toleration even, for me. I had no arts, but manly arts. On them I have stood, and, please God, in spite of the Duke of Bedford and the Earl of Lauderdale, to the last gasp will I stand.

Had his Grace condescended to enquire concerning the person, whom he has not thought it below him to reproach, he might have found, that in the whole course of my life, I have never, on any pretence of oeconomy, or on any other pretence, so much as in a single instance, stood between any man and his reward of service, or his encouragement in useful talent and pursuit, from the highest of those services and pursuits to the lowest. On the contrary I have, on an hundred occasions, exerted myself with singular zeal to forward every man's even tolerable pretensions. I have more than once had good-natured reprehensions from my friends for carrying the matter to something bordering on abuse. This line of conduct, whatever it's merits might be, was partly owing to natural disposition; but I think full as much to reason and principle. I looked on the consideration of publick service, or publick ornament, to be real and very justice: and I ever held, a scanty and penurious justice to partake of the nature of a wrong. I held it to be, in its consequences, the worst oeconomy in the world. In saving money, I soon can count up all the good I do; but when by a cold penury, I blast the abilities of a nation, and stunt the growth of it's active energies, the ill I may do is beyond all calculation. Whether it be too much or too little, whatever I have done has been general and systematick. I have never entered into those trifling vexations and

---

oppressive details, that have been falsely, and most ridiculously laid to my charge.

Did I blame the pensions given to Mr. Barré and Mr. Dunning between the proposition and execution of my plan? No! surely, no! Those pensions were within my principles. I assert it, those gentlemen deserved their pensions, their titles, all they had; and if more they had, I should have been but pleased the more. They were men of talents; they were men of service. I put the profession of the law out of the question in one of them. It is a service that rewards itself. But their *publick service*, though, from their abilities unquestionably of more value than mine, in it's quantity and in it's duration was not to be mentioned with it. But I never could drive a hard bargain in my life, concerning any matter whatever; and least of all do I know how to haggle and huckster with merit. Pension for myself I obtained none; nor did I solicit any. Yet I was loaded with hatred for every thing that was with-held, and with obloquy for every thing that was given. I was thus left to support the grants of a name ever dear to me,[15] and ever venerable to the world, in favour of those, who were no friends of mine or of his, against the rude attacks of those who were at that time friends to the grantees, and their own zealous partizans. I have never heard the Earl of Lauderdale complain of these pensions. He finds nothing wrong till he comes to me. This is impartiality, in the true modern revolutionary style.

Whatever I did at that time, so far as it regarded order and oeconomy, is stable and eternal; as all principles must be. A particular order of things may be altered; order itself cannot lose its value. As to other particulars, they are variable by time and by circumstances. Laws of regulation are not fundamental laws. The publick exigencies are the masters of all such laws. They rule the laws, and are not to be ruled by them. They who exercise the legislative power at the time must judge.

[15] [Burke's party leader, Charles Watson-Wentworth, Marquis of Rockingham.]

A LETTER TO A NOBLE LORD

It may be new to his Grace, but I beg leave to tell him, that mere parsimony is not oeconomy. It is separable in theory from it; and in fact it may, or it may not, be a *part* of oeconomy, according to circumstances. Expence, and great expence, may be an essential part in true oeconomy. If parsimony were to be considered as one of the kinds of that virtue, there is however another and an higher oeconomy. Oeconomy is a distributive virtue, and consists not in saving, but in selection. Parsimony requires no providence, no sagacity, no powers of combination, no comparison, no judgment. Meer instinct, and that not an instinct of the noblest kind, may produce this false oeconomy in perfection. The other oeconomy has larger views. It demands a discriminating judgment, and a firm sagacious mind. It shuts one door to impudent importunity, only to open another, and a wider, to unpresuming merit. If none but meritorious service or real talent were to be rewarded, this nation has not wanted, and this nation will not want, the means of rewarding all the service it ever will receive, and encouraging all the merit it ever will produce. No state, since the foundation of society, has been impoverished by that species of profusion. Had the oeconomy of selection and proportion been at all times observed, we should not now have had an overgrown Duke of Bedford, to oppress the industry of humble men, and to limit by the standard of his own conceptions, the justice, the bounty, or, if he pleases, the charity of the Crown.

His Grace may think as meanly as he will of my deserts in the far greater part of my conduct in life. It is free for him to do so. There will always be some difference of opinion in the value of political services. But there is one merit of mine, which he, of all men living, ought to be the last to call in question. I have supported with very great zeal, and I am told with some degree of success, those opinions, or if his Grace likes another expression better, those old prejudices which buoy up the ponderous mass of his nobility, wealth, and titles. I have omitted no exertion to prevent him and them from sinking to that level, to which the meretricious French faction, his Grace at least coquets with, omit no exertion to reduce both. I have done all I could to discountenance their enquiries into the fortunes of those, who hold large portions of wealth without any apparent merit of their own. I have strained every nerve to keep the Duke of Bedford in that situation, which alone makes him my superior. Your Lordship has been a witness of the use he makes of that pre-eminence.

But be it, that this is virtue! Be it, that there is virtue in this well selected rigour; yet all virtues are not equally becoming to all men and at all times. There are crimes, undoubtedly there are crimes, which in all seasons of our existence, ought to put a generous antipathy in action; crimes that provoke an indignant justice, and call forth a warm and animated pursuit. But all things, that concern, what I may call, the preventive police of morality, all things merely rigid, harsh and censorial, the antiquated moralists, at whose feet I was brought up, would not have thought these the fittest matter to form the favourite virtues of young men of rank. What might have been well enough, and have been received with a veneration mixed with awe and terrour, from an old, severe, crabbed Cato, would have wanted something of propriety in the young Scipios, the ornament of the Roman Nobility, in the flower of their life. But the times, the morals, the masters, the scholars have all undergone a thorough revolution. It is a vile illiberal school, this new French academy of the *sans culottes*. There is nothing in it that is fit for a Gentleman to learn.

Whatever it's vogue may be, I still flatter myself, that the parents of the growing generation will be satisfied with what is to be taught to their children in Westminster, in Eaton, or in Winchester: I still indulge the hope that no *grown* Gentleman or Nobleman of our time will think of finishing at Mr. Thelwall's lecture whatever may have been left incompleat at the old Universities of his country.[16] I would give to Lord

---

[16] [John Thelwall (1764–1834), who communicated Jacobin principles through his popular lectures on Roman history and other subjects, had recently been acquitted of sedition.]

A LETTER TO A NOBLE LORD

Grenville and Mr. Pitt for a motto, what was said of a Roman Censor or Praetor (or what was he), who in virtue of a Senatus consultum shut up certain academies,

"Cludere Ludum Impudentiae jussit."[17]

Every honest father of a family in the kingdom will rejoice at the breaking up for the holidays, and will pray that there may be a very long vacation in all such schools.

The awful state of the time, and not myself or my own justification, is my true object in what I now write; or in what I shall ever write or say. It little signifies to the world what becomes of such things as me, or even as the Duke of Bedford. What I say about either of us is nothing more than a vehicle, as you, my Lord, will easily perceive, to convey my sentiments on matters far more worthy of your attention. It is when I stick to my apparent first subject that I ought to apologize, not when I depart from it. I therefore must beg your Lordship's pardon for again resuming it after this very short digression; assuring you that I shall never altogether lose sight of such matter as persons abler than I am may turn to some profit.

The Duke of Bedford conceives, that he is obliged to call the attention of the House of Peers to his Majesty's grant to me, which he considers as excessive and out of all bounds.

I know not how it has happened, but it really seems, that, whilst his Grace was meditating his well-considered censure upon me, he fell into a sort of sleep. Homer nods; and the Duke of Bedford may dream; and as dreams (even his golden dreams) are apt to be ill-pieced and incongruously put together, his Grace preserved his idea of reproach to *me*, but took the subject-matter from the Crown-grants *to his own family*. This is "the stuff of which his dreams are made."[18] In that

---

[17] [*Senatûs consultum:* resolution of the Senate. *Cludere Ludum* . . . : "He ordered the closing of this training ground of impudence." Tacitus, *De Oratoribus,* 35]

[18] [See *The Tempest* IV.i.156-57.]

A LETTER TO A NOBLE LORD

way of putting things together his Grace is perfectly in the right. The grants to the House of Russel were so enormous, as not only to outrage oeconomy, but even to stagger credibility. The Duke of Bedford is the Leviathan among all the creatures of the Crown. He tumbles about his unwieldy bulk; he plays and frolicks in the ocean of the Royal bounty. Huge as he is, and whilst "he lies floating many a rood,"[19] he is still a creature. His ribs, his fins, his whalebone, his blubber, the very spiracles through which he spouts a torrent of brine against his origin, and covers me all over with the spray—every thing of him and about him is from the Throne. Is it for *him* to question the dispensation of the Royal favour?

I really am at a loss to draw any sort of parallel between the publick merits of his Grace, by which he justifies the grants he holds, and these services of mine, on the favourable construction of which I have obtained what his Grace so much disapproves. In private life, I have not at all the honour of acquaintance with the noble Duke. But I ought to presume, and it costs me nothing to do so, that he abundantly deserves the esteem and love of all who live with him. But as to publick service, why truly it would not be more ridiculous for me to compare myself in rank, in fortune, in splendid descent, in youth, strength, or figure, with the Duke of Bedford, than to make a parallel between his services, and my attempts to be useful to my country. It would not be gross adulation, but uncivil irony, to say, that he has any publick merit of his own to keep alive the idea of the services by which his vast landed Pensions were obtained. My merits, whatever they are, are original and personal; his are derivative. It is his ancestor, the original pensioner, that has laid up this inexhaustible fund of merit, which makes his Grace so very delicate and exceptious about the merit of all other grantees of the Crown. Had he permitted me to remain in quiet, I should have said 'tis his estate; that's enough. It is his by law; what have I to do with it or it's history? He would naturally have said on his side,

---

[19] [See *Paradise Lost* 1:196.]

'tis this man's fortune. He is as good now, as my ancestor was two hundred and fifty years ago. I am a young man with very old pensions; he is an old man with very young pensions—that's all?

Why will his Grace, by attacking me, force me reluctantly to compare my little merit with that which obtained from the Crown those prodigies of profuse donation by which he tramples on the mediocrity of humble and laborious individuals? I would willingly leave him to the Herald's College, which the philosophy of the Sans culottes (prouder by far than all the Garters, and Norroys and Clarencieux, and Rouge Dragons that ever pranced in a procession of what his friends call aristocrates and despots), will abolish with contumely and scorn. These historians, recorders, and blazoners of virtues and arms, differ wholly from that other description of historians, who never assign any act of politicians to a good motive. These gentle historians, on the contrary, dip their pens in nothing but the milk of human kindness. They seek no further for merit than the preamble of a patent, or the inscription on a tomb. With them every man created a peer is first an hero ready made. They judge of every man's capacity for office by the offices he has filled; and the more offices the more ability. Every General-officer with them is a Marlborough; every Statesman a Burleigh; every Judge a Murray or a Yorke. They, who alive, were laughed at or pitied by all their acquaintance, make as good a figure as the best of them in the pages of Gwillim, Edmonson, and Collins.

To these recorders, so full of good nature to the great and prosperous, I would willingly leave the first Baron Russel, and Earl of Bedford, and the merits of his grants. But the aulnager, the weigher, the meter of grants, will not suffer us to acquiesce in the judgment of the Prince reigning at the time when they were made. They are never good to those who earn them. Well then; since the new grantees have war made on them by the old, and that the word of the Sovereign is not to be taken, let us turn our eyes to history, in which great men have always a pleasure in contemplating the heroic origin of their house.

The first peer of the name, the first purchaser of the grants, was a Mr. Russel, a person of an ancient gentleman's family, raised by being a minion of Henry the Eighth. As there generally is some resemblance of character to create these relations, the favourite was in all likelihood much such another as his master. The first of those immoderate grants was not taken from the antient demesne of the Crown, but from the recent confiscation of the ancient nobility of the land. The lion having sucked the blood of his prey, threw the offal carcase to the jackall in waiting. Having tasted once the food of confiscation, the favourites became fierce and ravenous. This worthy favourite's first grant was from the lay nobility. The second, infinitely improving on the enormity of the first, was from the plunder of the church. In truth his Grace is somewhat excusable for his dislike to a grant like mine, not only in it's quantity, but in it's kind so different from his own.

Mine was from a mild and benevolent sovereign; his from Henry the Eighth.

Mine had not it's fund in the murder of any innocent person of illustrious rank,[20] or in the pillage of any body of unoffending men. His grants were from the aggregate and consolidated funds of judgments iniquitously legal, and from possessions voluntarily surrendered by the lawful proprietors with the gibbet at their door.

The merit of the grantee whom he derives from, was that of being a prompt and greedy instrument of a *levelling* tyrant, who oppressed all descriptions of his people, but who fell with particular fury on every thing that was *great and noble*. Mine has been, in endeavouring to screen every man, in every class, from oppression, and particularly in defending the high and

[20] See the history of the melancholy catastrophe of the Duke of Buckingham. Temp. Hen. 8. [The jealousy and suspicion which Henry VIII entertained of Edward Stafford (1478–1521), 3rd Duke of Buckingham, resulted in Buckingham's execution on groundless charges of treason. He was an enemy to Henry's powerful Cardinal, Thomas Wolsey (c. 1475–1530).]

eminent, who in the bad times of confiscating Princes, confiscating chief Governors, or confiscating Demagogues, are the most exposed to jealousy, avarice and envy.

The merit of the original grantee of his Grace's pensions, was in giving his hand to the work, and partaking the spoil with a Prince, who plundered a part of his national church of his time and country. Mine was in defending the whole of the national church of my own time and my own country, and the whole of the national churches of all countries, from the principles and the examples which lead to ecclesiastical pillage, thence to a contempt of *all* prescriptive titles, thence to the pillage of *all* property, and thence to universal desolation.

The merit of the origin of his Grace's fortune was in being a favourite and chief adviser to a Prince, who left no liberty to their native country. My endeavour was to obtain liberty for the municipal country in which I was born, and for all descriptions and denominations in it. Mine was to support with unrelaxing vigilance every right, every privilege, every franchise, in this my adopted, my dearer and more comprehensive country; and not only to preserve those rights in this chief seat of empire, but in every nation, in every land, in every climate, language and religion, in the vast domain that still is under the protection, and the larger that was once under the protection, of the British Crown.

His founder's merits were, by arts in which he served his master and made his fortune, to bring poverty, wretchedness and depopulation on his country. Mine were under a benevolent Prince, in promoting the commerce, manufactures and agriculture of his kingdom; in which his Majesty shews an eminent example, who even in his amusements is a patriot, and in hours of leisure an improver of his native soil.

His founder's merit, was the merit of a gentleman raised by the arts of a Court, and the protection of a Wolsey, to the eminence of a great and potent Lord. His merit in that eminence was by instigating a tyrant to injustice, to provoke a people to rebellion. My merit was, to awaken the sober part of the country, that they might put themselves on their guard against any one potent Lord, or any greater number of potent Lords, or any combination of great leading men of any sort, if ever they should attempt to proceed in the same courses, but in the reverse order, that is, by instigating a corrupted populace to rebellion, and, through that rebellion, introducing a tyranny yet worse than the tyranny which his Grace's ancestor supported, and of which he profited in the manner we behold in the despotism of Henry the Eighth.

The political merit of the first pensioner of his Grace's house, was that of being concerned as a counsellor of state in advising, and in his person executing the conditions of a dishonourable peace with France; the surrendering the fortress of Boulogne, then our out-guard on the Continent. By that surrender, Calais, the key of France, and the bridle in the mouth of that power, was, not many years afterwards, finally lost. My merit has been in resisting the power and pride of France, under any form of it's rule; but in opposing it with the greatest zeal and earnestness, when that rule appeared in the worst form it could assume; the worst indeed which the prime cause and principle of all evil could possibly give it. It was my endeavour by every means to excite a spirit in the house, where I had the honour of a seat, for carrying on with early vigour and decision, the most clearly just and necessary war, that this or any nation ever carried on;[21] in order to save my country from the iron yoke of it's power, and from the more dreadful contagion of it's principles; to preserve, while they can be preserved pure and untainted, the ancient, inbred integrity, piety, good nature, and good humour of the people of England, from the dreadful pestilence which beginning in France, threatens to lay waste the whole moral, and in a great degree the whole physical world, having done both in the focus of it's most intense malignity.

The labours of his Grace's founder merited the curses, not loud but deep, of the Commons of England, on whom *he*

[21] [Already at war with Austria, France declared war on England and Holland on February 1, 1793, less than two weeks after the execution of Louis XVI.]

and his master had effected a *compleat Parliamentary Reform*, by making them in their slavery and humiliation, the true and adequate representatives of a debased, degraded, and undone people. My merits were, in having had an active, though not always an ostentatious share, in every one act, without exception, of undisputed constitutional utility in my time, and in having supported on all occasions, the authority, the efficiency, and the privileges of the Commons of Great Britain. I ended my services by a recorded and fully reasoned assertion on their own journals of their constitutional rights, and a vindication of their constitutional conduct. I laboured in all things to merit their inward approbation, and (along with the assistants of the largest, the greatest, and best of my endeavours) I received their free, unbiassed, publick, and solemn thanks.

Thus stands the account of the comparative merits of the Crown grants which compose the Duke of Bedford's fortune as balanced against mine. In the name of common sense, why should the Duke of Bedford think, that none but of the House of Russel are entitled to the favour of the Crown? Why should he imagine that no King of England has been capable of judging of merit but King Henry the Eighth? Indeed, he will pardon me; he is a little mistaken; all virtue did not end in the first Earl of Bedford. All discernment did not lose it's vision when his Creator closed his eyes. Let him remit his rigour on the disproportion between merit and reward in others, and they will make no enquiry into the origin of his fortune. They will regard with much more satisfaction, as he will contemplate with infinitely more advantage, whatever in his pedigree has been dulcified by an exposure to the influence of heaven in a long flow of generations, from the hard, acidulous, metallick tincture of the spring. It is little to be doubted, that several of his forefathers in that long series, have degenerated into honour and virtue. Let the Duke of Bedford (I am sure he will) reject with scorn and horror, the counsels of the lecturers, those wicked panders to avarice and ambition, who would tempt him in the troubles of his country, to seek another enormous fortune from the forfeitures of another nobility, and the plunder of another church. Let him (and I trust that yet he will) employ all the energy of his youth, and all the resources of his wealth, to crush rebellious principles which have no foundation in morals, and rebellious movements, that have no provocation in tyranny.

Then will be forgot the rebellions, which, by a doubtful priority in crime, his ancestor had provoked and extinguished. On such a conduct in the noble Duke, many of his countrymen might, and with some excuse might, give way to the enthusiasm of their gratitude, and in the dashing style of some of the old declaimers, cry out, that if the fates had found no other way in which they could give a Duke of Bedford[22] and his opulence as props to a tottering world, then the butchery of the Duke of Buckingham might be tolerated; it might be regarded even with complacency, whilst in the heir of confiscation they saw the sympathizing comforter of the martyrs, who suffer under the cruel confiscation of this day; whilst they beheld with admiration his zealous protection of the virtuous and loyal nobility of France, and his manly support of his brethren, the yet standing nobility and gentry of his native land. Then his Grace's merit would be pure and new, and sharp, as fresh from the mint of honour. As he pleased he might reflect honour on his predecessors, or throw it forward on those who were to succeed him. He might be the propagator of the stock of honour, or the root of it, as he thought proper.

Had it pleased God to continue to me the hopes of succession, I should have been, according to my mediocrity, and the mediocrity of the age I live in, a sort of founder of a family; I should have left a son, who, in all the points in which personal merit can be viewed, in science, in erudition, in genius, in taste, in honour, in generosity, in humanity, in every liberal sentiment, and every liberal accomplishment, would not have shewn himself inferior to the Duke of Bedford, or to any of

[22] At si non aliam venturo fata Neroni, &c. ["If the Fates could find no other way to bring in Nero, etc." Lucan, *Pharsalia,* 1:33]

those whom he traces in his line. His Grace very soon would have wanted all plausibility in his attack upon that provision which belonged more to mine than to me. He would soon have supplied every deficiency, and symmetrized every disproportion. It would not have been for that successor to resort to any stagnant wafting reservoir of merit in me, or in any ancestry. He had in himself a salient, living spring, of generous and manly action. Every day he lived he would have repurchased the bounty of the crown, and ten times more, if ten times more he had received. He was made a publick creature; and had no enjoyment whatever, but in the performance of some duty. At this exigent moment, the loss of a finished man is not easily supplied.

But a disposer whose power we are little able to resist, and whose wisdom it behoves us not at all to dispute; has ordained it in another manner, and (whatever my querulous weakness might suggest) a far better. The storm has gone over me; and I lie like one of those old oaks which the late hurricane has scattered about me. I am stripped of all my honours; I am torn up by the roots, and lie prostrate on the earth! There, and prostrate there, I most unfeignedly recognize the divine justice, and in some degree submit to it. But whilst I humble myself before God, I do not know that it is forbidden to repel the attacks of unjust and inconsiderate men. The patience of Job is proverbial. After some of the convulsive struggles of our irritable nature, he submitted himself, and repented in dust and ashes. But even so, I do not find him blamed for reprehending, and with a considerable degree of verbal asperity, those ill-natured neighbours of his, who visited his dunghill to read moral, political, and oeconomical lectures on his misery. I am alone. I have none to meet my enemies in the gate. Indeed, my Lord, I greatly deceive myself, if in this hard season I would give a peck of refuse wheat for all that is called fame and honour in the world. This is the appetite but of a few. It is a luxury; it is a privilege; it is an indulgence for those who are at their ease. But we are all of us made to shun disgrace, as we are made to shrink from pain, and poverty, and disease. It is an instinct; and under the direction of reason, instinct is always in the right. I live in an inverted order. They who ought to have succeeded me are gone before me. They who should have been to me as posterity are in the place of ancestors. I owe to the dearest relation (which ever must subsist in memory) that act of piety, which he would have performed to me; I owe it to him to shew that he was not descended, as the Duke of Bedford would have it, from an unworthy parent.

The Crown has considered me after long service: the Crown has paid the Duke of Bedford by advance. He has had a long credit for any service which he may perform hereafter. He is secure, and long may he be secure, in his advance, whether he performs any services or not. But let him take care how he endangers the safety of that Constitution which secures his own utility or his own insignificance; or how he discourages those, who take up, even puny arms, to defend an order of things, which, like the Sun of Heaven, shines alike on the useful and the worthless. His grants are engrafted on the public law of Europe, covered with the awful hoar of innumerable ages. They are guarded by the sacred rules of prescription, found in that full treasury of jurisprudence from which the jejuneness and penury of our municipal law has, by degrees, been enriched and strengthened. This prescription I had my share (a very full share) in bringing to it's perfection.[23] The Duke of Bedford will stand as long as prescriptive law endures; as long as the great stable laws of property, common to us with all civilized nations, are kept in their integrity, and without the smallest intermixture of the laws, maxims, principles, or precedents of the Grand Revolution. They are secure against all changes but one. The whole revolutionary system, institutes, digest, code, novels, text, gloss, comment, are not only not the same, but they are the very reverse, and the reverse fundamentally, of all the laws, on which civil life has hitherto been upheld in all the govern-

---

[23] Sir George Savile's Act, called the *Nullum Tempus* Act.

ments of the world. The learned professors of the Rights of Man regard prescription, not as a title to bar all claim, set up against old possession—but they look on prescription as itself a bar against the possessor and proprietor. They hold an immemorial possession to be no more than a long continued, and therefore an aggravated injustice.

Such are *their* ideas; such *their* religion, and such *their* law. But as to *our* country and *our* race, as long as the well compacted structure of our church and state, the sanctuary, the holy of holies of that ancient law, defended by reverence, defended by power, a fortress at once and a temple,[24] shall stand inviolate on the brow of the British Sion—as long as the British Monarchy, not more limited than fenced by the orders of the State, shall, like the proud Keep of Windsor, rising in the majesty of proportion, and girt with the double belt of it's kindred and coeval towers, as long as this awful structure shall oversee and guard the subjected land—so long the mounds and dykes of the low, fat, Bedford level will have nothing to fear from all the pickaxes of all the levellers of France. As long as our Sovereign Lord the King, and his faithful subjects, the Lords and Commons of this realm, the triple cord, which no man can break; the solemn, sworn, constitutional frankpledge of this nation; the firm guarantees of each others being, and each others rights; the joint and several securities, each in it's place and order, for every kind and every quality, of property and of dignity—As long as these endure, so long the Duke of Bedford is safe: and we are all safe together—the high from the blights of envy and the spoliations of rapacity; the low from the iron hand of oppression and the insolent spurn of contempt. Amen! and so be it: and so it will be,

Dum domus Aeneae Capitoli immobile saxum
Accolet; imperiumque pater Romanus habebit.[25]

[24] Templum in modum arcis. Tacitus of the Temple of Jerusalem. [A temple in the form of a citadel. Tacitus, *Histories* 5.12]
[25] ["As long as the house of Aeneas dwells on the immovable rock of the Capitol, and the father of Rome maintains authority." Vergil, *Aeneid* 9:448–449]

A LETTER TO A NOBLE LORD

But if the rude inroad of Gallick tumult, with it's sophisti-
cal Rights of Man, to falsify the account, and it's sword as a
makeweight to throw into the scale, shall be introduced into
our city by a misguided populace, set on by proud great men,
themselves blinded and intoxicated by a frantick ambition, we
shall, all of us, perish and be overwhelmed in a common ruin.
If a great storm blow on our coast, it will cast the whales on the
strand as well as the periwinkles. His Grace will not survive
the poor grantee he despises, no not for a twelvemonth. If the
great look for safety in the services they render to this Gallick
cause, it is to be foolish, even above the weight of privilege
allowed to wealth. If his Grace be one of these whom they
endeavour to proselytize, he ought to be aware of the character of the sect, whose doctrines he is invited to embrace. With
them, insurrection is the most sacred of revolutionary duties
to the state. Ingratitude to benefactors is the first of revolutionary virtues. Ingratitude is indeed their four cardinal virtues compacted and amalgamated into one; and he will find it
in every thing that has happened since the commencement of
the philosophick revolution to this hour. If he pleads the merit of having performed the duty of insurrection against the
order he lives in (God forbid he ever should), the merit of
others will be to perform the duty of insurrection against him.
If he pleads (again God forbid he should, and I do not suspect
he will) his ingratitude to the Crown for it's creation of his
family, others will plead their right and duty to pay him in
kind. They will laugh, indeed they will laugh, at his parch-
ment and his wax. His deeds will be drawn out with the rest of
the lumber of his evidence room, and burnt to the tune of *ça
ira*[26] in the courts of Bedford (then Equality) House.

Am I to blame, if I attempt to pay his Grace's hostile reproaches to me with a friendly admonition to himself? Can I
be blamed, for pointing out to him in what manner he is like
to be affected, if the sect of the cannibal philosophers of
France should proselytize any considerable part of this peo-

[26] [The refrain of a Jacobin song that promised the hanging of all aristocrats.]

ple, and, by their joint proselytizing arms, should conquer that Government, to which his Grace does not seem to me to give all the support his own security demands? Surely it is proper, that he, and that others like him, should know the true genius of this sect; what their opinions are; what they have done; and to whom; and what (if a prognostick is to be formed from the dispositions and actions of men) it is certain they will do hereafter. He ought to know, that they have sworn assistance, the only engagement they ever will keep, to all in this country, who bear a resemblance to themselves, and who think as such, that *The whole duty of man*[27] consists in destruction. They are a misallied and disparaged branch of the house of Nimrod. They are the Duke of Bedford's natural hunters; and he is their natural game. Because he is not very profoundly reflecting, he sleeps in profound security: they, on the contrary, are always vigilant, active, enterprizing, and though far removed from any knowledge, which makes men estimable or useful, in all the instruments and resources of evil, their leaders are not meanly instructed, or insufficiently furnished. In the French Revolution every thing is new; and, from want of preparation to meet so unlooked for an evil, every thing is dangerous. Never, before this time, was a set of literary men, converted into a gang of robbers and assassins. Never before, did a den of bravoes and banditti, assume the garb and tone of an academy of philosophers.

Let me tell his Grace, that an union of such characters, monstrous as it seems, is not made for producing despicable enemies. But if they are formidable as foes, as friends they are dreadful indeed. The men of property in France confiding in a force, which seemed to be irresistible, because it had never been tried, neglected to prepare for a conflict with their enemies at their own weapons. They were found in such a situation as the Mexicans were, when they were attacked by the dogs, the cavalry, the iron, and the gunpowder of an handful of bearded men, whom they did not know to exist in nature.

[27] [The title of a popular work of practical devotion, published anonymously in 1658.]

This is a comparison that some, I think, have made; and it is just. In France they had their enemies within their houses. They were even in the bosoms of many of them. But they had not sagacity to discern their savage character. They seemed tame, and even caressing. They had nothing but *douce humanité*[28] in their mouth. They could not bear the punishment of the mildest laws on the greatest criminals. The slightest severity of justice made their flesh creep. The very idea that war existed in the world disturbed their repose. Military glory was no more, with them, than a splendid infamy. Hardly would they hear of self defence, which they reduced within such bounds, as to leave it no defence at all. All this while they meditated the confiscations and massacres we have seen. Had any one told these unfortunate Noblemen and Gentlemen, how, and by whom, the grand fabrick of the French monarchy under which they flourished would be subverted, they would not have pitied him as a visionary, but would have turned from him as what they call a *mauvais plaisant*.[29] Yet we have seen what has happened. The persons who have suffered from the cannibal philosophy of France, are so like the Duke of Bedford, that nothing but his Grace's probably not speaking quite so good French, could enable us to find out any difference. A great many of them had as pompous titles as he, and were of full as illustrious a race: some few of them had fortunes as ample; several of them, without meaning the least disparagement to the Duke of Bedford, were as wise, and as virtuous, and as valiant, and as well educated, and as compleat in all the lineaments of men of honour as he is: And to all this they had added the powerful outguard of a military profession, which, in it's nature, renders men somewhat more cautious than those, who have nothing to attend to but the lazy enjoyment of undisturbed possessions. But security was their ruin. They are dashed to pieces in the storm, and our shores are covered with the wrecks. If they had been

[28] [Sweet humanity.]
[29] [Sorry jester.]

aware that such a thing might happen, such a thing never could have happened.

I assure his Grace, that if I state to him the designs of his enemies, in a manner which may appear to him ludicrous and impossible, I tell him nothing that has not exactly happened, point by point, but twenty-four miles from our own shore. I assure him that the Frenchified faction, more encouraged, than others are warned, by what has happened in France, look at him and his landed possessions, as an object at once of curiosity and rapacity. He is made for them in every part of their double character. As robbers, to them he is a noble booty: as speculatists, he is a glorious subject for their experimental philosophy. He affords matter for an extensive analysis, in all the branches of their science, geometrical, physical, civil and political. These philosophers are fanaticks; independent of any interest, which if it operated alone would make them much more tractable, they are carried with such an headlong rage towards every desperate trial, that they would sacrifice the whole human race to the slightest of their experiments. I am better able to enter into the character of this description of men than the noble Duke can be. I have lived long and variously in the World. Without any considerable pretensions to literature in myself, I have aspired to the love of letters. I have lived for a great many years in habitudes with those who professed them. I can form a tolerable estimate of what is likely to happen from a character, chiefly dependent for fame and fortune, on knowledge and talent, as well in it's morbid and perverted state, as in that which is sound and natural. Naturally men so formed and finished are the first gifts of Providence to the World. But when they have once thrown off the fear of God, which was in all ages too often the case, and the fear of man, which is now the case, and when in that state they come to understand one another, and to act in corps, a more dreadful calamity cannot arise out of Hell to scourge mankind. Nothing can be conceived more hard than the heart of a thorough-bred metaphysician. It comes nearer to the cold malignity of a wicked spirit than to the frailty and passion of a

man. It is like that of the principle of Evil himself, incorpore-
al, pure, unmixed, dephlegmated, defecated evil. It is no easy
operation to eradicate humanity from the human breast.
What Shakespeare calls "the compunctious visitings of nature,"[30] will sometimes knock at their hearts, and protest
against their murderous speculations. But they have a means
of compounding with their nature. Their humanity is not dissolved. They only give it a long prorogation. They are ready to
declare, that they do not think two thousand years too long a
period for the good that they pursue. It is remarkable, that
they never see any way to their projected good but by the road
of some evil. Their imagination is not fatigued, with the con-
templation of human suffering thro' the wild waste of centuries added to centuries, of misery and desolation. Their humanity is at their horizon—and, like the horizon, it always flies
before them. The geometricians, and the chymists bring, the
one from the dry bones of their diagrams, and the other from
the soot of their furnaces, dispositions that make them worse
than indifferent about those feelings and habitudes, which are
the supports of the moral world. Ambition is come upon them
suddenly; they are intoxicated with it, and it has rendered
them fearless of the danger, which may from thence arise to
others or to themselves. These philosophers, consider men in
their experiments, no more than they do mice in an air pump,
or in a recipient of mephitick gas. Whatever his Grace may
think of himself, they look upon him, and every thing that
belongs to him, with no more regard than they do upon the
whiskers of that little long-tailed animal, that has been long the
game of the grave, demure, insidious, spring-nailed, velvet-
pawed, green-eyed philosophers, whether going upon two
legs, or upon four.

His Grace's landed possessions are irresistibly inviting to
an *agrarian* experiment. They are a downright insult upon
the Rights of Man. They are more extensive than the territory
of many of the Grecian republicks; and they are without com-

---

[30] [See *Macbeth* I.v.45.]

parison more fertile than most of them. There are now republicks in Italy, in Germany and in Swisserland, which do not possess any thing like so fair and ample a domain. There is scope for seven philosophers to proceed in their analytical experiments, upon Harington's seven different forms of republicks, in the acres of this one Duke.[31] Hitherto they have been wholly unproductive to speculation; fitted for nothing but to fatten bullocks, and to produce grain for beer, still more to stupify the dull English understanding. Abbé Sieyes has whole nests of pigeon-holes full of constitutions ready made, ticketed, sorted, and numbered; suited to every season and every fancy; some with the top of the pattern at the bottom, and some with the bottom at the top; some plain, some flowered; some distinguished for their simplicity; others for their complexity; some of blood colour; some of *boue de Paris*;[32] some with directories, others without a direction; some with councils of elders, and councils of youngsters; some without any council at all. Some where the electors choose the representatives; others, where the representatives choose the electors. Some in long coats, and some in short cloaks; some with pantaloons; some without breeches. Some with five shilling qualifications; some totally unqualified. So that no constitution-fancier may go unsuited from his shop, provided he loves a pattern of pillage, oppression, arbitrary imprisonment, confiscation, exile, revolutionary judgment, and legalised premeditated murder, in any shapes into which they can be put. What a pity it is, that the progress of experimental philosophy should be checked by his Grace's monopoly! Such are their sentiments, I assure him; such is their language when they dare to speak; and such are their proceedings, when they have the means to act.

Their geographers, and geometricians, have been some time out of practice. It is some time since they have divided their own country into squares. That figure has lost the

[31] [A reference to the political theories of James Harrington's *Commonwealth of Oceana* (1656).]

[32] [Dirt of Paris.]

A LETTER TO A NOBLE LORD

charms of it's novelty. They want new lands for new trials. It is not only the geometricians of the republick that find him a good subject, the chymists have bespoke him after the geometricians have done with him. As the first set have an eye on his Grace's lands, the chymists are not less taken with his buildings. They consider mortar as a very anti-revolutionary invention in it's present state; but properly employed, an admirable material for overturning all establishments. They have found that the gunpowder of *ruins* is far the fittest for making other *ruins*, and so *ad infinitum*. They have calculated what quantity of matter convertible into nitre is to be found in Bedford House, in Woburn Abbey, and in what his Grace and his trustees have still suffered to stand of that foolish royalist Inigo Jones, in Covent Garden. Churches, play-houses, coffee-houses, all alike are destined to be mingled, and equalized, and blended into one common rubbish; and well sifted, and lixiviated, to chrystalize into true democratick explosive insurrectionary nitre. Their Academy del *Cimento*[33] (per antiphrasin) with Morveau and Hassenfrats as it's head, have computed that the brave Sans-culottes may make war on all the aristocracy of Europe for a twelvemonth, out of the rubbish of the Duke of Bedford's buildings.[34]

[33] [The short-lived Accademia del Cimento (Academy of Experiment) was founded in 1657 as a protest against the medieval quadrivium. Burke refers here to two French chemists who participated in the Revolution.]

[34] There is nothing, on which the leaders of the Republick, one and indivisible, value themselves, more than on the chymical operations, by which, through science, they convert the pride of Aristocracy, to an instrument of it's own destruction—on the operations by which they reduce the magnificent ancient country seats of the nobility, decorated with the *feudal* titles of Duke, Marquis, or Earl, into magazines of what they call *revolutionary* gunpowder. They tell us, that hitherto things "had not yet been properly and in a *revolutionary* manner explored." . . . "The strong *chateaus*, those *feudal* fortresses, that *were ordered to be demolished*, attracted next the attention of your Committee. *Nature* there had *secretly* regained her *rights*, and had produced salt-petre for the *purpose*, as it should seem, *of facilitating the execution of your decree by preparing the means of destruction*. From these *ruins*, which *still frown* on the liberties of the Republick, we have extracted the means of producing good; and those piles, which have hitherto glutted the *pride of Despots*, and covered the plots of La Vendée, will soon furnish wherewithal to tame the traitors, and to overwhelm the disaffected." . . . "The *rebellious cities* also, have afforded a large quantity of salt-petre. *Commune Affranchie*

A LETTER TO A NOBLE LORD

While the Morveaux and Priestleys are proceeding with these experiments upon the Duke of Bedford's houses, the Sieyes, and the rest of the analytical legislators, and constitution-venders, are quite as busy in their trade of decomposing organization, in forming his Grace's vassals into primary assemblies, national guards, first, second and third requisitioners, committees of research, conductors of the travelling guillotine, judges of revolutionary tribunals, legislative hangmen, supervisors of domiciliary visitation, exactors of forced loans, and assessors of the maximum.

The din of all this smithery may some time or other possibly wake this noble Duke, and push him to an endeavour to save some little matter from their experimental philosophy. If he pleads his grants from the Crown, he is ruined at the outset. If he pleads he has received them from the pillage of superstitious corporations, this indeed will stagger them a little, because they are enemies to all corporations, and to all religion. However, they will soon recover themselves, and will tell his Grace, or his learned council, that all such property belongs to the *nation*; and that it would be more wise for him, if he wishes to live the natural term of a *citizen* (that is, according to Condorcet's calculation, six months on an average), not to pass for an usurper upon the national property. This is what the *Serjeants* at law of the Rights of Man, will say to the puny *apprentices* of the common law of England.

Is the Genius of Philosophy not yet known? You may as well think the Garden of the Tuileries was well protected with the cords of ribbon insultingly stretched by the National Assembly to keep the sovereign canaille from intruding on the retirement of the poor King of the French as that such flimsy cobwebs will stand between the savages of the Revolution and their natural prey. Deep Philosophers are no triflers; brave Sans culottes are no formalists. They will no more regard a Marquis of Tavistock than an Abbot of

(that is, the noble city of Lyons reduced in many parts to an heap of ruins), and Toulon will pay a *second* tribute to our artillery." Report 1st. February 1794.

A Letter to a Noble Lord

Tavistock; the Lord of Wooburn will not be more respectable in their eyes than the Prior of Wooburn: they will make no difference between the Superior of a Covent Garden of nuns and of a Covent Garden of another description. They will not care a rush whether his coat is long or short; whether the colour be purple or blue and buff. They will not trouble *their* heads, with what part of *his* head, his hair is cut from; and they will look with equal respect on a tonsure and a crop. Their only question will be that of their *Legendre*,[35] or some other of their legislative butchers, How he cuts up? how he tallows in the cawl or on the kidneys?

Is it not a singular phoenomenon, that whilst the Sans culotte Carcase Butchers, and the Philosophers of the shambles, are pricking their dotted lines upon his hide, and like the print of the poor ox that we see in the shop windows at Charing Cross, alive as he is, and thinking no harm in the world, he is divided into rumps, and sirloins, and briskets, and into all sorts of pieces for roasting, boiling, and stewing, that all the while they are measuring *him*, his Grace is measuring *me*; is invidiously comparing the bounty of the Crown with the deserts of the defender of his order, and in the same moment fawning on those who have the knife half out of the sheath— poor innocent!

> Pleas'd to the last, he crops the flow'ry food,
> And licks the hand just rais'd to shed his blood.[36]

No man lives too long, who lives to do with spirit, and suffer with resignation, what Providence pleases to command or inflict: but indeed they are sharp incommodities which beset old age. It was but the other day, that on putting in order some things which had been brought here on my taking leave of London for ever, I looked over a number of fine portraits, most of them of persons now dead, but whose socie-

[35] [Louis Legendre was a sans-culotte, friend of Danton, and a butcher.]
[36] [Pope, *An Essay on Man*, 1:83-84.]

A LETTER TO A NOBLE LORD

ty, in my better days, made this a proud and happy place. Amongst these was the picture of Lord Keppel.[37] It was painted by an artist worthy of the subject, the excellent friend of that excellent man from their earliest youth, and a common friend of us both, with whom we lived for many years without a moment of coldness, of peevishness, of jealousy, or of jar, to the day of our final separation.

I ever looked on Lord Keppel as one of the greatest and best men of his age; and I loved, and cultivated him accordingly. He was much in my heart, and I believe I was in his to the very last beat. It was after his trial at Portsmouth that he gave me this picture. With what zeal and anxious affection I attended him through that his agony of glory, what part my son in the early flush and enthusiasm of his virtue, and the pious passion with which he attached himself to all my connections, with what prodigality we both squandered ourselves in courting almost every sort of enmity for his sake, I believe he felt, just as I should have felt, such friendship on such an occasion. I partook indeed of this honour, with several of the first, and best, and ablest in the kindgom, but I was behind hand with none of them; and I am sure, that if to the eternal disgrace of this nation, and to the total annihilation of every trace of honour and virtue in it, things had taken a different turn from what they did, I should have attended him to the quarter-deck with no less good will and more pride, though with far other feelings, than I partook of the general flow of national joy that attended the justice that was done to his virtue.

Pardon, my Lord, the feeble garrulity of age, which loves to diffuse itself in discourse of the departed great. At my years

[37] [Sir Joshua Reynolds painted seven portraits of the naval commander Augustus, First Viscount Keppel (1725-1786). Keppel was tried and acquitted in 1779 on capital charges stemming from his conduct of an indecisive naval engagement the previous year with the French. Burke, along with other Rockingham Whigs, took a very active role in Keppel's defense. When Rockingham became Prime Minister in 1782, Keppel was appointed 1st Lord of the Admiralty and raised to the peerage shortly thereafter. He was Bedford's uncle.]

A LETTER TO A NOBLE LORD

we live in retrospect alone: and, wholly unfitted for the society of vigorous life, we enjoy, the best balm to all wounds, the consolation of friendship, in those only whom we have lost for ever. Feeling the loss of Lord Keppel at all times, at no time did I feel it so much as on the first day when I was attacked in the House of Lords.

Had he lived, that reverend form would have risen in its place, and with a mild, parental reprehension to his nephew the Duke of Bedford, he would have told him that the favour of that gracious prince, who had honoured his virtues with the government of the navy of Great Britain, and with a seat in the hereditary great council of his kingdom, was not undeservedly shewn to the friend of the best portion of his life, and his faithful companion and counsellor under his rudest trials. He would have told him, that to whomever else these reproaches might be becoming, they were not decorous in his near kindred. He would have told him that when men in that rank lose decorum, they lose every thing.

On that day I had a loss in Lord Keppel; but the publick loss of him in this aweful crisis—! I speak from much knowledge of the person, he never would have listened to any compromise with the rabble rout of this Sans Culotterie of France. His goodness of heart, his reason, his taste, his publick duty, his principles, his prejudices, would have repelled him for ever from all connection with that horrid medley of madness, vice, impiety, and crime.

Lord Keppel had two countries; one of descent, and one of birth. Their interests and their glory are the same; and his mind was capacious of both. His family was noble and it was Dutch: that is, he was of the oldest and purest nobility that Europe can boast, among a people renowned above all others for love of their native land. Though it was never shewn in insult to any human being, Lord Keppel was something high. It was a wild stock of pride, on which the tenderest of all hearts had grafted the milder virtues. He valued ancient nobility; and he was not disinclined to augment it with new honours. He valued the old nobility and the new, not as an excuse for inglorious sloth, but as an incitement to virtuous activity. He considered it as a sort of cure for selfishness and a narrow mind; conceiving that a man born in an elevated place, in himself was nothing, but every thing in what went before, and what was to come after him. Without much speculation, but by the sure instinct of ingenuous feelings, and by the dictates of plain unsophisticated natural understanding, he felt, that no great Commonwealth could by any possibility long subsist, without a body of some kind or other of nobility, decorated with honour, and fortified by privilege. This nobility forms the chain that connects the ages of a nation, which otherwise (with Mr. Paine) would soon be taught that no one generation can bind another. He felt that no political fabrick could be well made without some such order of things as might, through a series of time afford a rational hope of securing unity, coherence, consistency, and stability to the state. He felt that nothing else can protect it against the levity of courts, and the greater levity of the multitude. That to talk of hereditary monarchy without any thing else of hereditary reverence in the Commonwealth, was a low-minded absurdity; fit only for those detestable "fools aspiring to be knaves,"[38] who began to forge in 1789, the false money of the French Constitution—That it is one fatal objection to all *new* fancied and *new fabricated* Republicks (among a people, who, once possessing such an advantage, have wickedly and insolently rejected it), that the *prejudice* of an old nobility is a thing that *cannot* be made. It may be improved, it may be corrected, it may be replenished: men may be taken from it, or aggregated to it, but the *thing itself* is matter of *inveterate* opinion, and therefore *cannot* be matter of mere positive institution. He felt, that this nobility, in fact does not exist in wrong of other orders of the state, but by them, and for them.

[38] [See Pope, *Epilogue to the Satires*, 1:163-64.]

A LETTER TO A NOBLE LORD

I knew the man I speak of; and, if we can divine the future, out of what we collect from the past, no person living would look with more scorn and horrour on the impious parricide committed on all their ancestry, and on the desperate attainder passed on all their posterity, by the Orleans, and the Rochefoucaults, and the Fayettes, and the Viscomtes de Noailles,[39] and the false Perigords, and the long *et caetera* of the perfidious Sans Culottes of the court, who like demoniacks, possessed with a spirit of fallen pride, and inverted ambition, abdicated their dignities, disowned their families, betrayed the most sacred of all trusts, and by breaking to pieces a great link of society, and all the cramps and holdings of the state, brought eternal confusion and desolation on their country. For the fate of the miscreant parricides themselves he would have had no pity. Compassion for the myriads of men, of whom the world was not worthy, who by their means have perished in prisons, or on scaffolds, or are pining in beggary and exile, would leave no room in his, or in any well-formed mind, for any such sensation. We are not made at once to pity the oppressor and the oppressed.

Looking to his Batavian descent, how could he bear to behold his kindred, the descendants of the brave nobility of Holland, whose blood prodigally poured out, had, more than all the canals, meers, and inundations of their country, protected their independence, to behold them bowed in the basest servitude, to the basest and vilest of the human race; in servitude to those who in no respect, were superior in dignity, or could aspire to a better place than that of hangmen to the tyrants, to whose sceptered pride they had opposed an elevation of soul, that surmounted, and overpowered the loftiness of Castile, the haughtiness of Austria, and the overbearing arrogance of France?[40]

[39] [Noblemen who sympathized with the French Revolution to the point of renouncing their privileges as noblemen.]

[40] [By the time of this writing, the French revolutionary army had forced the Prince of Orange to flee to England and had established the Batavian Republic, dominated by France. In the next paragraph, Burke compares

A Letter to a Noble Lord

Could he with patience bear, that the children of that nobility, who would have deluged their country and given it to the sea, rather than submit to Louis XIV who was then in his meridian glory, when his arms were conducted by the Turennes, by the Luxembourgs, by the Boufflers; when his councils were directed by the Colberts, and the Louvois; when his tribunals were filled by the Lamoignons and the Daguessaus—that these should be given up to the cruel sport of the Pichegru's, the Jourdans, the Santerres, under the Rollands, and Brissots, and Gorsas, and Robespierres, the Reubels, the Carnots, and Talliens, and Dantons, and the whole tribe of Regicides, robbers, and revolutionary judges, that, from the rotten carcase of their own murdered country, have poured out innumerable swarms of the lowest, and at once the most destructive of the classes of animated nature, which like columns of locusts, have laid waste the fairest part of the world?

Would Keppel have borne to see the ruin of the virtuous Patricians, that happy union of the noble and the burgher, who with signal prudence and integrity, had long governed the cities of the confederate Republick, the cherishing fathers of their country, who, denying commerce to themselves, made it flourish in a manner unexampled under their protection? Could Keppel have borne that a vile faction should totally destroy this harmonious construction, in favour of a robbing Democracy, founded on the spurious rights of man?

He was no great clerk, but he was perfectly well versed in the interests of Europe, and he could not have heard with patience, that the country of Grotius, the cradle of the Law of Nations, and one of the richest repositories of all Law, should be taught a new code by the ignorant flippancy of Thomas Paine, the presumptuous foppery of La Fayette, with his stolen rights of man in his hand, the wild profligate intrigue and

the French military leaders under Louis XIV to the military and political leaders of the French National Convention.]

turbulency of Marat, and the impious sophistry of Condorcet, in his insolent addresses to the Batavian Republick?

Could Keppel, who idolized the house of Nassau, who was himself given to England, along with the blessings of the British and Dutch revolutions; with revolutions of stability; with revolutions which consolidated and married the liberties and the interests of the two nations for ever, could he see the fountain of British liberty itself in servitude to France? Could he see with patience a Prince of Orange expelled as a sort of diminutive despot, with every kind of contumely, from the country, which that family of deliverers had so often rescued from slavery, and obliged to live in exile in another country, which owes it's liberty to his house?

Would Keppel have heard with patience, that the conduct to be held on such occasions was to become short by the knees to the faction of the homicides, to intreat them quietly to retire? or if the fortune of war should drive them from their first wicked and unprovoked invasion, that no security should be taken, no arrangement made, no barrier formed, no alliance entered into for the security of that, which under a foreign name is the most precious part of England? What would he have said, if it was even proposed that the Austrian Netherlands (which ought to be a barrier to Holland, and the tie of an alliance, to protect her against any species of rule that might be erected, or even be restored in France) should be formed into a republick under her influence and dependent upon her power?

But above all, what would he have said, if he had heard it made a matter of accusation against me, by his nephew the Duke of Bedford, that I was the author of the war? Had I a mind to keep that high distinction to myself, as from pride I might, but from justice I dare not, he would have snatched his share of it from my hand, and held it with the grasp of a dying convulsion to his end.

It would be a most arrogant presumption in me to assume to myself the glory of what belongs to his Majesty, and to his Ministers, and to his Parliament, and to the far greater majority of his faithful people: But had I stood alone to counsel, and that all were determined to be guided by my advice, and to follow it implicitly—then I should have been the sole author of a war. But it should have been a war on my ideas and my principles. However let his Grace think as he may of my demerits with regard to the war with Regicide, he will find my guilt confined to that alone. He never shall, with the smallest colour of reason, accuse me of being the author of a peace with Regicide. But that is high matter; and ought not to be mixed with any thing of so little moment, as what may belong to me, or even to the Duke of Bedford.

I have the honour to be, &c.

EDMUND BURKE

INDEX

Aaron, 153
Academy del Cimento, 317, 317n
Adam, 171, 197–198
Addison, Joseph, 12n
Aeneid (Vergil), 159–162, 160n, 287n, 291n, 310n
Agricultural economy of France, 232
Algiers, 236
Ambassador, French
British fail to recognize, 248
Ambition in National Assembly, 233
American Revolution. *See* Revolution, American
Anarchy, 38–39
French Revolution described as, 36–41
Ancients
Burke allies with, against moderns, 28
Greeks, xiii, 23–24, 30, 42–43, 47, 75–76, 92, 102, 104, 162, 167, 188, 210, 212, 264, 267, 269n, 275n, 295n
Romans, 12n, 14, 90, 102, 196, 199, 222, 299
See also Cicero; Classical writings; Tacitus; Vergil
Anglicans. *See* Church of England
Anglo-Gallick clubs, 248
Anne (Queen of England), 74, 121, 121n, 133
Anti-Orange party
pro-French attitude of, 229
Antoinette, Marie (Queen of France), 43–46, 200, 203–204, 235n
British reaction to capture of, 73
Burke defends, 24–25
Burke predicts execution of, 44
pilloried, 45
promiscuity of, 19–20, 23–24
An Appeal from the New to the Old Whigs (Burke), x, xi–xii, xv, xvii, 28, 73–201

Argus, 94n
Aristocracy
and British Constitution, 101
curtailed by Louis XVI, 242
during revolutions, 191
French attempt to destroy, 52–54
House of Lords a pillar of, 149–150
importance of, to country, xvii–xviii
natural, ix–x, 66–67, 168, 175
natural versus hereditary, xviii–xix
nature of, 168
restored during Glorious Revolution, 145
seat of power and intelligence, 235
in Spain, 224–225
threatened in Holland, 229
threats to hereditary estates, 191
Army, British
leads to stability, 214–215
quality of, 57
Army, French
revolts against officers, 78
revolutionaries oppose, 56
Arragon, 225
Art
and human nature, 74–81
is man's nature, 168–169
Assassination, 55
Astraea Redux (Dryden), 197n
Atheists
establishment of atheism, 266–267
partisans of French, 212
similar to Epicureans, 237
sworn enemies to king, nobility and priesthood, 237–238
Athens, 212
"At His Arrival at Bristol" (Burke), 104–106
Augustine, St., 267
Aulick Council, 268
Aurelius, Marcus, 90
Aurora, 113
Austria, 203–204, 323, 325

INDEX

INDEX

INDEX

INDEX

INDEX

INDEX

INDEX

INDEX

INDEX

INDEX

The typeface used for this book is ITC New Baskerville, which was created for the International Typeface Corporation and is based on the types of English type founder and printer John Baskerville (1706–75). Baskerville is the quintessential "transitional" face: it retains the bracketed and obliqued serifs of "old-style" faces such as Caslon and Garamond, but in its increased lowercase height, lighter color, and enhanced contrast between thick and thin strokes, it presages "modern" faces.

This book is printed on paper that is acid-free and meets the requirements of the American National Standard for Permanence of Paper for Printed Library Materials, Z39.48, 1998.∞

Editorial services by Harkavy Publishing Service, New York, New York

Book design by Binns & Lubin/Martin Lubin, New York, New York

Typesetting by Alexander Typesetting, Inc., Indianapolis, Indiana

Index by Scholars Editorial Services, Inc., Madison, Wisconsin

Printed and bound by Sheridan Books, Chelsea, Michigan